Secure Continuous Delivery on Google Cloud

Implement an automated and secure software delivery pipeline on Google Cloud using native services

Giovanni Galloro

Nathaniel Avery

David Dorbin

Secure Continuous Delivery on Google Cloud

Group Product Manager: Preet Ahuja

Publishing Product Manager: Surbhi Suman

Book Project Manager: Ashwini Gowda

Senior Editor: Mohd Hammad

Technical Editor: Nithik Cheruvakodan

Copy Editor: Safis Editing

Proofreader: Mohd Hammad and Safis Editing

Indexer: Manju Arasan

Production Designer: Jyoti Kadam

DevRel Marketing Executive: Rohan Dobhal

First published: April 2024

Production reference: 1220324

Published by Packt Publishing Ltd.

Grosvenor House

11 St Paul's Square

Birmingham

B3 1RB, UK

ISBN 978-1-80512-928-8

www.packtpub.com

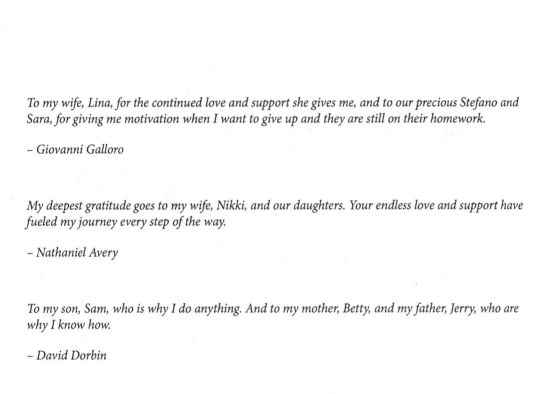

To my wife, Lina, for the continued love and support she gives me, and to our precious Stefano and Sara, for giving me motivation when I want to give up and they are still on their homework.

– Giovanni Galloro

My deepest gratitude goes to my wife, Nikki, and our daughters. Your endless love and support have fueled my journey every step of the way.

– Nathaniel Avery

To my son, Sam, who is why I do anything. And to my mother, Betty, and my father, Jerry, who are why I know how.

– David Dorbin

Foreword

We are what we repeatedly do. Excellence, then, is not an act but a habit.

– Will Durant

When you accomplish something for the first time, it's worth celebrating. Did you complete a marathon? Send the inaugural edition of your newsletter? Stay within your spending budget this month? Or ship v1 of your software to production? That's amazing, and you should be proud.

However, I'm even more impressed if you do it a second time. And a third, and fourth, and fifth time. This indicates that you've built a habit or technique to successfully perform the activity over and over again. That's hard to do, but it's what often characterizes those who are consistently excellent.

Shipping software is far from simple, especially in the modern era. You've got more complex application code, with dozens of referenced packages outside of the programming language's base libraries. The architecture is denser than it was a decade ago, with a mix of frontends, backends, APIs, databases, message queues, and so on. And this pile of software gets deployed to distributed infrastructure that you may not even own. With enough caffeine and manual effort, you can get modern software deployed the first time. But that's not sustainable. If you care about being responsive to customer needs, keeping systems up and running, and maintaining your sanity, you'll choose to automate the path to production.

Doing so isn't just nice to have; it's a precursor to better business performance. The research from the DevOps Research and Assessment (DORA) team at Google Cloud gave us trustworthy proof points that bear this out. Companies that are elite at managing short lead times, regular deployment frequencies, low change failure rates, and minimal time to restore service have better business outcomes and happier teams. Sounds great. How do you actually make it happen?

This book is the first publication that offers an end-to-end look at secure software delivery in Google Cloud. Public clouds can often feel like a set of powerful but loosely connected services. It's often left to the user to figure out the right way to stitch them together to achieve their desired outcome. But when it comes to securely delivering software in a repeatable way, we crave opinions from experts. Fortunately, that's the book you're holding in your hands right now.

Each of the authors brings years of engineering and implementation experience to this book. They've seen a wide range of environments and software delivery programs in their careers, and that colors their walk through the major stages of the software development life cycle. At each stage, you'll learn about the Google Cloud technologies that play a part and will have the opportunity to complete at least one exercise that helps you go from theoretical knowledge to practical wisdom.

Here's a warning. Many things in this book will feel foreign and maybe even a bit uncomfortable! Using declarative tools such as Skaffold for local, iterative builds? Coding in cloud-based development environments? Stashing dependent language packages in managed repositories versus directly using NPM or Maven Central? Relying on canary deployments that progressively roll out your software? Verifying container images with binary authorization? Some of these things you'll be doing for the first time. That's good. We're in a brave new world and need to challenge ourselves to uplevel our toolchain and skillset.

Look, I'm also a realist and expect that you might use many services from Google Cloud, but not all. You could have existing continuous integration product investments. Maybe you have a mature artifact repository and have no reason to change anything. That's OK. The authors also dedicate a chapter to thinking through integrations with existing product investments.

This book is a jumping-off point for a journey to evolve your software delivery process. It won't answer every question you have; there are always more configurations than available pages! But I'm confident that by digesting this content and getting hands-on with the embedded exercises, you'll be well on your way to developing fresh habits that predict future excellence. Enjoy the ride.

Richard Seroter

Chief Evangelist at Google Cloud

Contributors

About the authors

Giovanni Galloro has been working at Google since 2017 as a customer engineer specializing in container-based runtimes, DevOps tools, and application networking. He works with multiple organizations across EMEA, helping them to leverage these capabilities and improve their software delivery practices.

Giovanni is a community ambassador for the Continuous Delivery Foundation and is a frequent speaker at developer conferences.

Before Google, he worked at Microsoft, Red Hat, VMware, and HP, following the evolution of application platforms over the past 20 years.

Nathaniel Avery works at Google as an outbound product manager for the Google Cloud Application Ecosystem group, specializing in DevOps tools, and has spoken to many Fortune 500 companies about DevOps tooling solutions.

Before joining Google, Nate spent more than 20 years in IT designing, planning, and implementing complex systems, integrating custom-built and COTS applications for federal government customers.

Currently, he's working on better ways to build and use cloud resources to help customers deliver better products, safely and securely, without sacrificing velocity.

David Dorbin has been a technical writer for more than three decades. He's been with Google for more than a dozen years, documenting payment applications, internal tools, and Google Cloud DevOps products.

Before Google, he worked with numerous start-ups and established companies, documenting technologies in payment processing, digital publishing and rights management, consumer electronics, and cryptography for financial institutions.

In his free time, Dave enjoys playing bass and banjolele (but never at the same time), or doing more damage to his Achilles' heel on the streets and trails of northern New Jersey.

We are happy to donate the earnings from this book to Save the Children Italia.

About the reviewer

Richard Seroter is currently the chief evangelist at Google Cloud and leads the Developer Relations program. He's also an instructor at Pluralsight, a frequent public speaker, and the author of multiple books on software design and development. As chief evangelist at Google Cloud, Richard leads the team of developer advocates, developer engineers, outbound product managers, and technical writers who ensure that people find, use, and enjoy Google Cloud. Richard maintains a regularly updated blog (`seroter.com`) on the topics of architecture and solution design and can be found on Twitter/X as `@rseroter`.

Table of Contents

3

Developing and Testing with Cloud Code   37

4

Securing Your Code with Cloud Workstations   59

Part 2: Build and Package Your Application

5

6

Part 3: Deploy and Run Your Application

7

8

9

Securing Your Runtimes with Binary Authorization   177

Part 4: Hands-On Secure Pipeline Delivery and Looking Forward

10

Demonstrating an End-to-End Software Delivery Pipeline   203

11

Integrating with Your Organization's Workflows   225

12

Diving into Best Practices and Trends in Continuous Delivery   253

Preface

Continuous Delivery (CD) is a set of software engineering practices that enables teams to deliver software quickly and safely by automating the entire software release process through a deployment pipeline.

To build a continuous delivery pipeline, you typically need separate tools to perform the necessary tasks, including the following:

- Automate artifact builds and software tests
- Manage source code
- Store, secure, and distribute software artifacts
- Manage and automate deployment to different runtime environments

You can choose tools from different providers and different deployment or installation methods, and integrate them. Or you can use a set of managed services from the same cloud provider, reducing the setup, integration, and management effort, allowing you to focus on your code.

The goal of this book is to use hands-on exercises to show you how to build an end-to-end continuous delivery pipeline on Google Cloud using Google-managed services, covering not only how to get code from commit to production but also how you can optimize your inner development loop.

The book starts by introducing continuous delivery principles and best practices to implement them while protecting your artifacts from security threats. You'll then learn how to use Skaffold, Cloud Code, Duet AI, and Cloud Workstations to help stay in the flow and optimize feedback loops while you code. You'll experiment with automating your builds and tests and generating signed provenance for your artifacts using Cloud Build. You'll understand how to store your software artifacts and assess their security posture using Artifact Registry. You'll learn how to orchestrate deployments and promotions through different stages using Cloud Deploy, and release your software on GKE and Cloud Run. You'll also see how to use Binary Authorization to protect these runtime environments. Furthermore, we'll show some examples of integrating these tools with other services you may have.

After you learn about each tool or service, following the hands-on examples, we'll guide you through creating an end-to-end software delivery pipeline that represents a real production environment, with multiple actors involved, using all the aforementioned services together.

Lastly, we'll provide some additional best practices, as well as insights into some possible future trends.

By the end of this book, you'll be able to build a secure software delivery pipeline from development to production using Google Cloud's managed services and best practices.

Who this book is for

This book is mainly for technical practitioners, such as DevOps engineers and platform engineers, who manage application deployment, create continuous delivery pipelines, and want to automate workflows in a fully managed, scalable, and secure platform.

Another group who will find the book useful are software developers involved in application delivery, who are interested in learning how to leverage Google Cloud tools to optimize development flow status and feedback loop.

What this book covers

Chapter 1, Introducing Continuous Delivery and Software Supply Chain Security, describes continuous delivery principles and some of the practices and technical capabilities that drive the ability to implement them. The chapter also provides an overview of the security threats that a software supply chain can be exposed to and some practices that can mitigate them.

Chapter 2, Using Skaffold for Development, Build, and Deploy, describes Skaffold and how you can use it to test your application continuously while you develop it, build the container image containing your application, execute tests, and deploy it on different Kubernetes clusters.

Chapter 3, Developing and Testing with Cloud Code, demonstrates how to use Cloud Code, a Google-provided IDE add-on, to optimize the development flow state and feedback loops, and how to use Duet AI to get help while coding.

Chapter 4, Securing Your Code with Cloud Workstations, describes how an administrator can preconfigure Cloud Workstations, fully managed developer workstations hosted in Google Cloud, and how developers can use those workstations to work on code using their preferred IDE.

Chapter 5, Automating Continuous Integration with Cloud Build, describes Cloud Build, a managed service used to automate building artifacts, as well as other continuous integration (CI) tasks, and how you can use Cloud Build to build your application from source to a deployable container image.

Chapter 6, Securely Store Your Software on Artifact Registry, describes Artifact Registry, the Google-managed container and software artifact repository, and shows how to use it to store container images, application dependencies, and all of your software artifacts, scan them for vulnerabilities, and store vulnerabilities' metadata.

Chapter 7, Exploring Runtimes – GKE, GKE Enterprise, and Cloud Run, describes the main runtime environments into which you can deploy your applications using Google Cloud continuous delivery tooling. This chapter includes Google Kubernetes Engine (GKE) hosted on GCP as well as Cloud Run, and on-premises Kubernetes or hosted on other hyperscale cloud platforms.

Chapter 8, Automating Software Delivery Using Cloud Deploy, describes Cloud Deploy, a service you can use to automate how your application is delivered to a predetermined sequence of runtime environments. You'll learn how to create the software delivery pipeline that guides your application delivery to those target environments.

Chapter 9, Securing Your Runtimes with Binary Authorization, describes Binary Authorization, a service that lets you configure policies to control the execution of container-based applications on Google Cloud runtimes such as GKE and Cloud Run.

Chapter 10, Demonstrating an End-to-End Software Delivery Pipeline, shows how to use all the Google Cloud tools described in the previous chapters to create and run an end-to-end pipeline from code to production for an example application.

Chapter 11, Integrating with Your Organization's Workflows, demonstrates an example of how to integrate your pipeline with external systems present in your organization, such as source-code management systems or workflow management tools.

Chapter 12, Diving into Best Practices and Trends in Continuous Delivery, describes some best practices for continuous delivery on Google Cloud that we didn't cover exhaustively in previous chapters. This chapter also provides some hints on future improvements, directions, and developments in software delivery capabilities.

To get the most out of this book

To get the most out of this book, you'll need a basic understanding of software development and application packaging (basic project structure, builds, and unit tests), application deployment, Linux containers, Kubernetes, and the fundamentals of Google Cloud (Cloud APIs, IAM, etc.).

Software/hardware covered in the book	Operating system requirements
Cloud Shell	You can execute all the exercises in the book in Cloud Shell and the Google Cloud console. Cloud Shell supports the latest versions of Google Chrome, Mozilla Firefox, Microsoft Edge, Microsoft Internet Explorer 11+, and Apple Safari 8+. Safari in private browser mode is not supported.
Google Cloud console	You can use the Google Cloud console in the following browsers: Chrome, Safari, Firefox, and Edge.
gcloud CLI installed locally (optional)	Linux (Debian, Ubuntu, Red Hat/Fedora/CentOS), macOS, and Windows.
Skaffold installed locally (optional)	Linux (Debian, Ubuntu, Red Hat/Fedora/CentOS), macOS, and Windows.
Cloud Code installed locally (optional)	You need a supported IDE. Examples in the book are based mainly on Code OSS/VS Code.

All the tasks in the book that require a terminal or an editor can be performed with Cloud Shell (or Cloud Workstations), accessible with one of the aforementioned supported browsers. We suggest using Cloud Shell or Cloud Workstations because they have all the necessary tools already installed. If you prefer, you can install the gcloud CLI, Skaffold, and Cloud Code locally, following the requirements in the preceding table.

If you are using the digital version of this book, we advise you to type the code yourself or access the code from the book's GitHub repository (a link is available in the next section). Doing so will help you avoid any potential errors related to the copying and pasting of code.

Download the example code files

You can download the example code files for this book from GitHub at `https://github.com/PacktPublishing/Secure-Continuous-Delivery-on-Google-Cloud`. If there's an update to the code, it will be updated in the GitHub repository.

We also have other code bundles from our rich catalog of books and videos available at `https://github.com/PacktPublishing/`. Check them out!

Conventions used

There are a number of text conventions used throughout this book.

`Code in text`: Indicates code words in text, database table names, folder names, filenames, file extensions, pathnames, dummy URLs, user input, and Twitter handles. Here is an example: "A new build now runs, linked to the `scdbook-e2e-merge` trigger."

A block of code is set as follows:

```
[{
"id" : "upstream1",
"repository" : "projects/$PROJECT_ID/locations/us-central1/
repositories/python-local",
"priority" : 100
},
```

Any command-line input or output is written as follows:

```
gcloud artifacts repositories list --project=$PROJECT_ID \
--location=us-central1
```

Bold: Indicates a new term, an important word, or words that you see onscreen. For instance, words in menus or dialog boxes appear in **bold**. Here is an example: "To view the render logs, click the link next to **Render logs**, under **Rendering**."

> **Tips or important notes**
> Appear like this.

Get in touch

Feedback from our readers is always welcome.

General feedback: If you have questions about any aspect of this book, email us at customercare@packtpub.com and mention the book title in the subject of your message.

Errata: Although we have taken every care to ensure the accuracy of our content, mistakes do happen. If you have found a mistake in this book, we would be grateful if you would report this to us. Please visit www.packtpub.com/support/errata and fill in the form.

Piracy: If you come across any illegal copies of our works in any form on the internet, we would be grateful if you would provide us with the location address or website name. Please contact us at copyright@packtpub.com with a link to the material.

If you are interested in becoming an author: If there is a topic that you have expertise in and you are interested in either writing or contributing to a book, please visit authors.packtpub.com.

Share Your Thoughts

Once you've read *Secure Continuous Delivery on Google Cloud*, we'd love to hear your thoughts! Scan the QR code below to go straight to the Amazon review page for this book and share your feedback.

https://packt.link/r/1805129287

Your review is important to us and the tech community and will help us make sure we're delivering excellent quality content.

Download a free PDF copy of this book

Thanks for purchasing this book!

Do you like to read on the go but are unable to carry your print books everywhere?

Is your eBook purchase not compatible with the device of your choice?

Don't worry, now with every Packt book you get a DRM-free PDF version of that book at no cost.

Read anywhere, any place, on any device. Search, copy, and paste code from your favorite technical books directly into your application.

The perks don't stop there, you can get exclusive access to discounts, newsletters, and great free content in your inbox daily.

Follow these simple steps to get the benefits:

1. Scan the QR code or visit the link below

https://packt.link/free-ebook/978-1-80512-928-8

2. Submit your proof of purchase
3. That's it! We'll send your free PDF and other benefits to your email directly

Part 1:
Introduction and Code Your Application

This part is an overview of continuous delivery, its underlying principles and practices, and best practices for protecting software artifacts from security threats along the software supply chain. In this part, you'll also learn about Skaffold, Cloud Code, and Cloud Workstations, three tools that can help developers to be more productive, stay in the flow, and optimize their feedback loop.

This part has the following chapters:

- *Chapter 1, Introducing Continuous Delivery and Software Supply Chain Security*
- *Chapter 2, Using Skaffold for Development, Build, and Deploy*
- *Chapter 3, Developing and Testing with Cloud Code*
- *Chapter 4, Securing your Code with Cloud Workstations*

1

Introducing Continuous Delivery and Software Supply Chain Security

Most transactions and interactions today are digital or rely on digital services, so the ability to deliver software quickly, reliably, and securely is a critical competitive advantage. **Continuous delivery (CD)** is a software engineering practice that enables teams to achieve this goal by automating the entire software release process, from committing code to deploying to production. CD, properly done, empowers organizations to reduce their **time to market (TTM)**, improve software quality, and release new features and bug fixes more frequently.

The goal of this book is to share how to implement secure CD using Google Cloud services such as **Cloud Code**, **Cloud Workstations**, **Cloud Build**, **Artifact Registry**, **Cloud Deploy**, and others.

In this book, we describe each service and show how you can use them together to automate and secure your software delivery pipeline. But first, in this chapter, we introduce CD principles and some of the practices and technical capabilities that drive the ability to implement them.

This chapter also provides an overview of security threats that a software supply chain can face and some practices that can mitigate those threats.

This chapter includes the following sections:

- Introduction to CD
- Understanding continuous integration
- Understanding continuous testing
- Understanding deployment automation
- Securing your software delivery pipeline

We start this book by looking at what CD is.

Introduction to CD

CD is a set of practices and principles that aim to streamline and automate software delivery from commit to production. Teams and organizations practice with the goal of deploying software to production on demand at any time without impacting service availability. The main objective of CD is that software should always be in a deployable state and software release should be a fast, repeatable process.

This section is a quick overview of CD, what it consists of, and how it can help your organization achieve better and faster software delivery.

CD practices

Some of the practices that underpin CD are set out here:

- **CI**: CI means that code changes are integrated into the source code repository quickly and regularly. Automated builds and tests are triggered with each code commit, providing rapid feedback to developers. Consistent, reliable builds are at the foundation of a trustworthy CD process.

- **Continuous testing**: This includes unit tests, integration tests, and **end-to-end** (**E2E**) tests. Test suites are executed automatically during the pipeline to catch regressions early and increase your confidence in the quality of the system.

- **Small, frequent releases**: Instead of large, infrequent releases, CD tries to break down features and changes into small, manageable chunks that can be released more frequently. This reduces the risk of introducing regressions and makes it easier to identify and fix problems.

- **Trunk-based development**: A software development methodology in which developers divide their work into small batches and merge each batch into the trunk at least once a day. This approach is in contrast to more complex branching strategies such as feature branching or Gitflow, in which developers create separate branches for different features or bug fixes.

- **Deployment pipeline**: The entire release process, from building the code to deploying it to production, is automated using a **pipeline**. The automated pipeline can run such tasks as the following:

  - Compiling code

  - Executing unit tests

  - Building software artifacts as container images

  - Progressively deploying the app on different pre-production environments where different kinds of automated or manual tests can be performed

  - Finally releasing the application to production

The following diagram represents an example pipeline, starting when there is a new commit in the source code repository. The tasks represented in the diagram and the ones listed previously are examples. The exact pipeline sequence changes depending on factors such as the application itself, the programming language, and the framework, as well as specific organizational contexts:

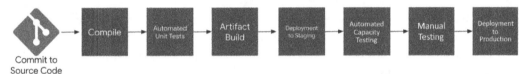

Figure 1.1 – A high-level look at a software delivery pipeline

That process, with those practices, can help you achieve improved software delivery performance, as described in the next section.

The impact of CD on software delivery performance

The **DevOps Research and Assessment** (**DORA**) research program has identified CD as one of the main capabilities driving software delivery performance, as measured by DORA's four key metrics.

The following list shows those four metrics and how they can help you improve your software delivery performance:

- **Deployment Frequency**: How often code changes are deployed to production.

  CD encourages more frequent deployments because it automates the deployment process and ensures that code changes are always production ready. Teams practicing CD can deploy changes to production on demand, often multiple times a day. Compare this to traditional approaches that might have longer release cycles.

- **Lead Time for Changes**: The time it takes to go from code commit to a production-ready release.

  CD streamlines the software development process, enabling faster development cycles and reducing delays. CD automates steps in the delivery pipeline, such as building, testing, and deploying, which reduces manual intervention and wait times.

  With CD, code changes are continuously integrated, tested, and delivered, shortening the time from development to production. Frequent, small releases accelerate TTM.

- **Change Failure Rate**: The percentage of changes or deployments that fail or require rollback.

  CD emphasizes continuous testing, including unit tests, integration tests, and acceptance tests. This reduces the chance that defects and errors make their way into production.

  Automation, in general, makes the release process repeatable and less error-prone because almost nothing is left to interpretation. Frequent, smaller releases make it easier to identify and fix issues early in the development process, reducing the likelihood of catastrophic failures in production.

- **Time to Restore Services**: The average time it takes to restore services after a production failure.

  CD practices typically include automated monitoring and alerting in production environments. This helps teams detect issues quickly. When issues do occur, CD enables rapid rollback or forward fixes. Automated deployments make it easier to apply fixes and quickly get the system back to a working state.

See `https://dora.dev/` for more info on DORA and the four key metrics.

In the rest of this chapter, we describe the most important underlying CD practices in more detail, starting with CI.

Understanding continuous integration

Continuous integration (CI) is a set of software development practices for frequently integrating code changes. Each time a developer integrates changes (usually at least daily), those changes are automatically verified and tested. This means that there is always an up-to-date build ready to deploy.

The practice of CI was created to solve integration and compatibility problems caused by the old approach of developers working in isolation for an extended period on their version of code and then attempting to merge their changes into a shared code base.

CI follows the counterintuitive principle that if something is painful, you can make it less painful by doing it more often. This is based on the understanding that the integration effort is exponentially proportional to the amount of time between integrations (as found on `https://martinfowler.com/articles/originalContinuousIntegration.html#TheMoreOftenTheBetter`).

The next section describes how to bring these principles to your software development process.

How to implement CI

Here is a list of fundamental practices that a team should consider following to implement CI:

- **Trunk-based development**: As described previously, developers divide their own work into small batches and merge that work into the main code branch (trunk) at least once a day.

- **Automated builds**: For every change committed to the repository, the application is automatically compiled, built, and tested without manual intervention. This helps ensure that the software is always in a state that can be deployed to production. Artifacts produced by the CI build should be used by all subsequent deployment tasks. An automatic build is run at least once a day.

- **Continuous testing**: Automated tests run every time a change is committed, including unit tests, integration tests, and other types of automated tests. This helps ensure that new code doesn't break existing functionality. Immediate feedback from these tests allows developers to fix issues quickly before those issues cause bigger problems. Tests should run successfully at least once a day, and if they fail, the team prioritizes fixing the problem.

- **Collaboration**: This is probably more a consequence of the previously listed elements than a principle to implement. With all team members committing to the shared repository regularly, there's a continual exchange of ideas and code. This openness not only improves the quality of the software but also enhances team dynamics, as everyone can see what others are working on. It also encourages developers, testers, and operations teams to work more closely together. This collaboration breaks down silos and promotes a more cohesive approach to software development, in which everyone is aware of the goals and challenges of the project.

Now that we've covered the main elements of CI, let's explore continuous testing.

Understanding continuous testing

Continuous testing automates as much of the testing as possible, running the tests frequently (before and after each build) as part of a CD pipeline.

This approach has the following benefits:

- Developers and the rest of the team get quick feedback on how the software is functioning and can immediately fix any issues.

- Tests' reliability is better than that of manual tests, which are repetitive and error-prone.

- Software can be released more frequently because the feedback loop is shorter.

Using continuous, automated testing doesn't mean you won't also run some manual tests, such as exploratory or usability testing, throughout the delivery process.

Now, let's look at the types of testing that are typically included in continuous testing.

Test types

The following are some test types typically used in continuous testing:

- **Unit tests**: These tests are building blocks, focusing on individual code units (functions, classes). Unit tests run quickly and provide fine-grained feedback.

- **Integration tests**: These tests verify how different parts of a system work together. Integration tests are crucial for identifying issues in the interactions between integrated components or systems. These are more likely to be run within your CI server where multiple code packages come together.

- **Acceptance tests**: These tests simulate real-world usage of a running application or service, verifying that essential functionality aligns with user expectations and business requirements. These may happen from your CI environment or other outside services that test applications running in a staging environment.

And now, let's see how to make continuous testing happen.

Implementing continuous testing

The following is a list of fundamental principles and practices for teams to implement continuous testing:

- **Test automation**: Automating unit tests, integration tests, and regression tests is essential for continuous testing. Automation allows the team to quickly identify and address issues, making the testing process more efficient.

- **Developer involvement in testing**: Developers should be the people primarily responsible for creating and maintaining automated test suites.

  This approach ensures that tests are always updated based on code changes and that developers write code that is relatively easy to test. The natural consequence and best realization of this approach is the **test-driven development** (TDD) practice, which is described next.

- **TDD**: A software development methodology in which tests are written before code. Initially, the developer writes an automated test for a new function or feature and then writes the actual code. This test defines how the new functionality should behave.

  The developer then writes the minimal amount of code necessary to make the test pass. After the test passes, the developer then refactors the code, which involves cleaning up and optimizing the code without changing its functionality.

- **Unit and acceptance tests' proportion**: One of the main goals of continuous testing is to detect and fix issues as soon as possible. Unit tests are typically faster than acceptance tests and are executed in the early phases, so the more issues are detected in unit tests, the sooner defects are detected and remediated.

  As much as possible, unit tests should do the work of detecting issues. When an error is found in acceptance tests or other manual tests, create an automated unit test for that behavior to ensure that this error is detected sooner if it occurs again.

Now that we've covered the main elements of continuous testing, we'll explore automated deployment in the next section.

Understanding deployment automation

Deployment automation allows software to be easily and automatically deployed to pre-production and production environments, at the push of a button. This is crucial for minimizing risks during production rollouts and results in rapid feedback on software quality. By enabling teams to perform extensive testing immediately after updates, deployment automation ensures prompt assessment and enhances overall software quality. Implementing deployment automation doesn't necessarily mean that you are doing *continuous deployment*. Continuous deployment is when you try to deploy every code change to production as soon as possible, and this can or cannot be applicable to your environment. You can do CD and automate your deployments but still have gated releases, feature flags, or even manual switches to formally light up the release.

An automated deployment process has the following inputs:

- Software artifacts (created by CI) that are ready for deployment in any environment, including production
- Configuration details unique to each environment
- Scripts for setting up the environment, deploying packages, and conducting deployment tests

Now, let's look at how to automate your deployments.

Implementing deployment automation

Here is a list of fundamental principles and practices that a team should follow to implement deployment automation:

- Implement a uniform deployment process across all environments, including production. This ensures the deployment method is thoroughly tested before it's used in production.
- Enable automated deployment of any artifact version to any environment by anyone with the right permissions. A process is not fully automated if it requires that someone file a ticket or manually prepare an environment.

- Use identical packages across all environments and maintain environment-specific configurations separately. This ensures packages deployed in production are the same as those tested.

- Ensure each environment's state can be re-created using version control. This makes deployment repeatable and enables deterministic production restoration in **disaster recovery (DR)** scenarios.

That covers deployment automation. In the next section, we introduce software delivery security.

Securing your software delivery pipeline

Software production and delivery can be viewed as a supply chain in which the same developer can be both a software producer (by developing software) and a consumer (by using existing software as a dependency for the app being developed).

This section is a high-level overview of some of the security threats against a software delivery pipeline, as well as some best practices that help protect against those threats. In later chapters, we describe how to implement some of the best practices, using Google Cloud-managed services.

First, let's look at the security of your source code.

Source code management threats and remediations

Threats to source code management systems affect the security of the source code. These threats can come from the code itself (for example, submitting source code that is unintentionally or intentionally vulnerable) or can be threats to the source control platform, which can be compromised in different ways. The next section lists some practices to help ensure your source code is safe.

Source code management security best practices

The following is a list of security best practices to protect the integrity of your source code:

- **Repository configuration**: Configure repositories using a secure, automated method that offers preconfigured templates based on the application's security level.

  Enforce centralized identity management with **multi-factor authentication (MFA)** for users, ensuring updated access privileges. Limit repository ownership to a few trusted employees, integrate identity management systems, and require dual approval for merges to enhance security.

- **Code reviews**: Code reviews are one of the most important practices to ensure software quality and security and should always be part of a secure software supply chain.

  Reviewers should be assigned to a repository application or a specific commit based on expertise in the programming language and relevant security risks. Perform code reviews on feature-branch pull requests as soon as developers are ready.

  In addition to human code reviews, implement static code analysis tools.

- **Merge approvals**: Establish a select group of trusted individuals to authorize merges into production branches. For applications with stricter security requirements, implement a process that requires more than one approver.

Now, let's look at security for your build process.

Build threats and remediations

The following are some examples of security threats to the artifact build process and tools:

- Builds that use modified source code (not from a trusted source control system)
- Compromise of the build system
- Artifacts built outside of the official build system and process
- Compromise of the artifact storage system

The following section lists some practices to help ensure the security of your build process.

Build security best practices

The **Supply-chain Levels for Software Artifacts** (**SLSA**) specification defines a set of build-security best practices. These are established by multiple software-industry organizations under the **Open Source Security Foundation** (**OpenSSF**) (https://openssf.org/).

SLSA (http://slsa.dev) is a specification meant to help you describe and improve your software supply chain security. It's structured as a series of tracks, each one covering an aspect of supply chain security, and levels, with each level offering progressively stronger security guidelines and requirements for each track.

At the time of this writing, the SLSA specification is at version 1.0, the first stable release of SLSA. SLSA v1.0 consists of only one track: **Build**. Future versions of SLSA will add tracks that cover other parts of the software supply chain.

Each level includes a set of requirements for the build process: lower-level requirements are easier to implement but provide lower security guarantees. Higher-level requirements are harder and usually more expensive to adopt but demonstrate that tougher security guidelines have been adopted for software build practices.

The level-based structure also allows you to incrementally adopt the guidelines, progressively improving the security posture of your software supply chain.

The primary goal of the SLSA Build track is to attest and verify that an artifact was built as expected. This is done mainly by generating build provenance, which software consumers can verify. The SLSA v1.0 Build track includes three levels: **L1** to **L3**. There is also an **L0** level, which refers to software that doesn't meet any SLSA requirements. The following table summarizes the build levels:

Track/Level	Requirements	Focus
Build L0	None	N/A
Build L1	Provenance showing how the package was built	Mistakes, documentation
Build L2	Signed provenance, generated by a hosted build platform	Tampering after the build
Build L3	Hardened build platform	Tampering during the build

Table 1.1 – SLSA v1 Build tracks

These security levels, and descriptions thereof, are from the SLSA specification, version 1.0, courtesy of the SLSA Working Group. You can find more details on the requirements for each level at `http://slsa.dev`.

In the next section, we'll talk about threats in your code's dependencies and some practices for remediating those threats.

Dependency threats and remediations

Dependency threats are vulnerabilities or intentionally malicious code in any software that your application depends on.

Dependency management best practices

The following is a list of security best practices for managing dependencies:

- **Scan dependencies for vulnerabilities**: Integrate a scanning tool into the development and build workflow that identifies vulnerabilities, using databases such as the **National Institute of Standards of Technology National Vulnerability Database (NIST NVD)**.

- **Store dependencies in a private registry**: A private registry offers the convenience of a public repository, with enhanced control over dependencies. It can provide capabilities such as access control, vulnerability scanning, and repository management.

- **Remove unused dependencies**: Regularly cleaning up unneeded dependencies keeps your application lean and nimble, improving its performance and reducing its attack surface. This proactive approach helps minimize potential security risks associated with outdated or irrelevant dependencies.

- **Use open source tools to track dependency insights**: Various tools can help you to get information on dependencies. Here are two examples:

  - **Open Source Insights** (`https://deps.dev/`): A website that provides information about software packages vulnerabilities and licenses.

  - **Open Source Vulnerability (OSV) Database** (`https://osv.dev/`): A searchable vulnerability database.

This section described how to secure your software delivery pipeline, including a look at how your code and its dependencies can face vulnerabilities.

Summary

In this chapter, you were introduced to CD principles and some of the practices and technical capabilities that underpin them, such as CI, continuous testing, deployment automation, and trunk-based development. You also learned how CD and these practices positively impact software delivery performance and achieve organization goals, as measured by DORA research.

In the second part of the chapter, we described some potential security threats to a software supply chain and some strategies to protect against them. We also provided an overview of the SLSA Build track specification.

This information should prepare you for the rest of the book, in which we show how to implement CD and software supply chain security best practices using Google Cloud-managed services.

The next chapter is a look at Skaffold, an open source tool for continuous development and CD that is used by several of the Google Cloud services described in this book.

2

Using Skaffold for Development, Build, and Deploy

Skaffold is an open source tool that helps developers write code iteratively and automate continuous delivery pipelines for their applications. It simplifies how you develop, build, test, push, and deploy container-based applications to multiple environments (such as local dev, test, staging, and production).

Typically, if you're developing a container-based application for Kubernetes, and you want to test how it will behave in the target environment, you need to do multiple tasks, such as building the image, pushing it to a registry, configuring manifests for each target, and deploy.

Skaffold helps to perform the preceding tasks with a single command line and a single configuration file, so you don't have to switch contexts too much.

In this chapter, we describe Skaffold and how you can use it to optimize your inner development loop, build and test your application, and deploy it to different target runtime environments.

In this chapter, we'll cover the following main topics:

- Skaffold's capabilities and architecture
- Installing Skaffold
- Using Skaffold with your application

Technical requirements

For this chapter, you will need the following:

- A GitHub account to access the repository used in this chapter (`https://github.com/PacktPublishing/Secure-Continuous-Delivery-on-Google-Cloud`) as well as the Skaffold installation files.

- A Google Cloud project, with billing or a free trial enabled, the default VPC network, and the following APIs enabled:

  - Google Compute Engine API

  - Google Kubernetes Engine API

  - Artifact Registry API

  - Container Scanning API

  - Cloud Resource Manager API

- A local Kubernetes cluster, such as minikube, or Docker Desktop. If you use Cloud Shell on Google Cloud, you will have minikube already installed in the environment.

Understanding Skaffold's capabilities and architecture

This section describes Skaffold and how it can help you develop and deliver your applications.

Whether you're working with a single-container or microservice application, Skaffold can help you do the following:

- **Optimize your inner development loop**: Skaffold can monitor your repository while you write code. It continuously deploys your changes to a designated development Kubernetes cluster so you can immediately see the results of your changes. Skaffold can also expose your application locally using kubectl and port forwarding, aggregate Pod logs, and provide debugging capabilities.

- **Manage how your container image is built**: Skaffold integrates with various tools and build environments.

- **Automate test execution for your application**: Skaffold lets you specify a container image to run to verify your deployment.

- **Manage how your application is deployed to different runtime environments**: Skaffold can apply different configurations for each environment using profiles.

You can do all of this using Skaffold with specific command-line parameters. You can also run a complete pipeline (build, test, and deploy) using skaffold run against a Skaffold configuration file called skaffold.yaml.

The Skaffold binary and `skaffold.yaml` are the two main Skaffold components. Cloud Code, described in *Chapter 3*, includes Skaffold as the underlying technology to optimize the continuous development loop and for debugging, and Cloud Deploy, described in *Chapter 9*, uses Skaffold to render manifests and to deploy your application into different environments.

Now that you know a little about what Skaffold does, let's take a closer look at Skaffold's architecture and how to use it to build and deploy your application.

Skaffold for building

Skaffold can build your container image using any of the following tools and environments:

- Dockerfile:

    - Locally with Docker

    - In-cluster with kaniko

    - In the cloud with Cloud Build

- Jib for Maven and Gradle:

    - Locally

    - In the cloud with Cloud Build

- Bazel, locally

- Cloud Native Buildpacks:

    - Locally with Docker

    - In the cloud with Cloud Build

- Custom script:

    - Locally

    - In-cluster

In `dev` mode, Skaffold can also upload file changes directly to a running Kubernetes Pod without you having to rebuild the image.

Skaffold for deploying

Skaffold can deploy to any Kubernetes cluster and to Cloud Run.

Skaffold can render (populate with specific deployment information, such as the image tag) and deploy manifests for Kubernetes deployment with the help of the following tools:

- kubectl
- Helm
- Kustomize
- kpt

Let's look at Skaffold's architecture now.

Skaffold's architecture

The following diagram, from the Skaffold documentation, shows Skaffold's capabilities and related tools:

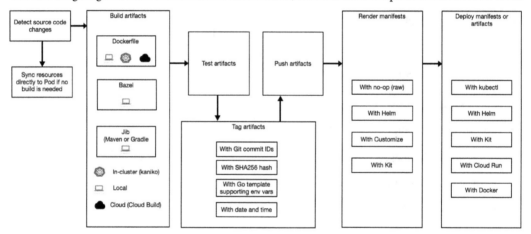

Figure 2.1 – Skaffold flow and interaction with other tools

Let's learn about installing Skaffold now.

Installing Skaffold

You can install Skaffold as a single binary to run from the command line, or you can use it as part of Cloud Code. Cloud Code is available from Google as a set of extensions to popular IDEs. You can also use it in the Google Cloud Shell IDE. Cloud Code is described in *Chapter 3*.

Skaffold is also used in Cloud Deploy to render manifests and apply them to deploy your application to various Google Cloud runtime environments. Cloud Deploy is described in *Chapter 8*.

The examples in the chapter are executed using the standalone Skaffold binary. Installing Skaffold as part of Cloud Code is described in *Chapter 3*.

The following command installs the Skaffold binary on an x86_64 Linux machine:

```
curl -Lo skaffold https://storage.googleapis.com/skaffold/releases/
latest/skaffold-linux-amd64 && sudo install skaffold /usr/local/bin/
```

For other platforms, follow the instructions listed at `https://skaffold.dev/docs/install/`.

Using Skaffold with your application

In this section, we demonstrate Skaffold's capabilities by using it on an example application.

Let's start by initializing our repository.

Initializing your repository using skaffold init

For this exercise, we use an example application written in Go, but Skaffold is language agnostic and supports any containerized application.

The sample application is an adaptation derived from the microservices example from the Skaffold GitHub repository and is contained in the ch2 folder in the book repository, available at `https://github.com/PacktPublishing/Secure-Continuous-Delivery-on-Google-Cloud`.

To initialize your repository, do the following:

1. Get the source code and change directory to see your local copy:

    ```
    git clone https://github.com/PacktPublishing/Secure-Continuous-
    Delivery-on-Google-Cloud
    \
    && cd ch2/single
    ```

2. Explore the content of the repository using the following command:

    ```
    ls -l
    ```

    The output will look like this:

    ```
    total 12
    -rw-r--r-- 1 galloro galloro  955 Feb 12 16:58 app.go
    -rw-r--r-- 1 galloro galloro  882 Feb 12 16:58 Dockerfile
    ```

    You can see the Go source file, a Dockerfile, and a folder. That folder contains the Kubernetes manifest that defines a Deployment and a Service object. Feel free to open the files in an editor to view their content.

The program prints text on a web page and writes to the standard output a string containing the environment where the application is running:

```
..
func handler(w http.ResponseWriter, r *http.Request) {
        fmt.Fprintf(w, "scd-on-gcp app running in target:
%s!!\n", os.Getenv("TARGET"))
}

func main() {
        log.Printf("scd-on-gcp app server ready, running in
target: %s", os.Getenv("TARGET"))
        http.HandleFunc("/", handler)
        http.ListenAndServe(":8081", nil)
}
```

The program reads from a TARGET variable defined as dev inside the kubernetes/ deployment.yaml file:

```
spec:
      containers:
      - name: scdongcp-app
        env:
          - name: TARGET
            value: dev
        image: scdongcp-app
        ports:
        - containerPort: 8081
          name: http
```

Because the repository doesn't have a Skaffold config file, you need to create one. You can use the following command to create one with a suggested base structure:

```
skaffold init
```

The skaffold init command looks for build configuration files in your project directory and suggests a possible configuration for your skaffold.yaml file, depending on the repository structure. For example, if Skaffold detects go.mod or package.json files, it suggests Cloud Native Buildpacks.

If Skaffold finds a repository with a Maven project, it suggests the Jib builder (https:// github.com/GoogleContainerTools/jib). If Skaffold finds a Dockerfile, it suggests the Docker builder.

In this case, because Skaffold finds a Dockerfile, it uses the Docker builder for the generated skaffold.yaml. Skaffold also names the image according to the existing Kubernetes manifest and uses it for deployment.

Here's the Skaffold config created by `skaffold init` in our case:

```
apiVersion: skaffold/v4beta2
kind: Config
metadata:
  name: single
build:
  artifacts:
  - image: scdongcp-app
    docker:
      dockerfile: Dockerfile
manifests:
  rawYaml:
  - kubernetes/deployment.yaml
```

3. Type y to accept the proposed configuration.

   If a `skaffold.yaml` file is already in the repository, you don't need to run `skaffold init`.

4. Open the `skaffold.yaml` file with any text or code editor to explore it.

   You can customize the proposed structure that `skaffold init` created. In this example, we will keep the suggested configuration, so close the file without saving any changes.

Now that your repository is initialized, let's try building and testing while writing code.

Testing your application while you code using skaffold dev

In this section, we'll show how to use Skaffold to watch your local code repository as you work, and immediately build changes and deploy them to a running Kubernetes cluster. In this way, you can continuously see the effects of your changes. The cluster can be running locally in your development workstation or remotely anywhere.

To enable continuous development, you need a target dev Kubernetes cluster to deploy to. The cluster can be a minimal local installation running on your developer workstation, such as Docker Desktop or minikube. In this example, we'll use minikube, which you can install using the instructions at `https://minikube.sigs.k8s.io/docs/start/`. You also need a container or virtual machine manager, such as Docker, Parallels, VirtualBox, or VMware Fusion/Workstation).

If you're using Google Cloud Shell, then minikube, Skaffold, kubectl, Cloud Code, and other tools are already installed.

Enable and use Skaffold continuous development mode using the following steps:

1. After you've installed Docker and enabled non-root Docker access on it, install minikube.

    The following command is for x86_64 Linux:

    ```
    curl -LO https://storage.googleapis.com/minikube/releases/
    latest/minikube-linux-amd64
    sudo install minikube-linux-amd64 /usr/local/bin/minikube
    ```

    Chapter 3 shows you how Cloud Code setup makes things easier, including installing Skaffold and minikube.

    Besides Skaffold and minikube, you also need to install kubectl. Follow the documentation for your platform provided here: https://kubernetes.io/docs/tasks/tools/.

    When you use a local cluster, as in this case, Skaffold doesn't push the built image to a remote registry. Skaffold can detect whether the target cluster is a local one from the kubectl context name or other files, as described here: https://skaffold.dev/docs/environment/local-cluster/.

    The push behavior can be changed within the build.local section of skaffold.yaml, as described in the skaffold.yaml reference: https://skaffold.dev/docs/references/yaml/.

2. After you install minikube, start it:

    ```
    minikube start
    ```

    Wait for minikube to start. When it's running, you'll see a line similar to this:

    ```
    * Done! kubectl is now configured to use "minikube" cluster and
    "default" namespace by default
    ```

    Because Skaffold automatically uses the minikube internal Docker daemon, you need to configure your Docker CLI to use minikube too, so Docker can access images built by Skaffold.

3. Configure Docker to use minikube:

    ```
    eval $(minikube -p minikube docker-env)
    ```

4. Configure Skaffold to consider the kubeconfig context created for minikube as local:

    ```
    skaffold config set --kube-context minikube local-cluster true
    ```

5. Start the continuous development loop:

    ```
    skaffold dev --port-forward
    ```

The `--port-forward` parameter automatically forwards the port exposed by the Kubernetes Service defined in your `kubernetes/deployment.yaml` file to a port on your `localhost`, so you can continually check how the application behaves. If you didn't have a Service object defined, you could have enabled port forwarding in `config.yaml`, adding a section similar to the following:

```
portForward:
  - resourceType: deployment
    resourceName: scdongcp-app
    port: http
    localPort: 4503
```

Skaffold builds your Docker image and deploys it on your minikube cluster. You can see the build commands and app output in the terminal:

```
Build [scdongcp-app] succeeded
Tags used in deployment:
 - scdongcp-app -> scdongcp-app:f35de13e08f6f57398467d8695f6f61f3f13cd5d13ae40241fdd2fabf4af5f7c
Starting deploy...
 - service/scdongcp-app created
 - deployment.apps/scdongcp-app created
Waiting for deployments to stabilize...
 - deployment/scdongcp-app is ready.
Deployments stabilized in 2.147 seconds
Port forwarding service/scdongcp-app in namespace default, remote port 80 -> http://127.0.0.1:4503
Listing files to watch...
 - scdongcp-app
Press Ctrl+C to exit
Watching for changes...
[scdongcp-app] 2023/02/12 11:19:19 scd-on-gcp app server ready, running in target: dev
```

Figure 2.2 – Output from the skaffold dev command

Skaffold also prints the exposed URL where the services have been forwarded on your host. Use that link to see your application web page. It should look like the following:

scd-on-gcp app running in target: dev!!

Next, we'll update the application and see the change immediately in the deployment on the cluster.

6. Open the `app.go` file and change the message on line 25 to the following:

```
fmt.Fprintf(w, "scd-on-gcp app updated in target: %s!!\n",
os.Getenv("TARGET"))
```

The build-and-deploy process starts immediately. At the end of the deployment, refresh your browser window with the application to see your change deployed:

scd-on-gcp app updated in target: dev!!

You tested how changes are immediately deployed in the target minikube cluster and are immediately visible. Now, we'll stop continuous development mode.

7. Press *Ctrl + C* to stop continuous development mode.

When you stop continuous development mode, Skaffold also cleans up the resources it created on the cluster:

```
^CCleaning up...
Service "scdongcp-app" deleted
Deployment.apps "scdongcp-app" deleted
```

We built *and* deployed our application according to the `skaffold.yaml` configuration, and then watched our files for changes. Now let's see how to just build our application and container image as part of a continuous delivery pipeline execution.

Building your application using skaffold build

We will build our app using the `skaffold build` command, which builds our artifacts following the statement inside the `build` section of our `skaffold.yaml` file. When you use the `--file-output` parameter, the `build` command writes the coordinates for build artifacts in an output JSON file, so you can reference this file from your deployment pipeline.

Skaffold can tag the container images it builds using different policies. The policy can be configured in the `tagPolicy` field in the `build` section of the `skaffold.yaml` configuration file. By default, the `gitCommit` policy is used, which tags the image according to the following rules:

- Skaffold uses the workspace's Git tag, if applicable, to tag images
- Skaffold uses the short commit if the workspace is on a Git commit instead of a tag
- Skaffold appends a `-dirty` suffix to the image tag if there are uncommitted changes

After the build, Skaffold can push the image to a remote registry or keep it only on the local cluster, depending on how you configure the `build` section of `skaffold.yaml`. If a local cluster is used, as in this case, there's no specific statement in the `build` section of the config file, and the image is not pushed to a remote registry but is stored in the local cluster Docker daemon cache.

Let's build our image:

1. Type the following command from your local repository directory:

    ```
    skaffold build --file-output artifacts.json
    ```

    If you open `artifacts.json`, you can see that despite the default tagging policy, the image is tagged using an immutable tag created from the image ID, not the short commit. This provides an immutable tag to reference the image, because the commit ID is not immutable. If the image were pushed to a remote registry, you could use the image digest instead.

2. Check the applied tags.

    Because in our case Skaffold is creating the image only locally, we use the following command:

    ```
    docker images
    ```

You can see in the output that Skaffold tagged the image with both the immutable tag and the short commit `sha` + `-dirty` suffix (because the workspace has uncommitted changes):

```
~/scdbook-skaffold$ docker images
REPOSITORY                     TAG                                                              IMAGE ID
scdongcp-app                   94745d90095b71346934d257f51e3d998a9c6ca7f2a7eff4244900b315ea99ea  94745d90095b
scdongcp-app                   df42591-dirty                                                    94745d90095b
```

Figure 2.3 – List of built images, with tags, in your repository

Now that you've built your application, it's time to test it, using Skaffold.

Testing your application using skaffold test

Skaffold can also run tests against your images after they're built and before they're deployed. Tests can be either of the following types:

- **Custom tests**: Any custom script as a unit test or a vulnerability scan on the image.

- **Container structure tests**: Validate the structural integrity of container images. See https://github.com/GoogleContainerTools/container-structure-test for more information.

Let's try a custom test:

1. Open your `skaffold.yaml` file and add the following section at the bottom:

   ```
   test:
   - image: scdongcp-app
     custom:
       - command: echo This is a custom test command
   ```

2. Execute this test using Skaffold:

   ```
   skaffold test --build-artifacts artifacts.json
   ```

   The test execution and the text are shown in the output:

```
galloro@cloudshell:~/scdbook-skaffold/single$ skaffold test --build-artifacts artifacts.json
Starting test...
Testing images...
Running custom test command: "echo This is a custom test command"
This is a custom test command
Command finished successfully.
```

Figure 2.4 – Output from the skaffold test command

Tests defined inside the `tests` section of the config file are also executed when you run `skaffold dev` or you execute the end-to-end pipeline with `skaffold run`, as we'll show later in this chapter.

Deploying your application using skaffold deploy

Now, let's see how to use Skaffold to deploy our applications.

The continuous development flow that you tried with `skaffold dev` already includes a deployment task to a dev environment, a local minikube cluster in our case, but you can use specific Skaffold functions after you build your application to manage deploying it using a continuous delivery pipeline:

1. Deploy the image to the minikube cluster:

   ```
   skaffold deploy -a artifacts.json
   ```

   This command does two things:

   - Hydrates the manifest in the `manifests` or `deployment` section of your `skaffold.yaml` file with the specific image tag from the `skaffold build` command you ran previously (present in the `artifacts.json` file in this case). This renders a final manifest.

   - Applies the rendered manifest to the target Kubernetes cluster (the local minikube cluster in this case).

2. Check that the image has been deployed successfully:

   ```
   kubectl get pods,deploy,svc
   ```

   This returns the following output:

```
galloro@cloudshell:~/scdbook-skaffold/single$ kubectl get pods,deploy,svc
NAME                               READY    STATUS      RESTARTS    AGE
pod/scdongcp-app-7745544966-nzmcn  1/1      Running     0           10s

NAME                             READY    UP-TO-DATE    AVAILABLE    AGE
deployment.apps/scdongcp-app     1/1      1             1            10s

NAME                        TYPE          CLUSTER-IP      EXTERNAL-IP    PORT(S)          AGE
service/kubernetes          ClusterIP     10.96.0.1       <none>         443/TCP          12m
service/scdongcp-app        LoadBalancer  10.109.137.0    <pending>      80:32255/TCP     10s
```

Figure 2.5 – Output from kubectl get pods, showing that the image is deployed

In this case, the image was deployed using kubectl because there's no `deploy` section in `skaffold.yaml`, only a `manifests` section pointing to the `rawYaml` manifest already in the application repository.

Deploying and rendering separately using skaffold render and skaffold apply

Besides directly deploying the image on a target runtime environment, you can also separate manifest rendering from app deployment. This technique is useful if you want to use a GitOps approach, where manifests are hydrated by Skaffold and committed to a Git repository, from which a GitOps tool applies them to target clusters.

Let's try that with our application:

1. Delete the previous deployment:

   ```
   skaffold delete
   ```

2. Render a hydrated Kubernetes resource file with the properly tagged image:

   ```
   skaffold render -a artifacts.json --output render.yaml
   ```

3. Open the render.yaml file to check that the container image is updated with the tag of the image we previously built, stored in the artifacts.json file.

4. Apply the rendered manifest directly:

   ```
   skaffold apply render.yaml
   ```

5. Check that the image has been deployed successfully:

   ```
   kubectl get pods,deploy,svc
   ```

   This returns the following output:

```
galloro@cloudshell:~/scdbook-skaffold/single$ kubectl get pods,deploy,svc
NAME                             READY   STATUS    RESTARTS   AGE
pod/scdongcp-app-7745544966-nzmcn  1/1   Running   0          10s

NAME                            READY   UP-TO-DATE   AVAILABLE   AGE
deployment.apps/scdongcp-app    1/1     1            1           10s

NAME                   TYPE           CLUSTER-IP      EXTERNAL-IP    PORT(S)        AGE
service/kubernetes     ClusterIP      10.96.0.1       <none>         443/TCP        12m
service/scdongcp-app   LoadBalancer   10.109.137.0    <pending>      80:32255/TCP   10s
```

Figure 2.6 – Output from kubectl get pods, showing that the image is deployed

Cloud Deploy uses this same separation between skaffold render and skaffold apply to separate release creation from rollout creation in each specific environment. We show this in detail in *Chapters 9* and *11*.

Running the end-to-end pipeline using skaffold run

Let's now see how to run the end-to-end pipeline (build, test, and deploy) with a single command—skaffold run:

1. Again, let's delete the previous deployment using the following command:

   ```
   skaffold delete
   ```

2. Delete the artifacts.json file:

   ```
   rm artifacts.json
   ```

3.   Run the pipeline:

```
skaffold run --tail
```

For the run command, we use the --tail option, so we can see the standard output:

```
Generating tags...
 - scdongcp-app -> scdongcp-app:62d1c30-dirty
Checking cache...
 - scdongcp-app: Found. Tagging
Starting test...
Testing images...
Running custom test command: "echo This is a custom test command"
This is a custom test command
Command finished successfully.
Tags used in deployment:
 - scdongcp-app -> scdongcp-app:f5e73de0662c088407021f7129a7ebd78715670d796c3f1aed6ebb5e4a62d126
Starting deploy...
 - service/scdongcp-app created
 - deployment.apps/scdongcp-app created
Waiting for deployments to stabilize...
 - deployment/scdongcp-app is ready.
Deployments stabilized in 1.149 second
Press Ctrl+C to exit
[scdongcp-app] 2023/02/12 17:15:51 scd-on-gcp app server ready, running in target: dev
```

Figure 2.7 – Output from the skaffold run command

4.   Press *Ctrl + C* to stop streaming log messages.

Now that you've run the build-test-deploy pipeline, let's look at how to manage your pipeline across different environments.

Managing deployment in different environments

This section describes how to use Skaffold to manage deploying your application through different environments, applying different configurations each time.

To do that, we use Kustomize, Skaffold profiles, two Google Kubernetes Engine clusters, and an Artifact Registry repository.

Introduction to Kustomize

As mentioned at the beginning of this chapter, Skaffold supports different deployers, such as kubectl, Helm, and Kustomize. For this example, we will use Kustomize.

Kustomize is a tool for Kubernetes that lets you customize resource manifest files without having to edit the original files. You create a kustomization file, which specifies the changes you want to make to the original YAML files, and Kustomize applies those changes, leaving the original files untouched.

With Kustomize, you can define a base configuration and then apply patches and transformations to generate customized configurations for different environments or use cases.

To see an example of how this works, let's move to another folder in our repository:

```
cd ../multi
```

This is another application repository. It's for an application that has the same code as the previous one but with different Skaffold and Kubernetes configurations for different environments.

Let's look at the file structure in the `kubernetes` folder. This time, the structure is more complex than the single file in the repository we used in previous examples. There are four folders—one `base` folder and one for each deployment environment: `dev`, `qa`, and `prod`:

Figure 2.8 – Repository folder structure under kubernetes

This is how Kustomize works—in each folder, there is a `kustomization.yaml` file defining how a target manifest for that folder is built. The `kustomization.yaml` file in the `base` folder looks like the following:

```
apiVersion: kustomize.config.k8s.io/v1beta1
kind: Kustomization
resources:
  - deployment.yaml
```

This means that for anything using Kustomize, the `deployment.yaml` file defines Kubernetes resources in this folder. That file contains all the specifications to define the Kubernetes Deployment and Service resources, as in the previous example, except that the `TARGET` environment variable is missing in this case.

Let's look at the `kustomization.yaml` file inside the qa folder:

```
apiVersion: kustomize.config.k8s.io/v1beta1
kind: Kustomization
bases:
  - ../base
patches:
 - path: target.yaml
```

In this case, the resulting manifest for this folder is the result of merging what's in the `base` folder with the `target.yaml` file in the qa folder. This adds the `TARGET` variable with the value qa to the Deployment. This variable is printed by the app on the web page and logged to standard output:

```
apiVersion: apps/v1
kind: Deployment
metadata:
  name: scdongcp-app
spec:
  template:
    spec:
      containers:
        - name: scdongcp-app
          env:
            - name: TARGET
              value: qa
```

The `kustomization.yaml` file inside the prod folder has exactly the same contents, so for this folder also, the Kubernetes Deployment configuration will be the merge of `target.yaml` with the contents of the base folder. Let's look at `target.yaml` in the prod folder:

```
apiVersion: apps/v1
kind: Deployment
metadata:
  name: scdongcp-app
spec:
  replicas: 3
  template:
    spec:
      containers:
        - name: scdongcp-app
```

```
        env:
          - name: TARGET
            value: prod
```

Here, you can see that the TARGET variable has the value prod, and the number of replicas for the deployment is 3, while the number of replicas in the Deployment in the base folder is 1. This shows how you might need a different capacity configuration in production.

The target.yaml file in the dev folder adds the TARGET variable with the value dev as we had in the original file in the repository used in previous sections.

Skaffold profiles

You can use Skaffold profiles to apply different configurations to different environments. You can also use it to have multiple ways to perform a task, which you select using a command-line parameter.

You configure profiles in the profiles section of skaffold.yaml. Each profile has its own build, test, and deploy sections.

You can activate a profile using the -p command-line option, or by specifying a kubeconfig context, environment variable, or skaffold command defined inside the profile in skaffold.yaml.

Let's look at the skaffold.yaml file contained in the multi folder we are in:

```
apiVersion: skaffold/v4beta3
kind: Config
build:
  artifacts:
    - image: scdongcp-app
      docker:
        dockerfile: Dockerfile
manifests:
  kustomize:
    paths:
      - kubernetes/dev
profiles:
  - name: qa
    manifests:
      kustomize:
        paths:
          - kubernetes/qa
  - name: prod
    manifests:
      kustomize:
        paths:
          - kubernetes/prod
```

As you can see, it's similar to the one we generated when we initialized the previous repository. But this file includes a `deploy` section that uses Kustomize with the resources in the `kubernetes/dev` folder (used by default if no `profile` parameter is used). This configuration also has two profiles, `qa` and `prod`, which use Kustomize to leverage the manifests in the qa and `prod` folders, respectively. The manifests are hydrated using the Kustomize merge behavior we explained.

Google Cloud resources you need

For this example, we need two remote clusters, in addition to our minikube cluster. We're using Google Kubernetes Engine for this, plus a remote container repository in Artifact Registry.

You can create the two clusters from command line using the gcloud CLI. If you don't have it, you can install it as described here—`https://cloud.google.com/sdk/docs/install`:

1. After you install the gcloud CLI, authenticate it with your account.
2. Set your default Google Cloud project and region/zone.
3. Create the clusters:

```
gcloud container clusters create qa-cluster --zone=us-central1-b
--async && gcloud container clusters create prod-cluster
--zone=us-central1-b --async
```

This command uses the `us-central1-b` zone, but you can use whatever Google Cloud zone has Google Kubernetes Engine capacity.

4. Create your Artifact Registry repository:

```
gcloud artifacts repositories create scdbook-repo --repository-
format=docker --location us-central1 --description "Docker
repository for Secure Continuous Delivery Book"
```

This command uses the `us-central1` region, but you can use whatever Google Cloud region works for you.

5. Configure Docker authentication to Artifact Registry:

```
gcloud auth configure-docker us-central1-docker.pkg.dev
```

6. Check that your clusters have been provisioned:

```
gcloud container clusters list
```

Rerun this command until you see that both clusters have STATUS RUNNING.

7. Export your project ID:

```
export PROJECT_ID=$(gcloud config get-value project)
```

8. Get credentials and create kubeconfig contexts for your clusters:

```
gcloud container clusters get-credentials qa-cluster --zone
us-central1-b --project $PROJECT_ID
gcloud container clusters get-credentials prod-cluster --zone
us-central1-b --project $PROJECT_ID
```

9. Get the kubeconfig contexts:

```
kubectl config get-contexts
```

This command produces the following output:

```
galloro@cloudshell:~/scdbook-skaffold/multi$ kubectl config get-contexts
CURRENT   NAME                                           CLUSTER                                        AUTHINFO                                       NAMESPACE
*         gke_galloro-demos_us-central1-b_prod-cluster   gke_galloro-demos_us-central1-b_prod-cluster   gke_galloro-demos_us-central1-b_prod-cluster
          gke_galloro-demos_us-central1-b_qa-cluster     gke_galloro-demos_us-central1-b_qa-cluster     gke_galloro-demos_us-central1-b_qa-cluster
          minikube                                       minikube                                       minikube                                       default
```

Figure 2.9 – Output from kubectl command, showing Kubernetes contexts

The contexts for the clusters you just created are named with the formats gke_$PROJECT_ID_ us-central1-b_qa-cluster and gke_$PROJECT_ID_us-central1-b_prod-cluster.

Deploying your application to different environments

To deploy your application to a progression of different runtime environments, perform the following steps:

1. Build the image again from the current source:

```
skaffold build --file-output artifacts.json --default-repo
us-central1-docker.pkg.dev/$PROJECT_ID/scdbook-repo
```

The --default-repo parameter tells Skaffold to push our image to the repository we created, because we're not using a local cluster this time.

2. Deploy your app in your qa-cluster using the qa profile:

```
skaffold deploy -a artifacts.json -p qa --kube-
context=gke_${PROJECT_ID}_us-central1-b_qa-cluster
```

The -p option tells Skaffold to use the qa profile defined in the file, so it hydrates the manifests using the Kustomize configuration in the qa folder. The --kube-context parameter tells Skaffold to deploy to qa-cluster.

3. Check whether the application has been deployed:

```
kubectl --context=gke_${PROJECT_ID}_us-central1-b_qa-cluster get
pods,svc
```

This command produces the following output:

```
galloro@cloudshell:~/scdbook-skaffold/multi (galloro-demos)$ kubectl --context=gke_${PROJECT_ID}_us-central1-b_qa-cluster get pods,svc
NAME                                  READY   STATUS    RESTARTS   AGE
pod/scdongcp-app-779d54c57d-dcql5     1/1     Running   0          6m32s

NAME                       TYPE           CLUSTER-IP     EXTERNAL-IP       PORT(S)        AGE
service/kubernetes         ClusterIP      10.16.0.1      <none>            443/TCP        13h
service/scdongcp-app       LoadBalancer   10.16.15.124   104.154.160.160   80:32475/TCP   6m34s
```

Figure 2.10 – Output from kubectl get pods, showing that the image is deployed in qa

4. Get the EXTERNAL-IP value of service/scdongcp-app (104.154.160.160, in this example), and access it using your browser or curl.

    The output will be as follows:

    ```
    scd-on-gcp app running in target: qa!!
    ```

    This output shows qa!! because the TARGET variable has the value qa.

5. Promote the application to the production environment using a command similar to the last one, but using the prod profile and targeting prod-cluster:

    ```
    skaffold deploy -a artifacts.json -p prod --kube-
    context=gke_${PROJECT_ID}_us-central1-b_prod-cluster
    ```

6. Check whether the application has been deployed:

    ```
    kubectl --context=gke_${PROJECT_ID}_us-central1-b_prod-cluster
    get pods,svc
    ```

    This command produces the following output:

```
galloro@cloudshell:~/scdbook-skaffold/multi (galloro-demos)$ kubectl --context=gke_${PROJECT_ID}_us-central1-b_prod-cluster get pods,svc
NAME                                  READY   STATUS    RESTARTS   AGE
pod/scdongcp-app-895dc775c-8r7hn      1/1     Running   0          4m33s
pod/scdongcp-app-895dc775c-dnfhq      1/1     Running   0          4m33s
pod/scdongcp-app-895dc775c-pck67      1/1     Running   0          4m33s

NAME                       TYPE           CLUSTER-IP    EXTERNAL-IP     PORT(S)        AGE
service/kubernetes         ClusterIP      10.40.0.1     <none>          443/TCP        13h
service/scdongcp-app       LoadBalancer   10.40.8.200   34.29.220.243   80:30537/TCP   4m35s
```

Figure 2.11 – Output from kubectl get pods, showing that the image is deployed in prod

    This time, the deployment has three Pods, because the Kustomize configuration added replicas: 3 for prod.

7. Get the EXTERNAL-IP value of service/scdongcp-app (34.29.220.243, in this example), and access it using your browser or curl.

    The output will be as follows:

    ```
    scd-on-gcp app running in target: prod!!
    ```

    This time, it shows prod!! because the TARGET variable has the value prod.

You've now seen how Skaffold can use profiles and Kustomize to apply different configurations to deploy the same application to different environments. This understanding is important because Cloud Deploy also uses Skaffold profiles and Kustomize, or Helm, to promote your release across different environments.

Cleaning up

In the following chapters, you will need the GCP project, the Artifact Registry repository you created, and the local copy of the book's Git repository, so we suggest you keep them. We suggest that you just delete your Kubernetes clusters to avoid incurring costs and, if you prefer and are not using Google Cloud Shell, clean up your local environment.

Deleting your Google Kubernetes Engine clusters

Use the following to delete the Google Kubernetes Engine clusters:

```
gcloud container clusters delete qa-cluster --zone=us-central1-b
--async && gcloud container clusters delete prod-cluster --zone=us-
central1-b --async
```

Cleaning up your local environment

How you clean up your local environment depends on your operating system and whether you will reuse the environment for the exercises in the following chapters:

1. Stop minikube:

    ```
    minikube stop
    ```

2. Uninstall minikube (only if you're not using Google Cloud Shell and you don't need minikube anymore):

    ```
    minikube stop; minikube delete
    ```

3. If you are not using Google Cloud Shell and will not use the same local machine for the following chapters, you can delete your local copy of the repository:

    ```
    cd ~
    rm -rf   Secure-Continuous-Delivery-on-Google-Cloud
    ```

Let us summarize the chapter now.

Summary

You've now seen Skaffold's capabilities and architecture, and you've practiced how to build, test, and deploy using Skaffold, including doing so continuously while coding, in order to immediately see the results of each change you made.

Because Skaffold is used behind the scenes by Cloud Code and Cloud Deploy, and we use it throughout the book to manage various aspects of a continuous delivery pipeline, the information in this chapter is foundational for the rest of this book.

In the next chapter, we will look at how to use Cloud Code for software development.

3

Developing and Testing with Cloud Code

Cloud Code is a set of extensions for popular **integrated development environments (IDEs)**. Cloud Code gives developers a suite of tools to build, test, and deploy applications on Google Cloud, making it easy for developers to write, debug, and deploy their applications without having to leave their IDE.

As an IDE extension, Cloud Code is at the beginning of your secure source-to-production workflow. Skaffold, which you learned about in the previous chapter, is an integrated component of Cloud Code.

In this chapter, you will learn how to use Cloud Code to do the following:

- Continuously deploy and test locally while you code
- Create a GKE cluster from your editor
- Continuously deploy and test a Kubernetes app remotely while you code
- Debug

Technical requirements

The instructions in this chapter are based on Cloud Code for Cloud Shell. To perform them, you need the Google Cloud project and resources you created in *Chapter 2*. In addition to that, you should enable the Cloud AI Companion APIs.

The code used in this chapter is available in the folder named ch3 of the book repository at https://github.com/PacktPublishing/Secure-Continuous-Delivery-on-Google-Cloud.

For this chapter, we will use an application written in Java using Spring Boot.

About Cloud Code

Cloud Code is available as an extension for Visual Studio Code and JetBrains IDEs, such as IntelliJ IDEA, PyCharm, and GoLand. In addition to being an extension to each of those popular IDEs, Cloud Code is built into the Cloud Shell editor, a web-based IDE built on **Theia** (`https://theia-ide.org`). Also, it's available in Visual Studio Code and JetBrains IDEs from within Cloud Workstations, which we describe in *Chapter 4*.

Cloud Code helps these IDEs support the full development cycle, from writing code to continuously building and deploying the application on Kubernetes or Cloud Run. Cloud Code includes ready-to-use code and configuration samples and works with many popular programming languages.

Cloud Code uses Skaffold to run and debug your application, but with Cloud Code, you interact with these capabilities through your IDE as opposed to by using Skaffold commands directly.

With Cloud Code, you can deploy your application to Kubernetes, Cloud Run, or Cloud Functions. In this chapter, we'll deploy to Kubernetes.

Cloud Code's capabilities include the following:

- **YAML authoring support**: Cloud Code includes inline documentation, snippets, code completion, and schema validation.

- **Remote debugging**: You can place breakpoints and step through the code, hover over variables to view their properties, and view container logs.

- **Productivity improvements**: Cloud Code includes *explorers* for Kubernetes, Cloud Run, and Cloud Functions to help you visualize, monitor, and view information about your cluster or service without having to run CLI commands.

To start, let's see what it's like to write code while Cloud Code redeploys the application for each change we make, so we can test the results.

Continuously deploying and testing locally while you code

Similarly to what we did in *Chapter 2*, let's now use Cloud Code to deploy an app locally, and test it as we write code:

1. Open Google Cloud Shell from the Google Cloud console or at `shell.cloud.google.com`.

    Be sure to authenticate with an account that has permission to create and manage **Google Kubernetes Engine (GKE)** and Artifact Registry resources.

2. If you didn't use Cloud Shell for the exercises in *Chapter 2*, you need to clone the code for the exercise:

```
git clone https://github.com/PacktPublishing/Secure-Continuous-
Delivery-on-Google-Cloud
cd Secure-Continuous-Delivery-on-Google-Cloud-/ch3
```

3. To open the Cloud Shell editor and add the application folder to this workspace, run the following command from the ch3 folder:

```
cloudshell workspace .
```

The Cloud Shell Editor opens, with the file system **EXPLORER** in the left pane, so you can browse the app folder content:

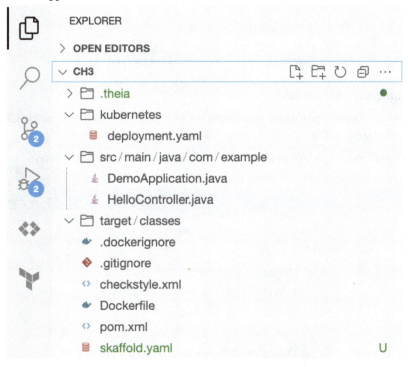

Figure 3.1 – The Cloud Code EXPLORER view

The folder contains code, project files, a Dockerfile, and a Kubernetes manifest for a Java-based application using Spring Boot.

The program prints on a web page the text scd-on-gcp app running in target:: %s, where %s is a TARGET variable that is defined as dev inside the kubernetes/deployment.yaml file.

4.   Click **Cloud Code** in the status bar and then select **Control minikube**:

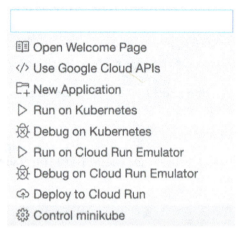

Figure 3.2 – Cloud Code status bar menu

5.   Select **minikube** and then **Start**.

6.   If prompted to authorize Cloud Code to use your credentials to call the Google Cloud API, click **Authorize**, and wait for minikube to finish starting.

7.   Click **Cloud Code**, again in the status bar, and then select **Run on Kubernetes**:

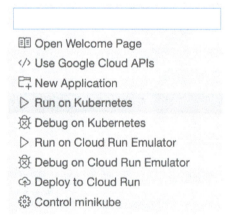

Figure 3.3 – Cloud Code status bar menu

This feature uses skaffold dev to continuously deploy your application on a target Kubernetes cluster (minikube in this case), as you saw in *Chapter 2*. Because the application folder we're using doesn't have a skaffold.yaml file, a configuration page is displayed asking you to choose your preferred builder and its settings. Keep the defaults, which use a local Docker builder using the provided Dockerfile, deploy to the minikube cluster, and enable port forwarding.

8. Click **Run**.

    If prompted, confirm that you want to use the current minikube context. You will see the build and deployment progress in the **DEVELOPMENT SESSIONS** view in the **CLOUD CODE** section of the left pane:

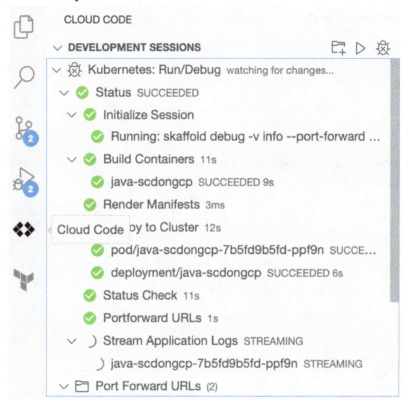

Figure 3.4 – The DEVELOPMENT SESSIONS view

Clicking different nodes in the **DEVELOPMENT SESSIONS** view displays logs, in the output pane, pertaining to the selected deployment phase.

9. After your **Deploy to Cluster**, **Status Check**, and **Portforward URLs** nodes are green, click on **service | java-scdongcp-external** in the **Port Forward URLs** folder.

    You will see the app web page:

scd-on-gcp app running in target: dev !!

Figure 3.5 – Web page output showing that the app is successfully deployed to dev

Now, let's try to update the application to see the change implemented immediately in the deployment on the minikube cluster:

10. Click on the **EXPLORER** section on the left pane.

11. Open the `HelloController.java` file inside `src/main/java/com/example`, and change the message on line 16 to the following:

```
        return String.format("scd-on-gcp app updated in target:
%s !!", target);)
```

12. Navigate again to the **Cloud Code** section to see the nodes updating.

13. Refresh the browser tab with the application page to see that the text is updated:

```
scd-on-gcp app updated in target: dev!!
```

This is the same flow you saw in *Chapter 2*. In fact, Cloud Code uses `skaffold dev` to watch your code and build and redeploy it if any change occurs. But with Cloud Code, you do that directly from your IDE.

Checking application logs from your editor

Now, let's look at the application logs from within your editor:

1. Click **Cloud Code** in the status bar, then select **Open Deployment Logs**.

   This view allows you to filter and navigate the logs for your app:

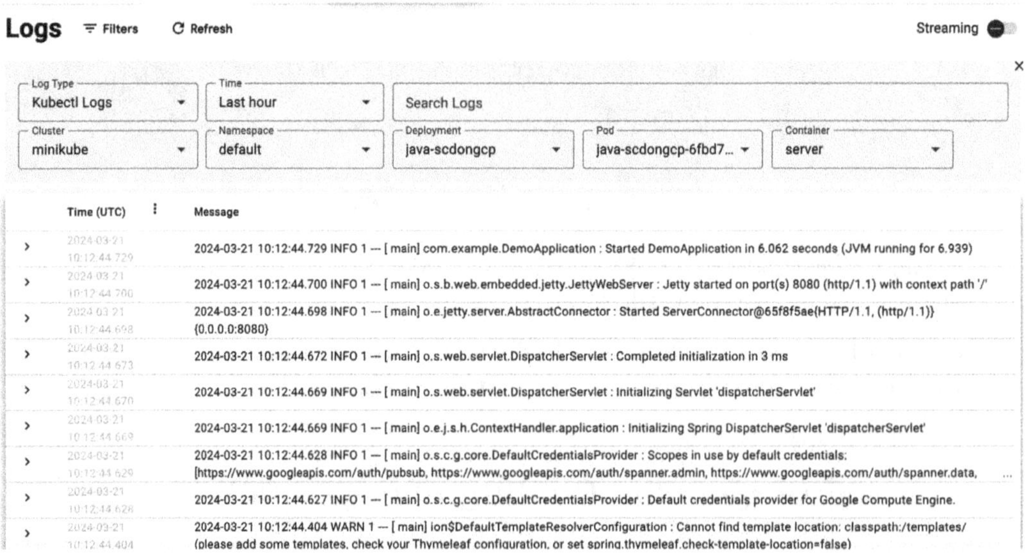

Figure 3.6 – Web page output showing that the updated app is successfully redeployed

2. Click on **Run | Stop** to stop Cloud Code from watching your code for changes:

Figure 3.7 – Stop Cloud Code from watching for changes

3. Click **Yes** when prompted to clean up resources.

Now that we've tried continuously deploying and testing locally while coding, let's start working with remote resources on Google Cloud. First, we'll create a GKE cluster.

Creating a GKE cluster from your editor

With Cloud Code, you can not only run the `skaffold dev` flow directly from your IDE but also interact directly with Google Cloud resources, so you don't need to switch context too much while you're coding.

In this section, you'll create a GKE cluster to deploy your application to:

1. In the Cloud Shell terminal pane, set your current project:

    ```
    gcloud config set project PROJECT_ID
    ```

    PROJECT_ID is the ID of the Google Cloud project you're using for this chapter.

2. Create the GKE cluster:

    A. In the **Kubernetes** section, in Cloud Code, click on the + sign to add a cluster to the **KubeConfig**:

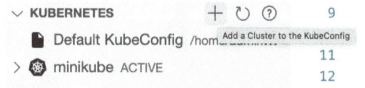

Figure 3.8 – Kubernetes sub-menu

B. Click **Google Kubernetes Engine**:

Choose a Platform (1/2)

|

Minikube

Google Kubernetes Engine

Other

Figure 3.9 – Kubernetes platform options

C. In **Select a Google Cloud Project**, select the project you want to use, then select + to create a new GKE cluster. You can choose between **Standard** and **Autopilot**. For our purposes, let's choose **Autopilot**:

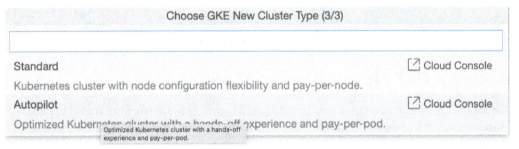

Choose GKE New Cluster Type (3/3)

Standard   ☐ Cloud Console
Kubernetes cluster with node configuration flexibility and pay-per-node.
Autopilot   ☐ Cloud Console
Optimized Kubernetes cluster with a hands-off experience and pay-per-pod.

Figure 3.10 – Kubernetes cluster type options

The Google Cloud console opens.

D. Choose the cluster name and region and click **CREATE**. Cluster creation takes a few minutes:

Cluster basics

Create an Autopilot cluster by specifying a name and region. After the cluster is created, you can deploy your workload through Kubernetes and we'll take care of the rest, including:

✓ **Nodes:** Automated node provisioning, scaling, and maintenance

✓ **Networking:** VPC-native traffic routing for public or private clusters

✓ **Security:** Shielded GKE Nodes and Workload Identity

✓ **Telemetry:** Cloud Operations logging and monitoring

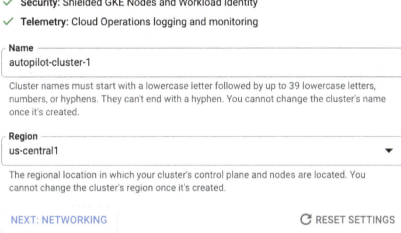

Figure 3.11 – Cluster creation, shown in the Google Cloud console

3. After the cluster is created, go back to the **Cloud Shell Editor** tab, and click **Refresh**.

4. When the cluster you created appears, select it.

    It's added to your `kubeconfig` file (and the **KUBERNETES** section in Cloud Code) as the active context:

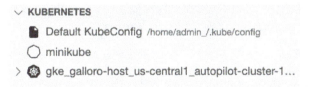

Figure 3.12 – Kubernetes platform options

Now that you have a remote GKE cluster, let's try continuously deploying to that remote cluster while you write code.

Continuously deploying and testing a Kubernetes app remotely while you code

Follow these steps to see the results of your work while you write code:

1. Click **Cloud Code** in the status bar and then select **Run on Kubernetes**.

2. When prompted, click **Use current context**. This should be the context of your newly created GKE cluster:

> The current context has changed since this config was last used.
>
> Use current context (gke_galloro-host_us-central1_autopilot-cluster-1)
>
> Switch current context

Figure 3.13 – Selecting the Kubernetes context

3. In **Choose Image Repository**, type the path of the Artifact Registry repository you created:

> Choose Image Repository (1/1)
>
> |
>
> Enter the address of an image repository
>
> Specify a custom address such as docker.io or non-Google Cloud registries

Figure 3.14 – Choose Image Repository

This will be `us-central1-docker.pkg.dev/PROJECT_ID/scdbook-repo`, where PROJECT_ID is your Google Cloud project ID:

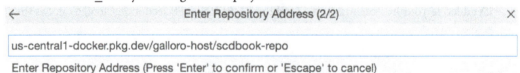

Figure 3.15 – Repository address

The build starts and the application is deployed to the GKE cluster you created. For a newly created GKE Autopilot cluster, this could take a couple of minutes while Autopilot allocates the needed resources.

4. After your **Deploy to Cluster**, **Status Check**, and **Portforward URLs** nodes are green, in the `Port Forward URLs` folder, click on **service | java-scdongcp-external**:

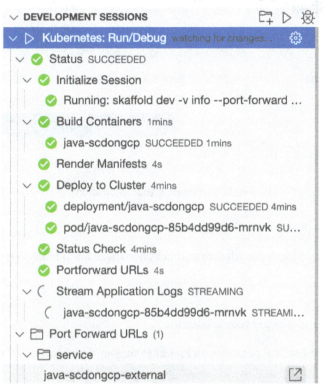

Figure 3.16 – Session information

You will see the app web page:

scd-on-gcp app running in target: dev !!

Figure 3.17 – Web page output showing that the app is deployed in dev

If you change your code, your app is immediately rebuilt and deployed, as you saw in the previous example using minikube.

5.   Click on **Run | Stop** to stop Cloud Code from watching your code for changes:

 Cloud Shell Editor

Figure 3.18 – Stopping your application

6.   Click **Yes** when prompted to clean up resources.

Now that we've tried continuous development for a Kubernetes application, let's look at debugging.

Debugging

You can use Cloud Code to debug your application:

1.   Click **Cloud Code** in the status bar, and select **Debug on Kubernetes**:

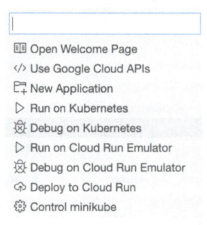

Figure 3.19 – Selecting the Debug on Kubernetes option

Cloud Code deploys your app in debug mode to your GKE cluster, remembering the choices you made before.

2. In the `HelloController.java` file, set a breakpoint at line 16 by clicking the blank space to the left of the line number.

    Line 16 is the line that has the return statement you updated previously. A red indicator shows that the breakpoint is set.

```
 HelloController.java  ×

src  >  main  >  java  >  com  >  example  >   HelloController.java  >   HelloController  >   hello()
  1     package com.example;
  2
  3     import org.springframework.web.bind.annotation.GetMapping;
  4     import org.springframework.web.bind.annotation.RestController;
  5     import org.springframework.beans.factory.annotation.Value;
  6
  7     @RestController
  8     public class HelloController {
  9
 10         @Value("${target:local}")
 11         String target;
 12
 13         @GetMapping("/")
 14         public String hello()
 15         {
●16             return String.format("scd-on-gcp app updated in target: %s !!", target);
 17         }
 18     }
 19
```

Figure 3.20 – A Java file with a breakpoint

3. Go back to the **Cloud Code** section, and in the `Port Forward URLs` folder, click on **service | java-scdongcp-external**.

Important note

The debugger stops the process at the breakpoint so you can investigate the variables and state of the application:

---

4.   Show the **DEBUG** view.

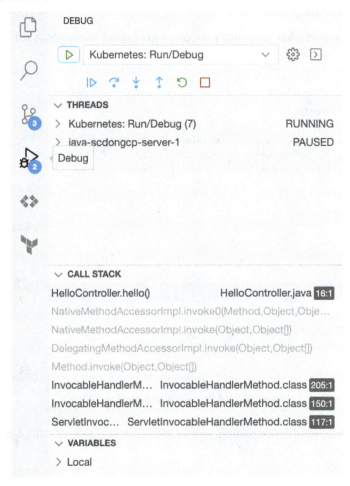

Figure 3.21 – The Debug view in Cloud Code

5. Click down into the **VARIABLES** section until you find the `target` variable:

Figure 3.22 – Available variables

Notice that the current value is dev. This is from the `deployment.yaml` manifest file.

6. Double-click the variable name target, and in the popup, change the value to Debug. Click **OK**.

Figure 3.23 – Set a value for your variable

7. Click **Continue** in the **DEBUG** control panel:

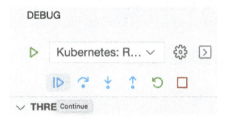

Figure 3.24 – Click to continue debugging

8. Refresh your browser to see the updated value:

scd-on-gcp app updated in target: Debug !!

Figure 3.25 – Web page output showing that the app is updated in Debug

9. Remove the breakpoint by clicking the red indicator to the left of the line number.

10. Click **Stop** in the **DEBUG** control panel to stop your debug session.

Figure 3.26 – DEBUG control panel

We've tried using Cloud Code for local and remote continuous deployment, and we've tried debugging on the remote cluster. Next, let's see how you can code using assistance from Duet AI.

Code with AI assistance

In this section, you will experiment with some ways to use Duet AI for Developers in Cloud Code to get help and generate code. At the time of writing, Duet AI for Developers is in preview and is still not enabled in Cloud Shell, so we will use the Cloud Code extension on a locally installed Visual Studio Code.

At the time of writing, Duet AI for Developers must be explicitly enabled in Cloud Code. If this is still the case for you, you will need to navigate to **Settings** | **Extensions** | **Cloud Code** and enable it.

Getting help to understand code

Let's ask Duet AI to explain existing code to us:

1. Clone the book repository in your local environment and add the ch3 folder to your Visual Studio Code workspace.

2. In Visual Studio Code, open the `HelloController.java` file inside `src/main/java/com/example`. Select the **@GetMapping** method, click on the lightbulb, and select **Explain this**.

Figure 3.27 – Duet AI smart actions: Explain this

The chat pane will open on the left and Duet AI will provide an explanation of the code, like the following one:

The code you provided is a simple Spring Boot controller. It has a single method, `hello`, which is annotated with `@GetMapping("/")`. This means that the method will be called when a GET request is made to the root URL of the application.

The `hello` method returns a String. The String is formatted using the `String.format()` method. The first argument to `String.format()` is a format string. The format string contains a placeholder for the value of the `target` variable. The second argument to `String.format()` is a variable number of arguments that are used to replace the placeholders in the format string.

In this case, the format string is "%s !!". The first argument to `String.format()` is the value of the `target` variable. The value of the `target` variable is "local". So, the String that is returned by the `hello` method is "scd-on-gcp app running in target: local !!".

Figure 3.28 – Example of Duet AI code explanation

3. It's also possible to open or close Duet AI chat directly from the activity bar of Visual Studio Code, click on the Duet AI icon to close it, then click it again to reopen it.

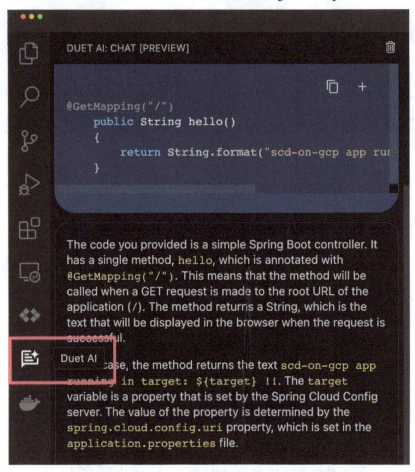

Figure 3.29 – Duet AI icon in the activity bar

4. In the chat prompt, write `generate tests for my code`. Duet AI will propose some test code, as you can see in the following example screenshot (your result might be different):

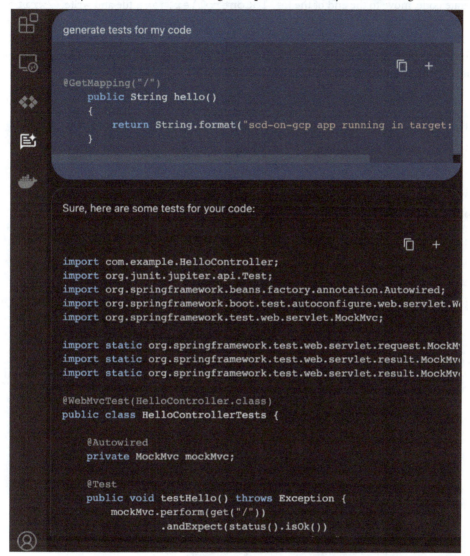

Figure 3.30 – Example test code generated by Duet AI

In this section, we saw how Duet AI can help you to better understand existing code and generate tests for it. Now, let's see how Duet AI can generate code.

Generating code

To generate code, move to the end of the `HelloController.java` file and write `//write a class to get the value of the target variable from the input in a form`. Then, press *Enter*. Grayed-out code should start to appear below. If you are satisfied with it, press *Tab* to accept it. Additional code will be generated. Press *Tab* until class generation completes, as in the following example (your result might be different):

```
//write a class to get the value of the target variable from the input
in a form
// Form.java
package com.example;


import org.springframework.stereotype.Controller;
import org.springframework.ui.Model;
import org.springframework.web.bind.annotation.GetMapping;
import org.springframework.web.bind.annotation.PostMapping;


@Controller
public class Form {


    @GetMapping("/")
    public String form(Model model) {
        model.addAttribute("target", "local");
        return "form";
    }


    @PostMapping("/")
    public String form(Model model, String target) {
        model.addAttribute("target", target);
        return "form";
    }
}
```

You have now seen some of the ways AI can help you in coding.

Cleaning up

To avoid incurring costs, delete the GKE cluster you created. You can do that on your `autopilot-cluster-1` using the same command you used in the *Cleaning up* section in *Chapter 2*, or by following the documentation at `https://cloud.google.com/kubernetes-engine/docs/how-to/deleting-a-cluster`.

Summary

You've now seen what Cloud Code can do. You've seen how to continuously deploy and test an application on a local Kubernetes installation while you write code. You've also seen how to deploy the app remotely. You've also tried debugging and getting assistance from Duet AI for your code.

In the next chapter, we'll show how to secure your code using Cloud Workstations.

4

Securing Your Code with Cloud Workstations

Cloud workstations are fully managed developer workstations hosted on Google Cloud. Cloud engineers or administrators can centrally create, manage, and update these workstations and make them accessible to developers from any device.

In this chapter, we describe how an administrator can preconfigure Cloud workstations, and how developers can use them to work on their code using their preferred IDE.

This chapter includes the following sections:

- Introduction to Cloud Workstations
- Configuring workstations for developers
- Customizing Cloud workstations
- Coding in Cloud Workstations

Technical requirements

To perform the tasks in this chapter, you need a Google Cloud project with billing or a free trial enabled. You can reuse the project you created in *Chapter 2*. In this case, you need to enable the Cloud Workstations API, in addition to the APIs you already enabled.

Your Google account needs the Cloud Workstations Admin or Project Editor role in that project, which you should have from following the instructions in the previous chapters.

The code used in this chapter is available in the ch4 folder of the book repository: `https://github.com/PacktPublishing/Secure-Continuous-Delivery-on-Google-Cloud/tree/main/ch4`.

Introduction to Cloud Workstations

Administrators create and configure Cloud workstations using the Google Cloud console, Google Cloud SDK, or Cloud Workstations API. Developers access their workstations remotely through a web browser or other means, as described in this chapter. With this approach, developers can be productive quickly, access pre-assembled environments for their language of choice, and have enough horsepower when they need it, while at the same time, operators can provide secure and consistent environments.

To start, let's take a look at the components of the **Cloud Workstations** service.

Cloud Workstations architecture

The main architectural components of Cloud Workstations are as follows:

- **Workstations** are backed by Compute Engine VM instances running in your project and your VPC.

  The creation, life cycle, and software deployment for these VMs are managed by a component called a controller. Software inside Cloud Workstation VMs is deployed in a container image.

- **Workstation clusters** define a group of workstations in a particular region and the VPC network they're attached to. Each cluster includes a controller and a gateway.

- **The controller** manages the life cycle of the VMs on which Cloud Workstations runs.

- **Gateway** receives traffic from clients and forwards it to a VM gateway component, running as a container inside each VM, through Private Service Connect.

- **Workstation configuration** holds common settings for a group of workstations.

- **Persistent disks** are mapped to the workstation user's home directory to persist data because the workstation's boot disk is ephemeral.

The following diagram shows the components of the Cloud Workstations service and how they fit together:

Cloud Workstations Architecture

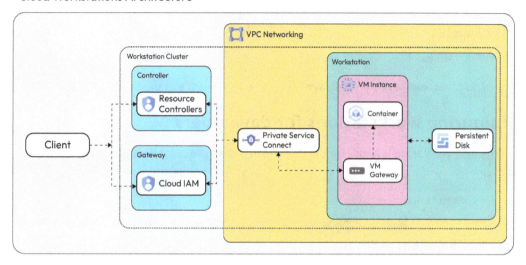

Figure 4.1 – Cloud Workstations architecture

Because Cloud Workstations runs inside your Google Cloud project and VPC, you can easily enable access for developers to your organization resources running inside them.

Cloud Workstations provides several container images that include the following preconfigured **Integrated Development Environments (IDEs)**:

- Base Editor: Built on top of Code-OSS with Cloud Code extensions, accessible using a web browser or SSH

- JetBrains IDEs, with Cloud Code extensions, accessible through JetBrains Gateway:

  - IntelliJ IDEA Ultimate IDE

  - PyCharm Professional IDE

  - GoLand IDE

  - WebStorm IDE

- JetBrains IDEs, without Cloud Code extensions, accessible through JetBrains Gateway:

  - CLion IDE

  - PhpStorm IDE

  - Rider IDE

  - RubyMine IDE

Cloud workstations can be customized, as we will show in the next sections.

Configuring workstations for developers

In this section, you'll learn how to create and configure workstations for developers. There are three main steps:

1. Create a workstation cluster.

2. Create two workstation configurations, with common settings for two different developer teams.

3. Create one or more workstations.

Let's start with the first step, which is creating the workstation cluster.

Creating a workstation cluster

In this section, you will see how to create a workstation cluster:

1. To start creating a cluster, go to the **Google Cloud Console** menu, and select **Cloud Workstations | Cluster management** and click on + **CREATE**.

2. Type a cluster name in the **Name** field. For the name selection, consider that clusters define a group of workstations in a particular region, the VPC network they're attached to, and whether they're accessible from the internet (public gateway) or only from the VPC network they are attached to (private gateway). For our example, we will use the name us-central-default-public.

3. Select a region in the **Region** field under **Location**. In our case, this is us-central1 (Iowa).

4. In the **Labels** section, if you click + **ADD LABEL**, you can add labels to your clusters that propagate to underlying Compute Engine resources and are also visible in billing so can be helpful to attribute costs to different departments or teams. Do not set any label.

5. In the **Network** section, under **Network settings**, fill the **Network** field with the name of your VPC and the subnet you want your workstations to attach to.

6. Under **Gateway type**, choose **Public gateway** to make your workstations accessible from the internet, or **Private gateway** to make them accessible only from the VPC they're connected to.

Choose **Public gateway** for this example. If you were to choose **Private gateway**, you would need to create a Private Service Connect endpoint to connect your cluster to your VPC, as described in the Cloud Workstations documentation: `https://cloud.google.com/workstations/docs/configure-vpc-service-controls-private-gateway#connecting_to_workstations`.

Your final configuration will look like the following:

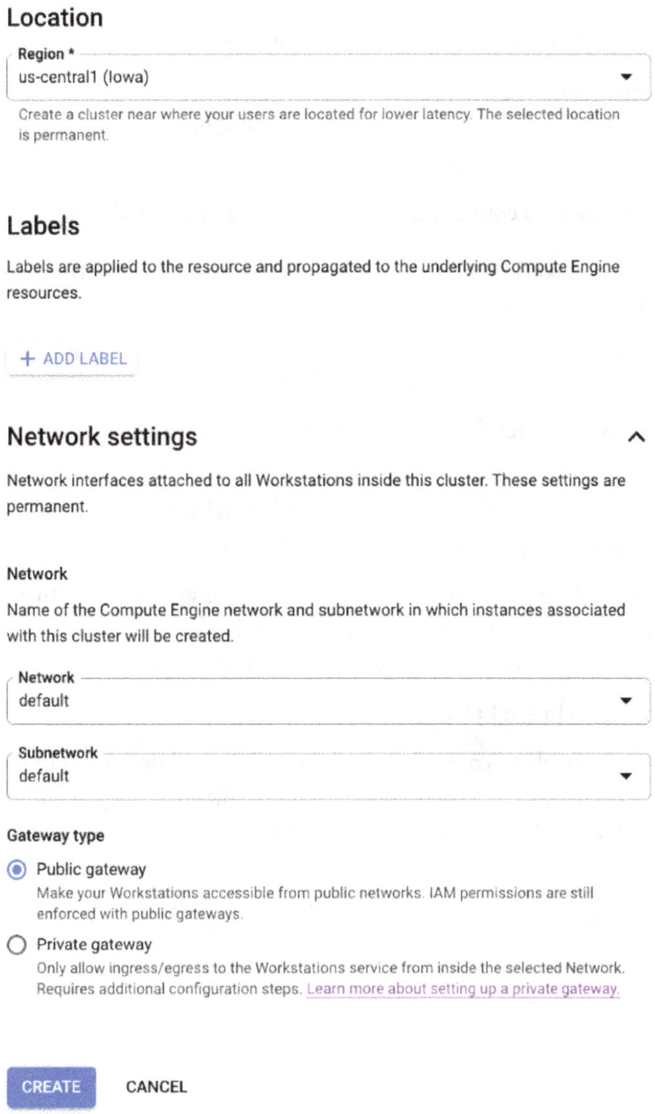

Location

Region *

us-central1 (Iowa)

Create a cluster near where your users are located for lower latency. The selected location is permanent.

Labels

Labels are applied to the resource and propagated to the underlying Compute Engine resources.

+ ADD LABEL

Network settings ^

Network interfaces attached to all Workstations inside this cluster. These settings are permanent.

Network

Name of the Compute Engine network and subnetwork in which instances associated with this cluster will be created.

Network

default

Subnetwork

default

Gateway type

⦿ Public gateway
Make your Workstations accessible from public networks. IAM permissions are still enforced with public gateways.

○ Private gateway
Only allow ingress/egress to the Workstations service from inside the selected Network. Requires additional configuration steps. Learn more about setting up a private gateway.

CREATE   CANCEL

Figure 4.2 – The Create workstation cluster screen in the Google Cloud console

7. Click **CREATE** to create the workstation cluster. The **Cluster management** screen displays while the cluster is created. Cluster creation takes between 10 and 20 minutes. During that time, you will see the status as **Updating**.

Wait for the cluster creation to finish before moving on to create workstation configurations.

Creating a workstation configuration for the base editor

The next step for configuring workstations for developers is to create one or more workstation configurations.

Workstation configurations hold common settings for similar workstations. Typically, you would create a different configuration for each development team, or if for any other reason, you want a configuration set to be used for multiple workstations.

To create a Cloud Workstations configuration using the base editor, follow these steps:

1. In the Google Cloud console, select **Cloud Workstations | Workstations configurations**, and click + **CREATE**.

2. In the **Basic information** section, type a configuration name in the **Name** field. For this example, let's call the configuration `base-editor-public`.

3. In the **Workstation cluster** field, select the cluster you created: `us-central-default-public (us-central1)`.

4. Under **Quick start workstations**, keep the default, **Enabled**, and the pool size of `1`. Keeping a number of VMs running means that workstations start up faster for developers.

    Based on the size of the pool, they get an already-running VM rather than waiting for one to start. The controller keeps the number of VMs in **Quick start pool size** running. If you choose **Disabled**, the VM starts each time a developer starts a workstation.

5. Don't add any labels in the **Labels** section.

    If you were to add labels to your configuration, they would propagate to the underlying GCE resources and would also be visible in `Billing`, which can help attribute costs to different departments or teams. Your **Basic information** section should now look like the following:

Basic information

Name *

base-editor-public

Workstation cluster *

us-central-default-public (us-central1)   ▼   ❓

Quick start workstations ❓

◉ Enabled (faster workstation startup)

○ Disabled (lower cost)

   ⓘ   Enabling this feature will improve startup times for workstations. Be
          aware that you will be billed for 1 instance, even if it is not being used.

Quick start pool size

1

Number of resources kept in a pre-started state. The project is billed for these resources.
As users start their workstations, the system refills the pool of pre-started resources. Start
with very low values and increase later, if necessary.

Labels

Labels are applied to the resource and propagated to the underlying Compute Engine
resources.

\+ ADD LABEL

CONTINUE

Figure 4.3 – Basic information form for your workstation configuration

6.   Click **CONTINUE**.

7.   In the **Machine settings** section, choose **E2** and **e2-standard-2**.

8.   In **Auto-sleep** under **Cost savings**, keep the default of **After 2 hours of inactivity (default)**.
    This determines the length of idle time before the VMs backing these workstations power off.

9.   Expand the **Advanced options** section. Here, you can set security-related configurations:

You can disable public IP addresses. In this case, workstations can't connect to the internet
directly. This improves your workstation's security posture if your developers don't need access
to internet services. If you were to select this, you would need to set up Private Google Access
(`https://cloud.google.com/vpc/docs/private-google-access`) to make
Google services such as Artifact Registry accessible from the VMs or set up Google Cloud NAT
(`https://cloud.google.com/nat/docs/overview`) in your network.

You can choose shielded VM features such as Secure Boot, vTPM, and Integrity Monitoring.

You can set encryption options to manage encryption for workstation disks with a **customer-managed encryption key** (**CMEK**) in place of the default Google-managed encryption key.

10. Leave all the advanced options set to their defaults and close the **Advanced options** section. Your **Machine settings** section should be configured as follows:

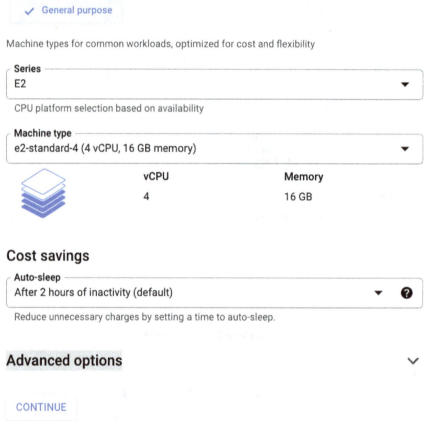

Figure 4.4 – Machine settings for your workstation configuration

11. Click **CONTINUE**.

12. In the **Environment settings** section, keep the default options with **Base Editor (Code OSS)**. This section lets you choose the container image to deploy on your workstations. If you keep the default **Code editors on base images** option selected, you can choose one of the preconfigured container images that Cloud Workstations provides:

Figure 4.5 – Environment settings showing available editors

Choosing **Custom container image** lets you specify (by URL) a custom image or select an image from an Artifact Registry repository in your project.

13. Under **Storage settings**, keep the default settings. This section lets you choose the disk type (**Standard, Balanced**, or **SSD**) and size of the persistent disk mapped to your workstation user's home directory. You can also choose the reclaim policy for whether the disk is deleted or retained when your workstation is deleted.

14. In the **Advanced container options** section, keep the default settings. In this section, you can set parameters to pass to the container running in the workstation, such as `Working directory`, `User`, `Command`, and arguments or environment variables.

15. Close the **Advanced container options** section. Your configuration should look like the following:

Environment settings

Select the code editor for workstations that use this configuration. If needed, you can preload tools and configurations using a custom container.

● Code editors on base images

○ Custom container image

Code editors
Base Editor (Code OSS)   ▼   ❓

Service account   ▼

The service account that will be used on VM instances to support this config. If a custom container image is used, this service account must have permissions to pull the container image (or if this is not set, the image should be publicly accessible).

Storage settings

A persistent disk stores the workstation home directory between sessions. Disk type and disk size cannot be modified after creation.

Disk type *
Standard   ▼

Disk size *
200 GB   ▼

Reclaim policy
Delete   ▼   ❓

Advanced container options   ⌄

Figure 4.6 – Environment settings for your workstation configuration

16. Click **CREATE** to create the configuration.

The configuration is created and the **workstation configurations** screen is displayed.

Creating a workstation configuration for the IntelliJ IDEA Ultimate IDE

In this step, we will create a second workstation configuration – this time, using the IntelliJ IDEA Ultimate IDE. To do that, follow the steps from the *Creating a workstation configuration for the base editor* section, but with the following changes:

- In the **Name** field in **Basic information**, type intellij-public
- In the **Code editors** field in **Environment settings**, choose **IntelliJ IDEA Ultimate**

You've created your workstation cluster and two workstation configurations. Next, let's create the workstations themselves.

Creating workstations and assigning them to developers

Follow these steps to create workstations that use the configurations you just created:

1. In the Google Cloud console, select **Cloud Workstations | Workstations**, and click **+ CREATE**.
2. In the **Name** field, type code-oss-wks.
3. In the **Configuration** field, select **base-editor-public**.

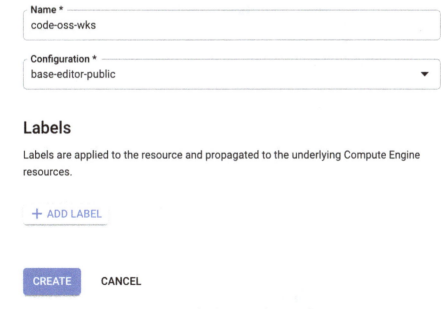

Figure 4.7 – The Create workstation form

4. Click **CREATE**.

5. Repeat *steps 1-4* to create another workstation, but this time, name the second workstation `intellij-wks` and choose the configuration named **intellij-public**. You'll see the two workstations on the **Workstations** page in the Google Cloud console:

Figure 4.8 – The Workstations page

You should be able to see the newly created workstation in both the **All workstations** pane and the **My workstations** pane because you have high-level permissions. The normal step, at this point, to assign a workstation to a user would be to click on the three dots at the end of the workstation line and click on **Add Users**, then assign the **Cloud Workstation User** role to the account of the user you want to assign the workstation to:

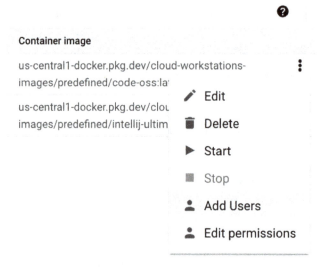

Figure 4.9 – Add Users, from the list of available container images

Now that you've created the cluster, two workstation configurations, and two workstations that use those configurations, let's customize the workstations.

Customizing Cloud Workstations

Because software in Cloud Workstations is deployed in container images, an effective way to customize workstations, while centrally managing, updating, and protecting them from vulnerabilities, is to create custom container images with the software and configurations that the users need, using one of the preconfigured images as the base image.

Creating a custom image and workstation configuration

In this section, you'll create a custom container image for Java developers, starting from the base editor preconfigured image, and then create another workstation configuration to use it. The configuration will include Maven and some Java extensions for VS Code.

To do this, you need a machine that can build container images, such as Docker, and that can push images to the Artifact Registry. For convenience, you can use Cloud Code for Cloud Shell, as described in *Chapter 3*, which has Docker already configured to authenticate to your existing Artifact Registry repository with your account.

Execute the following steps to build a custom image with Java tools, and a workstation configuration to go with that image:

1. Run the following command to create a directory for your custom image and move into that directory:

    ```
    mkdir java-tools && cd java-tools
    ```

2. Use your preferred editor to create a Dockerfile with the following content:

    ```
    FROM us-central1-docker.pkg.dev/cloud-workstations-images/
    predefined/code-oss:latest

    RUN sudo apt update
    RUN sudo apt install -y maven

    RUN wget https://open-vsx.org/api/vscjava/vscode-java-
    debug/0.40.1/file/vscjava.vscode-java-debug-0.40.1.vsix && \
    unzip vscjava.vscode-java-debug-0.40.1.vsix "extension/*" &&\
    mv extension /opt/code-oss/extensions/java-debug

    RUN wget https://open-vsx.org/api/vscjava/vscode-java-
    dependency/0.19.1/file/vscjava.vscode-java-dependency-
    0.19.1.vsix && \
    unzip vscjava.vscode-java-dependency-0.19.1.vsix "extension/*"
    &&\
    mv extension /opt/code-oss/extensions/java-dependency
    ```

```
RUN wget https://open-vsx.org/api/redhat/java/1.6.0/file/redhat.
java-1.6.0.vsix && \
unzip redhat.java-1.6.0.vsix "extension/*" &&\
mv extension /opt/code-oss/extensions/redhat-java

RUN wget https://open-vsx.org/api/vscjava/vscode-maven/0.35.2/
file/vscjava.vscode-maven-0.35.2.vsix && \
unzip vscjava.vscode-maven-0.35.2.vsix "extension/*" &&\
mv extension /opt/code-oss/extensions/java-maven
```

This Dockerfile installs Maven using `apt`, and downloads the Code-OSS extensions for Java development and makes them available during the build.

3. Run the following command to build your image:

    ```
    docker build -t us-central1-docker.pkg.dev/galloro-host/scdbook-
    repo/java-tools .
    ```

4. Run the following command to push your image to the Artifact Registry repository:

    ```
    docker push us-central1-docker.pkg.dev/galloro-host/scdbook-
    repo/java-tools
    ```

5. Follow the instructions in the *Creating a workstations configuration for the base editor* section earlier in this chapter to create a configuration using the custom image you built:

Select container image

ARTIFACT REGISTRY   CONTAINER REGISTRY

Project: galloro-host   CHANGE

▼   us-central1-docker.pkg.dev/galloro-host/scdbook-repo

   ▼   java-tools

         b5c5341ccf   **latest**   2 minutes ago

▶   europe-docker.pkg.dev/galloro-host/demos

SELECT   CANCEL

Figure 4.10 – Selecting a container image for your workstation configuration

6. Name the configuration `java-tools-public`.

7. In the **Environment settings** section, choose **Custom container image** and select the image you just created.

8. In the **Service account** field, select **Compute Engine default service account**:

Environment settings

Select the code editor for workstations that use this configuration. If needed, you can preload tools and configurations using a custom container.

○ Code editors on base images

◉ Custom container image

Container image URL
us-central1-docker.pkg.dev/galloro-host/scdbook-repo/java-tools@:   ❓   SELECT

You can customize Cloud Workstations with container images hosted on any container registry. Learn how to extend our base images.

Service account
Compute Engine default service account   ▼

The service account that will be used on VM instances to support this config. If a custom container image is used, this service account must have permissions to pull the container image (or if this is not set, the image should be publicly accessible).

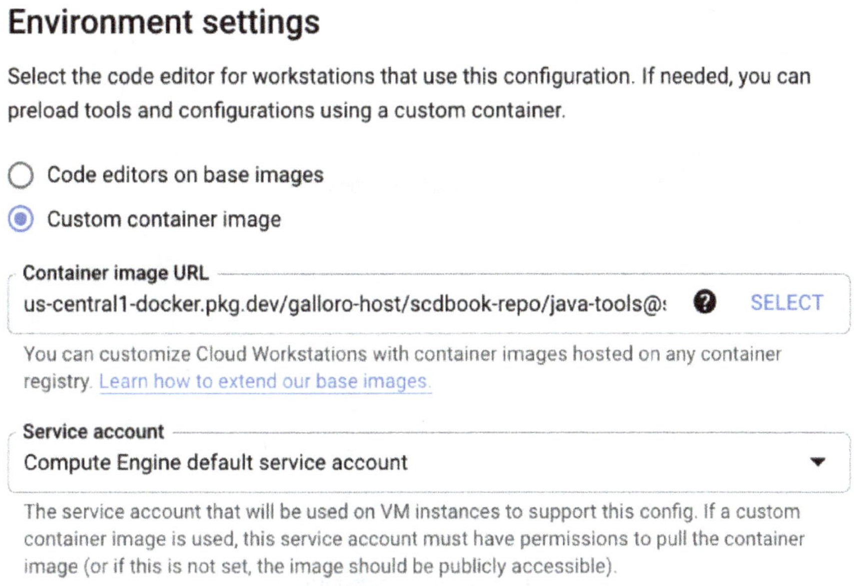

Figure 4.11 – Environment settings for workstation configuration

9. Follow the instructions in the *Creating workstations and assigning them to developers* section to create a workstation named `java-tools-wks`, using the `java-tools-public` configuration you just created:

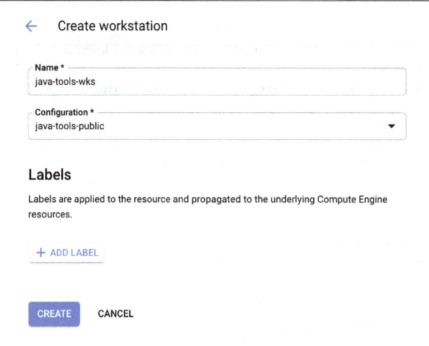

Figure 4.12 – The Create workstation form

Now, let's see the best approach to update your Cloud workstations.

Updating Cloud workstations

The preconfigured base images provided by Google are updated weekly, so when you rebuild your custom image, you will get the latest base image with all the OS updates. In addition to that, you will get the latest Maven version at each rebuild, and you can follow a similar approach for any software component that you have in your custom workstation image.

To maintain control, persistence, and repeatability, you should always rebuild your workstation configuration image to update your workstations and avoid updating running workstations directly. Already created workstations will get the updated image after a restart.

Now we have seen how to customize and update your workstations, let's see in the next section how developers will use them.

Coding on Cloud Workstations

You now have several workstation configurations and workstations, including one with a custom container image for Java development. Now, let's find out how to use them.

In this section, you'll learn how a developer connects to and uses Cloud Workstations. We include instructions for accessing a workstation that uses the base editor and instructions for accessing a workstation that uses the JetBrains IntelliJ IDE.

The following sections describe how to access a workstation that uses the base editor and a workstation that uses the JetBrains IntelliJ IDE.

Accessing a Cloud workstation configured with the base editor

The following steps describe how to launch a workstation configured to use the base editor:

1. In the Google Cloud console, select **Cloud Workstations | Workstations**.

2. Under **My workstations**, click **Launch** in the **java-tools-wks** workstation. This is the workstation you customized before, still based on the Code-OSS editor. Your browser will access the **Code OSS for Cloud Workstations** welcome page. Code OSS is the same IDE you worked on in *Chapter 3*, and it has the Cloud Code extension installed.

3. Click **Clone Git Repository**.

4. Click **Clone from GitHub**, then click **Allow** if you get a request to sign in to GitHub.

5. In the next dialog, click **Copy & Continue to GitHub**.

6. For **Do you want Code OSS - Cloud Workstations to open the external website?**, click **Open**.

7. Paste the code in the GitHub **Device Activation** page.

8. In the page that follows, click **Authorize Visual-Studio-Code**.

   You'll be required to sign in with your GitHub account.

9. Navigate back to the Cloud Workstations welcome page and type the following in the repository field: `https://github.com/PacktPublishing/Secure-Continuous-Delivery-on-Google-Cloud`

10. In the **Choose a folder to clone** request, accept the default folder, `/home/user`.

11. In the **Would you like to open the cloned repository?** dialog, click **Open**. You are in a Code OSS workspace similar to the one you used in *Chapter 3*, but now you're using a Cloud workstation hosted in your GCP project and VPC and preconfigured by you. In a real-world situation, an administrator from your organization (not Google Cloud) would typically preconfigure this.

Now, let's access the workstation configured with IntelliJ IDEA.

Accessing a Cloud workstation configured with a JetBrains IDE

The following steps describe how to install JetBrains Gateway and set up the connection to use Cloud Workstations with the JetBrains IntelliJ IDEA Ultimate IDE:

1. Download and install the latest version of JetBrains Gateway: `https://www.jetbrains.com/remote-development/gateway/`.

2. Open **JetBrains Gateway**.

3. In the **Install More Providers** section, click **Install** under **Google Cloud**:

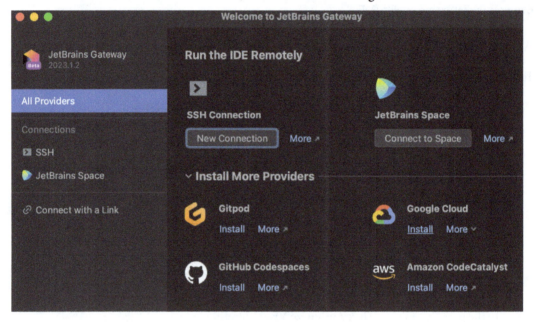

Figure 4.13 – JetBrains Gateway

4. After installing, click **Connect to Google Cloud** under **Cloud Workstations** in the **Run the IDE Remotely** section.

    This opens a browser-based authentication flow. Authenticate using your Google account with permissions on the project.

5. Back in the **JetBrains Gateway** window, in **Google Cloud Project**, click on the folder icon and then select your Google Cloud project:

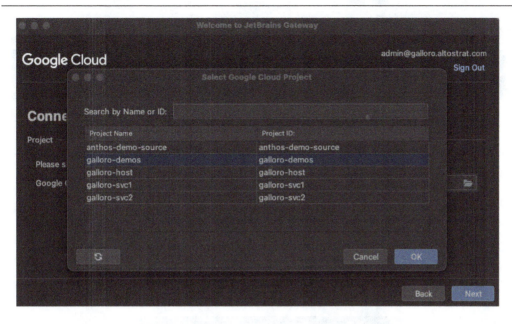

Figure 4.14 – Select Google Cloud Project from JetBrains

6. In the **Cloud Workstation** field, under **Workstation**, select your **intellij-wks** workstation and click **Next**:

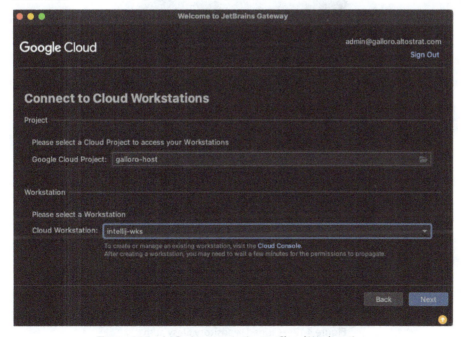

Figure 4.15 – JetBrains connection to Cloud Workstations

7. In the **Choose IDE and Project** window, click on the **open an SSH terminal** link:

Figure 4.16 – Choose IDE window, showing the open an SSH terminal link

This is because you still don't have an application project on your workstation, so you can clone the sample repository.

8. In the terminal, type the following command to clone the sample repository:

    ```
    git clone https://github.com/PacktPublishing/Secure-Continuous-
    Delivery-on-Google-Cloud
    ```

9. Close the terminal window.

10. In the **IDE project on remote host** field, browse and select the ch4 folder inside the repository you cloned:

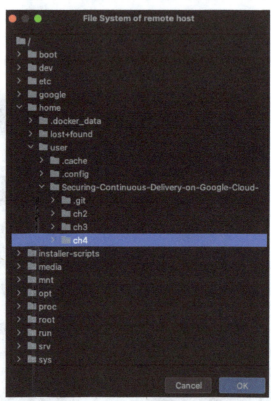

Figure 4.17 – Cloned repository filesystem

11. Click **Connect**; your connection will be set up, and you can access IntelliJ IDEA on your workstation:

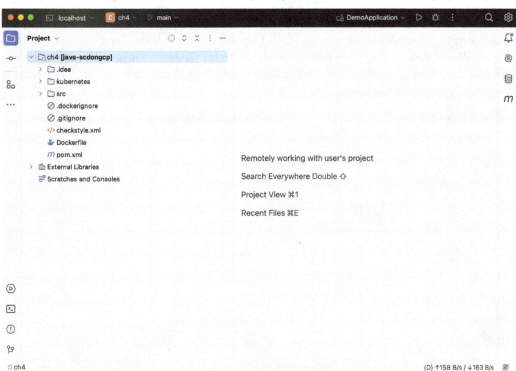

Figure 4.18 – IntelliJ IDEA on a Cloud Workstation

You've seen how to access and use Cloud Workstations to write code for your applications. Now, let's see how to clean up your resources.

Cleaning up

The workstations you created will shut down automatically after the idle time passes (2 hours). To avoid incurring additional costs, you can delete your workstations, workstation configurations, and workstation clusters following the instructions on this documentation page: `https://cloud.google.com/workstations/docs/delete-resources`.

Summary

You've seen how you can configure Cloud Workstations centrally, using Google-provided base images or customizing it for specific developers' needs. You've also learned how developers can access and use Cloud Workstations using a web browser or the JetBrains Gateway. You're now ready to use a Cloud workstation for yourself or create and centrally configure and manage a fleet of workstations for your development team or teams.

In the next chapter, you will see how to automate continuous integration tasks with Cloud Build.

Part 2:
Build and Package
Your Application

In this part, you'll learn how to use Cloud Build to automate artifact builds and other **continuous integration** (**CI**) tasks, including how to build your application from source to a deployable container image, how to store the resulting artifacts on **Artifact Registry**, and how to scan those artifacts for security vulnerabilities.

This part has the following chapters:

- *Chapter 5, Automating Continuous Integration with Cloud Build*
- *Chapter 6, Securely Store Your Software on Artifact Registry*

5

Automating Continuous Integration with Cloud Build

Cloud Build is a managed service that you can use to automate building artifacts as well as perform other **continuous integration** (**CI**) tasks. In this chapter, we describe the Cloud Build architecture and capabilities and how you can use it to build your application from source to a deployable container image.

Knowing how to use Cloud Build will help you feel confident about one of the most important parts of your secure software delivery toolchain.

In this chapter, we cover the following main topics:

- Cloud Build architecture and capabilities
- Building your application manually
- Customizing your build workers
- Generating security information for your build
- Automating builds

Technical requirements

To perform the tasks in this chapter, you need a Google Cloud project, with billing or free trial enabled, and an Artifact Registry repository. You can reuse the project and repository you created in *Chapter 2*.

Also, in addition to the APIs you enabled in previous chapters, you need to enable the following APIs:

- Cloud Build
- Artifact Analysis
- Secret Manager
- Service Networking

Your Google account needs to have the Cloud Build Editor or Project Editor roles in that project, which you should still have from previous chapters.

You also need a personal GitHub account that you will connect to Cloud Build to configure automatic build execution. If you can't provide that, you can use other supported repositories, but the detailed procedure may be different from the one described in the chapter.

The code used in this chapter is available in the `ch5` folder of the book repository at `https://github.com/PacktPublishing/Secure-Continuous-Delivery-on-Google-Cloud`.

First, let's take a look at what Cloud Build consists of and what it can do.

Cloud Build architecture and capabilities

Cloud Build is a Google-managed service that lets you automate build tasks such as dependency downloads, code compilation, automated test execution, artifact build as a container image, and artifact upload to your repository.

You can define how these tasks are linked together in your build through a build config specification in which each task is defined as a **build step**.

Cloud Build runs each step on Google-managed infrastructure as a container that exists only for the time that the step runs. There's no CI software to install and update or server to manage, and no build artifacts are left on the infrastructure when the build process finishes.

The steps of the same build have access to a common storage space, named a workspace, so they can share intermediate artifacts among them.

Your build can be linked to a source code repository so that your source code is cloned in your workspace as part of your build, and **triggers** can be configured to run the build automatically when a specific event occurs. In this chapter, we trigger based on events in your repository.

The following diagram summarizes that flow:

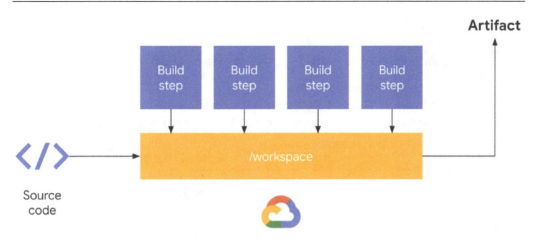

Figure 5.1 – Cloud Build architecture

As you can see in this diagram, the source code is loaded into the workspace, and each configured build step runs against it. The output from the build process in the workspace is the build artifact or artifacts.

Now that you know a little bit about how Cloud Build works, let's try a manual build.

Building your application manually

In this section, you'll build an example application with Cloud Build. Follow these steps:

1. To start, set an environment variable to your project ID using the following command:

    ```
    export PROJECT_ID=$(gcloud config get-value project)
    ```

2. If you don't already have the book repository cloned locally, clone it now.

3. cd into the ch5 folder.

    In that folder, you'll find the code and assets of the same Java application used in the previous chapters but with some differences, as this folder includes a cloudbuild.yaml file, an example build specification defining the steps of your build.

4. Open the file in a text editor to see the following contents:

    ```
    steps:
    - name: maven:3-eclipse-temurin-17
      entrypoint: mvn
      args: ["package", "-Dmaven.test.skip=true"]
      id: package
    - name: 'gcr.io/cloud-builders/docker'
      args: ['build', '.', '-t', 'us-central1-docker.pkg.
    dev/$PROJECT_ID/scdbook-repo/scdongcp-app', '-f', 'Dockerfile']
      id: build
    ```

```
    waitFor: ['package']
  images:
  - us-central1-docker.pkg.dev/$PROJECT_ID/scdbook-repo/scdongcp-
  app
```

Cloud Build runs each step of this build configuration in a container in its managed environment. This build configuration file includes two steps to be executed, identified by the `id` attribute:

- `package`: Compiles and packages the source code, producing a Java artifact
- `build`: Builds a Docker image, using the Dockerfile contained in the folder, and tags it as `us-central1-docker.pkg.dev/$PROJECT_ID/scdbook-repo/scdongcp-app`

Here are some other things you can find in this configuration file:

- In the `name` field for each step, you can specify a container image (referred to as a *builder image*) to run that specific step. Cloud Build provides some supported builder images at `https://cloud.google.com/build/docs/cloud-builders`, but you can use a custom image too.
- In the `entrypoint` field, you can specify an entry point for the builder.
- In the `args` field, you can put arguments for the builder image.
- If the image provides an entry point (or you defined one) these will be the arguments to that entry point. Otherwise, the first argument will be the entry point used when the container is executed.
- You can use the `id` field to set a unique identifier for the step.
- You can use this in conjunction with the `waitFor` field to set the order of execution for the steps. If `waitFor` isn't defined for a step, that step will wait for all preceding steps in the build config to complete before starting.
- The `images` section specifies that the image produced will be pushed to the Artifact Registry.

With a build configuration in place, you can now invoke the build from the command line.

Running a simple build from the command line

To run a build from the command line, follow these steps:

1. From the `ch5` folder in your clone of the repository for this book, execute the following command:

    ```
    gcloud builds submit --region=us-central1 --config cloudbuild.
    yaml
    ```

    This command uses the `us-central1` region, but you can use whichever Google Cloud region works for you.

Cloud Build uses the `cloudbuild.yaml` file to execute the defined build steps and to push the resulting container image to the target repository.

Wait for this build to finish executing.

2. From the Google Cloud console main menu, select **Cloud Build | History**, and select `us-central1` from the **Region** drop-down menu.

3. Click on the most recent build (at the top) to see the **Build details** page.

    This page shows a **Build Summary** and a line for each executed step (two, in this case) in the left pane and a **BUILD LOG** in the right pane:

Figure 5.2 – Build log output from your first build

You can scroll through the right pane to read the build log.

4. Select the **EXECUTION DETAILS** tab in the right pane to see information on the build, such as region, duration, storage bucket, and image built:

BUILD LOG	EXECUTION DETAILS	BUILD ARTIFACTS

Build id	2b67824c-a239-4ddc-b2a4-67b99e4e46e8
Status	Successful
Region	us-central1
Timing	
Created	March 21, 2024 at 5:51:51 PM UTC+1
Started	March 21, 2024 at 5:51:51 PM UTC+1
Finished	March 21, 2024 at 5:52:33 PM UTC+1
Queued time	0 sec
Total build time	41 sec
Fetch source	3 sec
Build step(s)	29 sec
Push	7 sec
Timeout	1 hr
Source	gs://galloro-host_cloudbuild/source/1711039910.564565-4583c8ee9f8b45a5b19765eccd08dfa4.tgz
Image	us-central1-docker.pkg.dev/galloro-host/scdbook-repo/scdongcp-app ☑
Service Account	688191958103@cloudbuild.gserviceaccount.com
Built-in substitutions	
BUILD_ID	2b67824c-a239-4ddc-b2a4-67b99e4e46e8
LOCATION	us-central1
PROJECT_ID	galloro-host
PROJECT_NUMBER	688191958103

Figure 5.3 – Execution details for your build

5.   Click on the **BUILD ARTIFACTS** tab to access links to download your build log and to see your image in Artifact Registry:

BUILD LOG	EXECUTION DETAILS	BUILD ARTIFACTS

≡ Filter   Enter property name or value

Artifact Name	Type		Security Insights
gs://688191958103.cloudbuild-logs.googleusercontent.com/log-2b67824c-a239-4ddc-b2a4-...	Build log	⬇	-
us-central1-docker.pkg.dev/galloro-host/scdbook-repo/scdongcp-app	Image	☑	**VIEW**
us-central1-docker.pkg.dev/galloro-host/scdbook-repo/scdongcp-app:latest	Image	☑	**VIEW**

Figure 5.4 – List of build artifacts from your build

Now that you've configured and run a build, let's add some tests.

Adding automated tests to your build

In the ch5 folder of our GitHub repository for this book, we added some sample test code to the Java application. With the editor of your choice, open the DemoApplicationTests.java file inside the src/test/java/com/example. There is some simple Spring Boot test code that checks that your application responds to HTTP requests without errors and returns a specific string: "scd-on-gcp app running in target: local !!".

Now, let's add a step to our build configuration to run this test before packaging and building our app:

1. In the editor of your choice, open the cloudbuild.yaml file and add, before the existing steps, a test step that runs the mvn test.

    You can also add a waitFor field to the package step so that it's executed after the test.

    The file will now look like this:

    ```
    steps:
    - name: maven:3-eclipse-temurin-17
      entrypoint: mvn
      args: ["-Dtest=DemoApplicationTests","test"]
      id: test
    - name: maven:3-eclipse-temurin-17
      entrypoint: mvn
      args: ["package", "-Dmaven.test.skip=true"]
      id: package
      waitFor: ['test']
    - name: 'gcr.io/cloud-builders/docker'
      args: ['build', '.', '-t', 'us-central1-docker.pkg.
    dev/$PROJECT_ID/scdbook-repo/scdongcp-app', '-f', 'Dockerfile']
      id: build
      waitFor: ['package']
    images:
    - us-central1-docker.pkg.dev/$PROJECT_ID/scdbook-repo/scdongcp-
    app
    ```

2. Run the build again, using the following command:

    ```
    gcloud builds submit --region=us-central1 --config cloudbuild.
    yaml
    ```

    Wait for this command to finish executing. It will take more time than the previous build command because it executes the automated unit test before running the package and build steps.

3. From the Google Cloud console main menu, select **Cloud Build | History**, and click on the last build under us-central1.

You can see on the **Build details** page that the build executed three steps:

Steps		Duration
✅	**Build Summary** 3 Steps	00:01:23
✅	0: test mvn -Dtest=DemoApplicationTests test	00:00:37
✅	1: package mvn package -Dmaven.test.skip=true	00:00:26
✅	2: build build . -t us-central1-docker.pkg.dev/galloro-demos…	00:00:05

Figure 5.5 – Build summary of the steps run for your build

4.   If you click on the **test** step (step **0**), you can explore the log. At the end of it, you will find test execution details.

Cloud Build can use various *builders*, which are containers that offer the build functionality you need. One such builder is **Skaffold**. Let's learn more about using Skaffold to run your build.

Building your application using Skaffold

Cloud Build can run any container image as a cloud builder. For example, you can use Skaffold to build your container image instead of running Docker directly. If you build with Skaffold, you can standardize your **continuous delivery** (CD) pipeline on the Skaffold configuration file and save your image details in the Skaffold-produced `artifacts.json` file (as described in *Chapter 2*. This way, you can use them in subsequent steps of your pipeline.

Let's see an example of how to do that: the `ch5` folder in this book's repository already contains a basic `skaffold.yaml` file. This is like the one we used in *Chapter 4*, so you don't need to generate one. Follow these steps:

1.   In your text editor, open the `cloudbuild.yaml` file and replace the `build` step with a `skaffold-build` step.

The file now looks like this:

```
steps:
- name: maven:3-eclipse-temurin-17
  entrypoint: mvn
  args: ["-Dtest=DemoApplicationTests","test"]
  id: test
- name: maven:3-eclipse-temurin-17
```

```
      entrypoint: mvn
      args: ["package", "-Dmaven.test.skip=true"]
      id: package
      waitFor: ['test']
  - name: gcr.io/k8s-skaffold/skaffold
      args:
        - skaffold
        - build
        - '--interactive=false'
        - '--file-output=/workspace/artifacts.json'
        - '--default-repo=us-central1-docker.pkg.dev/$PROJECT_ID/
scdbook-repo'
        - '--push=true'
      id: skaffold-build
      waitFor: ['package']
  images:
  - us-central1-docker.pkg.dev/$PROJECT_ID/scdbook-repo/scdongcp-
app
```

2. Run the build again, using the following command:

```
gcloud builds submit --region=us-central1 --config cloudbuild.
yaml
```

3. Wait for execution to complete, then in the console, select **Cloud Build | History**, and click on the last build, us-central1.

On the **Build details** page, you can see that the build executed skaffold-build as the third step:

Steps	Duration
✅ **Build Summary** 3 Steps	00:03:02
✅ 0: test mvn -Dtest=DemoApplicationTests test	00:00:39
✅ 1: package mvn package -Dmaven.test.skip=true	00:00:25
✅ 2: skaffold-build skaffold build --interactive=false --file-output=/work...	00:01:47

Figure 5.6 – Build steps for the Skaffold build

Now that you've run a build using the Skaffold builder, let's learn how to pass values using substitutions.

Using substitutions

Substitutions let you use variables in your build config that can be replaced by specific values at build time. This way, you can make your configuration more portable and reusable.

Cloud Build provides built-in substitutions, or you can define your own. An example of built-in substitution is the $PROJECT_ID environment variable that we're using in our build file from the first exercise. Other built-in substitutions are available for automatic builds invoked by triggers. We will see an example of them in the section dedicated to triggers, later in this chapter.

Let's see an example of using user-defined substitutions.

Once again, edit your cloudbuild.yaml file as follows:

1. Change each occurrence of the Artifact Registry repository name from scdbook-repo to $_REPO.

2. Change the image name from scdongcp-app to $_IMAGE.

3. Change the us-central1 part of the Artifact Registry repository name to $_REGION.

    The file should look like this:

    ```
    steps:
    - name: maven:3-eclipse-temurin-17
      entrypoint: mvn
      args: ["-Dtest=DemoApplicationTests","test"]
      id: test
    - name: maven:3-eclipse-temurin-17
      entrypoint: mvn
      args: ["package", "-Dmaven.test.skip=true"]
      id: package
      waitFor: ['test']
    - name: gcr.io/k8s-skaffold/skaffold
      args:
        - skaffold
        - build
        - <--interactive=false>
        - <--file-output=/workspace/artifacts.json'
        - <--default-repo=$_REGION-docker.pkg.dev/$PROJECT_ID/$_
    REPO'
        - <--push=true>
      id: skaffold-build
      waitFor: ['package']
    images:
    - $_REGION-docker.pkg.dev/$PROJECT_ID/$_REPO/$_IMAGE
    ```

4. Run the build again, providing values for the substitutions:

```
gcloud builds submit --region=us-central1 --config cloudbuild.
yaml --substitutions=_REPO="scdbook-repo",_IMAGE="scdongcp-
app",_REGION="us-central1"
```

5. From the Google Cloud console main menu, select **Cloud Build | History**, and click on the last build under us-central1. In **Build details**, you'll see that the build executed the same steps as the previous run.

6. Click on **EXECUTION DETAILS** in the right pane; among other information, you will see **User substitutions** values:

User substitutions	
_REPO	scdbook-repo
_IMAGE	scdongcp-app
_REGION	us-central1

Figure 5.7 – Substitution variable values from the executed build

In the preceding steps, you replaced values in your build config with substitution variables, then ran the build and saw that Cloud Build replaced the variables with the correct values. Next, let's learn about Cloud Build workers, worker pools, and how to customize them.

Customizing your build workers

By default, Cloud Build runs its builds in a Google-managed hosted environment with access to the public internet. The builds are executed as Linux containers on workers that are **virtual machines** (**VMs**) allocated for that specific build. At the time of writing, Cloud Build uses an e2-standard-2 machine with 2 vCPUs and 8 GB memory as the default worker.

In the sections that follow, we'll show you how to choose a custom machine type for your build workers and how to use private worker pools.

Custom machine types

You can customize the machine type using the machineType option in the build config file. At the time of writing, in addition to the default machine type, you can select one of the additional high-CPU machine types listed on the page available here: https://cloud.google.com/build/docs/api/reference/rest/v1/projects.builds#machinetype.

Custom machine types have more CPU power, but they take longer to provision compared to the default.

Let's modify our build to use a high-CPU custom machine type:

1. Edit your `cloudbuild.yaml` file and add an `options` section at the end of it, as shown:

    ```
    options:
      machineType: 'E2_HIGHCPU_8'
    ```

2. Run the build again.

    You still need to provide values for the substitutions. Use the following command to do so:

    ```
    gcloud builds submit --region=us-central1 --config cloudbuild.
    yaml --substitutions=_REPO="scdbook-repo",_IMAGE="scdongcp-
    app",_REGION="us-central1"
    ```

    Provisioning the custom machine can delay the start of the build.

3. From the console main menu, select **Cloud Build | History**, and click on the last build under `us-central1`.

4. Click on **EXECUTION DETAILS** in the right pane.

    Among other information, you will see the machine type set to `e2-highcpu-8`.

In this section, you've selected a custom machine type for the workers that perform your build. Next, you'll configure a private worker pool.

Private worker pools

In addition to custom machine types, you can use private worker pools to customize where your builds run. With private pools, you not only can choose different hardware configurations (you have more machine types than the ones available with the `machineType` option), but you can also connect your workers directly to your **Virtual Private Cloud** (**VPC**) network and assign a private IP range to them.

Google hosts the service producer network that runs your private pool. You can create a VPC peering connection between your VPC network and the service producer network so that your builds can access resources inside your VPC.

Let's see how you can create private worker pools and use them in your build. The following procedure assumes you have a VPC network available in your project:

1. From the Google Cloud console main menu, select **VPC network**, and click on the VPC that you want to connect to the private-pool network.

2. Select the **PRIVATE SERVICE CONFIGURATION** tab.

3. Under **ALLOCATED IP RANGES FOR SERVICES**, click **ALLOCATE IP RANGE**.

4. In the **Allocate an internal IP range** dialog, type `scd-pool-range` in the **Name** field, select **Automatic** for **IP range**, type `24` in the **Prefix length** field, and click **ALLOCATE**:

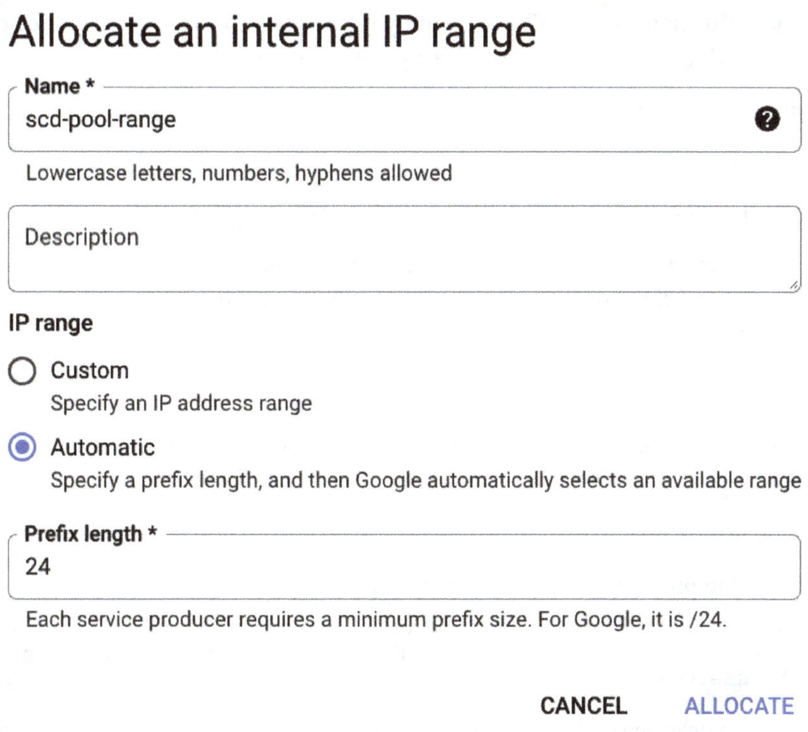

Allocate an internal IP range

Name *

scd-pool-range   ❓

Lowercase letters, numbers, hyphens allowed

Description

IP range

⚪ Custom

Specify an IP address range

🔘 Automatic

Specify a prefix length, and then Google automatically selects an available range

Prefix length *

24

Each service producer requires a minimum prefix size. For Google, it is /24.

CANCEL   ALLOCATE

Figure 5.8 – Allocating an internal IP range for a private worker pool

5. The range will be shown under **ALLOCATED IP RANGES FOR SERVICES**.

6. Now, select the **PRIVATE CONNECTIONS TO SERVICES** sub-tab, and click **CREATE CONNECTION**.

7. In the **Create a private connection** dialog, select `scd-pool-range` under **Assigned allocation** and click **CONNECT**.

    A private connection will be created between the Google producer network and your VPC.

8. Wait for the connection to be created, then select **Cloud Build | Settings | WORKER POOL** from the main menu, and click **CREATE**.

9. On the **Create private pool** page, enter the following settings:

    - **Name:** `scdbook-pool`

    - **Region:** `us-central1`

    - **Machine type:** `e2-standard-4`

    - **Available disk size:** `100 GB`

    - **Project:** Your project ID

- **Network**: The name of the VPC network you peered with the Google service producer network. This is the network your private pools will connect to.

- **Assign external IPs**: Leave selected

10. Click **CREATE**.

After the private pool is created, you will see the pool on the page.

11. In the `options` section of your `cloudbuild.yaml` file, replace the line that contains the `machineType` field with the option to run that build in this private pool. The `options` section will look like this:

```
options:
  pool:
    name: 'projects/$PROJECT_ID/locations/us-central1/
workerPools/scdbook-pool'
```

12. Run the build again.

You still need to provide values for the substitutions, like so:

```
gcloud builds submit --region=us-central1 --config cloudbuild.
yaml --substitutions=_REPO="scdbook-repo",_IMAGE="scdongcp-
app",_REGION="us-central1"
```

There may be a delay in starting the build because the private-pool worker is being provisioned.

13. From the Google Cloud console main menu, select **Cloud Build | History**, and click on the last build under `us-central1`.

14. Click on **EXECUTION DETAILS**.

Among other information, you will see **Worker pool** information:

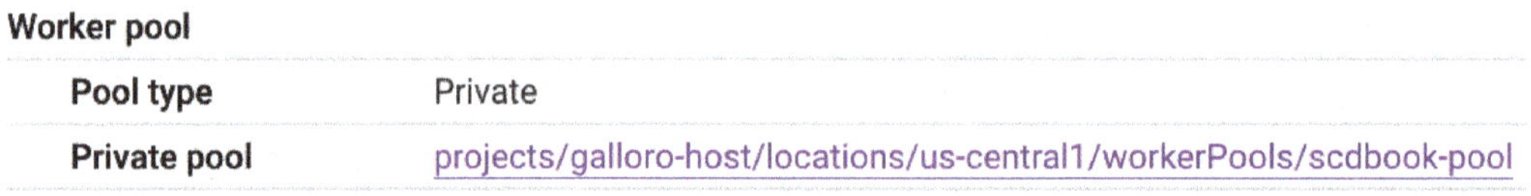

Worker pool

Pool type	Private
Private pool	projects/galloro-host/locations/us-central1/workerPools/scdbook-pool

Figure 5.9 – Information about your worker pool

The build can access resources inside your VPC directly using private IPs from the range you allocated. You can also remove public IP addresses to prevent the worker from accessing the internet.

In the next section, we learn how to get and use security information for your application.

Generating security information for your build

Cloud Build can provide security-related information for each build when the produced artifact (container image or Java, Python, or Node.js package) is stored in the Artifact Registry. The following information is provided:

- Vulnerability scanning report
- **Supply-chain Levels for Software Artifacts (SLSA)**-compliant digitally signed provenance

Cloud Build stores both of these as metadata in the Artifact Registry. The vulnerability scanning requires that the Artifact Analysis API is enabled.

The first thing we'll provide is **provenance** information.

Producing digitally signed provenance

In order to generate provenance metadata for builds running in regional or private pools, you need to add a `requestedVerifyOption` setting to your build config file:

1. In the `options:` section of your `cloudbuild.yaml` file, add the `requestedVerifyOption: VERIFIED` setting.

   The section will look like this:

   ```
   options:
     requestedVerifyOption: VERIFIED
     pool:
       name: 'projects/$PROJECT_ID/locations/us-central1/
   workerPools/scdbook-pool'
   ```

2. Execute the following command to run the build again, still providing values for the substitutions:

   ```
   gcloud builds submit --region=us-central1 --config cloudbuild.
   yaml --substitutions=_REPO="scdbook-repo",_IMAGE="scdongcp-
   app",_REGION="us-central1"
   ```

Next, we'll view the provenance and the generated vulnerability report.

Viewing vulnerability reports and provenance

Use the following procedure to view a vulnerability report for your build, including provenance information:

1. Go to **Cloud Build | History**, and click on the last build.
2. Click on **BUILD ARTIFACTS** in the right pane.
3. Click on **VIEW**, under the **Security Insights** column, for one of the image tags.

You will see the **Security insights** pane, which provides the following information:

- SLSA build-level certification for your build

- A list of vulnerabilities found in your image by Artifact Analysis

- Build information as a link to build logs

- SLSA-compliant provenance:

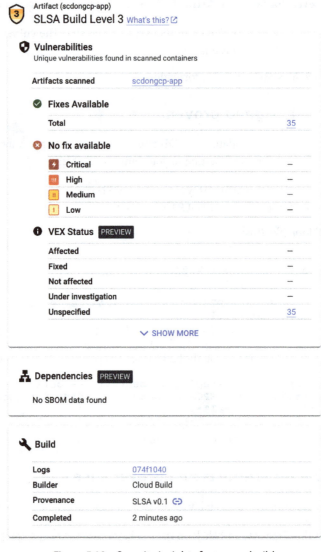

Figure 5.10 – Security insights from your build

4. Click the link icon next to **Provenance**.

You will see the provenance metadata in SLSA-compliant, in-toto format. SLSA metadata is stored in Artifact Registry and is also accessible using the Google Cloud CLI or an SLSA-compliant tool such as the slsa-verifier: `https://github.com/slsa-framework/slsa-verifier`.

Now that you've seen how to enhance the security of your application, let's learn about using Cloud Build triggers to automate your builds.

Automating builds

In the previous examples, we manually executed builds. Cloud Build can also start a build automatically using triggers (for example, a new commit to your source code repository).

Besides being invoked by repository-specific events, you can invoke triggers manually. You can link a trigger to a Pub/Sub topic so that the trigger runs upon receipt of a message on that topic. You can also expose a webhook URL for invocation.

In this section, we focus primarily on running builds after a specific repository event. To do that, you need to connect Cloud Build to a repository, as described next.

Creating your source code repository

Before connecting Cloud Build to a repository to automate builds when code is committed, you need a repository to which you will commit your code.

Perform the following steps to create a repository from the ch5 folder in this book's repository:

1. Create a new repository in your GitHub account, called scdbook-ch5.

2. Export your GitHub account to the GIT_ACCOUNT variable as follows:

    ```
    export GIT_ACCOUNT=yourgithubaccount
    ```

    Here, yourgithubaccount is the account name for your GitHub account.

3. Run the following commands to copy the content of the book repository ch5 folder as the content of your new repository and to initialize this new repository.

    From the ch5 folder of your local copy of the repository, run the following commands:

    ```
    cd ..
    cp -r ch5 ../scdbook-ch5
    cd ../scdbook-ch5
    git init
    git add .
    git commit -m "commit to new source repo"
    git branch -M main
    git remote add origin https://github.com/$GIT_ACCOUNT/
    scdbook-ch5.git
    git push -u origin main
    ```

You've now created a new GitHub repository and populated it with the contents of our ch5 folder. Next, you'll establish a connection between Cloud Build and that repo.

Connecting your source code repository to Cloud Build

Cloud Build allows you to create connections to source code repositories to do the following:

- Clone repositories in your build environment (storing data in the workspace)
- Link triggers to the repositories so that a build can be invoked from a repository event

There are two options for creating repository connections:

- **Cloud Build repositories (1st gen)**: The original way to connect Cloud Build to source code repositories. It supports integrations with the following:

  - GitHub
  - GitHub Enterprise
  - Bitbucket Server
  - Bitbucket Data Center
  - Google Cloud Source Repositories

- **Cloud Build repositories (2nd gen)**: A newer way to connect Cloud Build to source code repositories, allowing you to programmatically create and manage repository connections.

  You can set up a single connection for a repository and use the authentication data from that connection to set up additional connections across regions and projects. You can also use Terraform, the Google Cloud console, the gcloud command-line tool, and the Cloud Build API to set up connections.

  Cloud Build repositories (2nd gen) support integrations with the following repositories:

  - GitHub
  - GitHub Enterprise
  - GitLab
  - GitLab Enterprise Edition

In this section, you'll set up a connection to GitHub using **Cloud Build repositories 2nd gen** to automate your build.

Before you link repositories, you need to create a host connection. Here's how to do so:

1. From the Google Cloud console main menu, select **Cloud Build | Repositories**, and select the **2ND GEN** tab.

2. Click **Create host connection**.

3. On the **Configure Connection** page, select us-central1 from the **Region** dropdown, and
    in the **Name** field, enter Github:

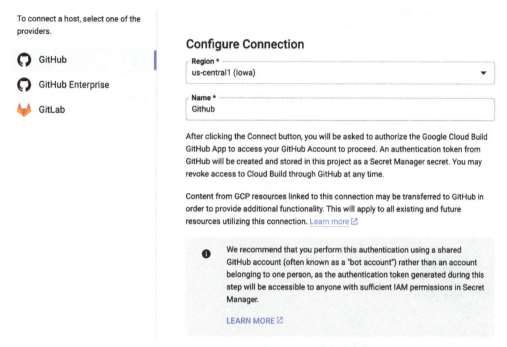

Figure 5.11 – Configuring a connection to a GitHub repository

4. Click on the **CONNECT** button at the bottom of the **Configure Connection** page.

    You are prompted to log in to your GitHub account in order to authorize the Cloud Build
    GitHub app to access it. Cloud Build stores the resulting authorization token as a secret in
    Secret Manager in your project.

5. Log in to your GitHub account.

    After the authorization flow, the connection is listed on the **Repositories and connections** page:

Figure 5.12 – Your connected repository, listed with your Cloud Build connections

6. Click **LINK REPOSITORY**.

7. In the **Link repositories** pane, for the **Connection** field, select the host connection you just created, and for the **Repository** field, select the repository named `scdbook-ch5` that you created in the previous section, as shown in the following screenshot:

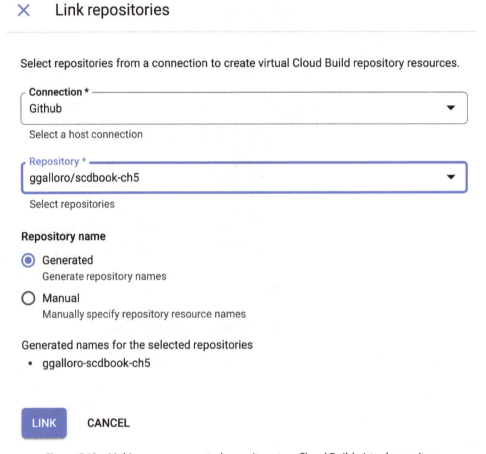

Figure 5.13 – Linking your connected repository to a Cloud Build virtual repository

8. Click **LINK**.

Your repository will be listed under the connection on the **Repositories and connections** page. Next, you'll create a trigger so that changes to this repository cause Cloud Build to run a build.

Creating a trigger for your build

Before you create a trigger, you need to modify the build config file to tag the image with the `git commit` repository short SHA, using the `$SHORT_SHA` built-in substitution that is available when a build is invoked from a trigger. Here's how to do so:

1. Add the `$SHORT_SHA` variable to the image value in the `cloudbuild.yaml` file for your newly created repository.

    The `images:` section will look like this:

    ```
    images:
    - $_REGION-docker.pkg.dev/$PROJECT_ID/$_REPO/$_IMAGE:$SHORT_SHA
    ```

2. Commit and push the changes to your repository using the following commands:

    ```
    git add .
    git commit -m "Added short_sha substitution"
    git push
    ```

    Now, your build is configured so that your image gets tagged with the `commit` SHA when the build is triggered by a push to the repository.

3. From the Google Cloud console main menu, select **Cloud Build | Triggers** and click **CREATE TRIGGER**.

4. On the **Create trigger** page, enter the following settings:

    *   **Name**: `scdbook-trigger`

    *   **Region**: `us-central1`

    *   **Event**: Select **Push to a branch**

    *   **Source**: Select **2nd gen**, and in the **Repository** field, select the repository you connected previously

    *   **Branch**: Leave the default, `^main$`:

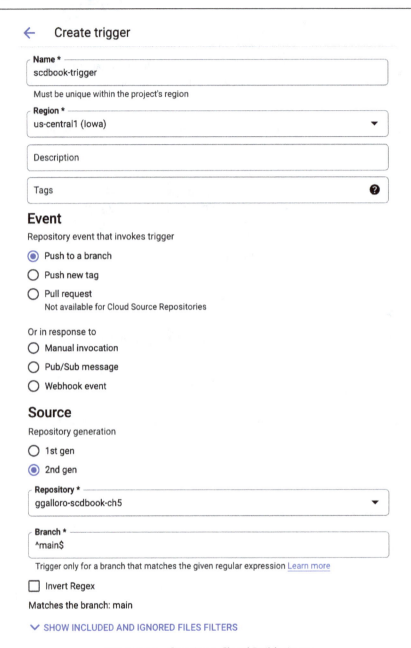

Figure 5.14 – Creating a Cloud Build trigger

5.   In the **Configuration** section, check the following settings:

  ▪   **Type** is set to **Cloud Build configuration file (yaml or json)**

  ▪   **Location** is **Repository**

- **Cloud Build configuration file location** points to the `cloudbuild.yaml` build config file in your repository:

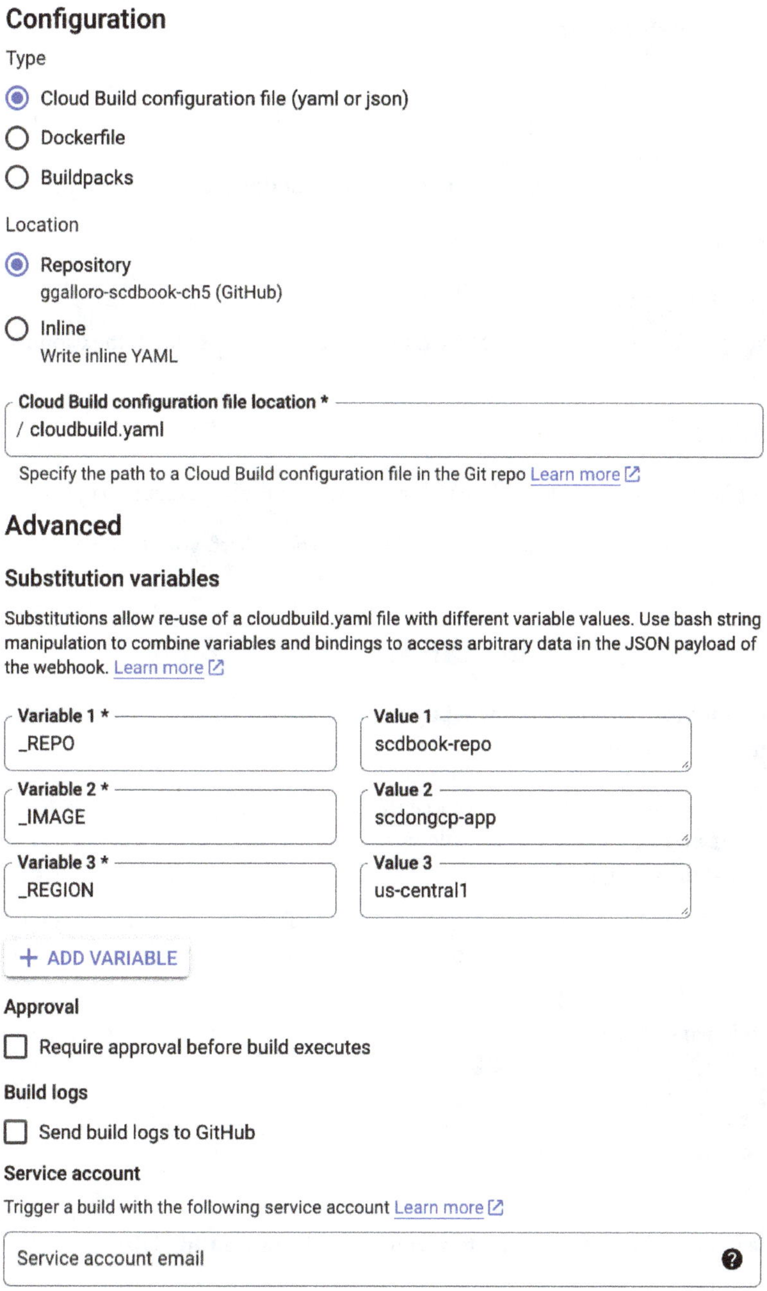

Configuration

Type

- ● Cloud Build configuration file (yaml or json)
- ○ Dockerfile
- ○ Buildpacks

Location

- ● Repository
  ggalloro-scdbook-ch5 (GitHub)
- ○ Inline
  Write inline YAML

Cloud Build configuration file location *
/ cloudbuild.yaml

Specify the path to a Cloud Build configuration file in the Git repo Learn more ☑

Advanced

Substitution variables

Substitutions allow re-use of a cloudbuild.yaml file with different variable values. Use bash string manipulation to combine variables and bindings to access arbitrary data in the JSON payload of the webhook. Learn more ☑

Variable 1 *	Value 1
_REPO	scdbook-repo

Variable 2 *	Value 2
_IMAGE	scdongcp-app

Variable 3 *	Value 3
_REGION	us-central1

+ ADD VARIABLE

Approval

☐ Require approval before build executes

Build logs

☐ Send build logs to GitHub

Service account

Trigger a build with the following service account Learn more ☑

Service account email   ❷

Figure 5.15 – Advanced configuration for your trigger

6. In the **Advanced** section, click + **ADD VARIABLE** and add the three user-defined substitution variables that our build config needs:

   - `_REPO=scdbook-repo`
   - `_IMAGE=scdongcp-app`
   - `_REGION=us-central1`

7. Explore the other options in the **Advanced** section but don't change anything:

   - You can require approvals to execute the build.
   - You can send your build logs to GitHub.
   - You can define the service account used to run the build (by default, the Cloud Build service account is used).

8. Click **CREATE**.

When the trigger is created, you can see it listed on the Cloud Build **Triggers** page.

You've now automated your build, including adding a trigger. Next, you'll trigger the build from a code commit.

Running an automated build after a code commit

With your Cloud Build trigger, you're now set up to invoke a build upon a commit to the repository. To do so, perform the following steps:

1. In the local folder of your newly created `scdbook-ch5` repository, open the `HelloController.java` source file in `src/main/java/com/example` and change *line 16* so that the string reads as `"scd-on-gcp app updated in target: %s !!"`.

2. Make the same change in the `DemoApplicationTests.java` file inside `src/test/java/com/example` so that the string in *line 26* is the same as in the previous step. If the strings aren't the same, your automated test will fail.

3. Run the following commands to commit your changes and push them to your forked repository on GitHub:

```
git add .
git commit -m "app updated"
git push
```

4. From the Google Cloud console main menu, select **Cloud Build | History**.

At the top of the build history, you should see the build running (or momentarily queued):

☐   ↺   ffe74273   ggalloro/scdbook-ch5 ☒

Figure 5.16 – Your automatically generated build listed in your Cloud Build history

5. Click on the build.

    You will see that the build executes the same three steps we saw in the manual execution (`test`, `package`, `skaffold-build`). But this time, the build was started automatically after committing the code to the repository. With this configuration, you can have each commit trigger an automatic build and an automated test execution.

6. Click on **BUILD ARTIFACTS** in the right pane.

    You can see that the image has been tagged with the commit short SHA:

us-central1-docker.pkg.dev/galloro-host/scdbook-repo/scdongcp-app:6fdaa29   Image ☒ **VIEW**

Figure 5.17 – Your container image with the sort SHA appended

7. Click on the **View artifact (external)** button.

    You are directed to the image in the Artifact Registry repository.

You've now configured and used a Cloud Build trigger to automatically run a build when you commit code to your repository. This follows the work you did to build your application, generate security information for it, create a repository, connect it to Cloud Build, and customize your build workers.

Summary

You've learned about Cloud Build architecture and capabilities. You've seen how you can define a build configuration to test, package, and build your application and how you can customize the workers that run your build. You've seen how to generate SLSA-compliant security metadata. And finally, you've learned how to automate your build so that it runs each time code is committed to your source code repository.

All of this contributes to an automated software build process that's reliable and secure. This is essential for security software delivery, allowing you to safely provide services to your users.

In the next chapter, you'll read about Artifact Registry and how to use it to securely store your application artifacts.

6

Securely Store Your Software on Artifact Registry

This chapter describes **Artifact Registry**, the Google-managed container and software artifact repository, and shows you how to use it to store container images, application dependencies, and all of your software artifacts. With Artifact Registry, you can also scan your artifacts for vulnerabilities, and you can store vulnerability metadata with those artifacts.

The following are the types of things you can store in Artifact Registry:

- Container images, such as Docker v2 or Helm 3
- Language packages, such as Java, Node.js, Python, or Go
- Operating system packages, such as Debian or RPM

This chapter will help you understand how to use Artifact Registry to store software artifacts. If you're performing the exercises in the rest of this book, you have artifacts generated by Google Cloud products, and you can deploy artifacts from Artifact Registry to Google Cloud and other runtimes. Artifact Registry also supports other CI/CD systems.

In this chapter we'll cover the following main topics:

- Manage container images using Artifact Registry
- Manage language packages
- Use virtual repositories and remote repositories
- Scan artifacts for vulnerabilities

Technical requirements

Before proceeding with this chapter, make sure you have enabled the Artifact Registry API. Additionally, be sure to install the **Google Cloud CLI**, if it's not already installed.

The GitHub repository for this book, in the `ch6` folder, contains examples for use with this chapter, and it can accessed using this link: `https://github.com/PacktPublishing/Secure-Continuous-Delivery-on-Google-Cloud-/tree/main/ch6`

In the first section, we'll show you how to use Artifact Registry to manage your container images.

Managing container images with Artifact Registry

This section includes several exercises that demonstrate how to use Artifact Registry to store and manage your containers:

- Create a repository to store images
- View role-based access control on the repository
- List the available repositories for a project
- Upload a container
- View container images
- Pull a container image or package

Creating an Artifact Registry repository to store your image

You can create an Artifact Registry repository using either the Google Cloud console or the command line. A repository is a centralized storage system for the software components and build outputs generated throughout the development process. It enables organized management, version control, and secure distribution of these artifacts. This example uses the command line to create a repository to store Docker images. In *Chapter 5*, we also worked with Docker images.

When you create an artifact repository, you'll specify the format, location, and a description:

```
gcloud artifacts repositories create \
continuous-delivery-container-repo \
--repository-format=docker \
--location=us-central1 \
--description="Docker repository example"
```

Here's the output from that example:

```
create request issued for: [continuous-delivery-container-repo]
Waiting for operation [projects/riccardo-blog-test-v1/locations/
us-central1/operations/73244659-77dc-481b-8253-26bd475ac3bf] to
complete...done.
Created repository [continuous-delivery-container-repo].
```

> **Important note**
>
> Artifact Registry requires that a Google Cloud region be specified. Artifact Registry supports using a single region or multi-regions. Multi-regions use multiple data centers to store the data and support large geographic regions such as the US, Europe, and Asia. Google Cloud recommends selecting a region location close to those who will consume the artifacts.

Now that you have an Artifact Registry repository, we'll show you how to control access to that repository.

Viewing role-based access control on a repository

Artifact Registry uses **role-based access controls** for permissions, through Google Cloud **Identity and Access Management (IAM)**.

Follow these steps to view permissions on a repository using the Google Cloud console and command line, respectively:

- To view permissions using the Google Cloud console, follow these steps:

  I.   From the Google Cloud console main menu, select **Artifact Registry | Repositories**, then select the repository by activating its checkbox, as shown in the following figure.

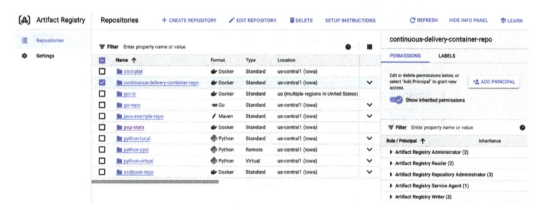

Figure 6.1 – List of repositories info panel

  II. Select the **PERMISSIONS** tab in the right panel, as seen in the previous figure.

  III. Expand the role to see which principals have been granted that role.

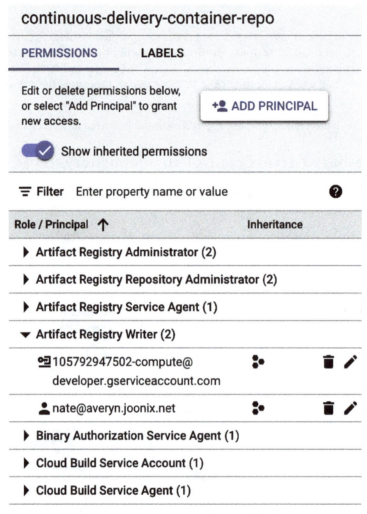

Figure 6.2 – Permissions tab showing principals for the selected role

- To view permissions using the command line, run the following command:

```
gcloud projects get-iam-policy $PROJECT_ID
```

This is an example output:

```
auditConfigs:
- auditLogConfigs:
  - logType: ADMIN_READ
  - logType: DATA_READ
  - logType: DATA_WRITE
  service: artifactregistry.googleapis.com
```

```
bindings:
- members:
  - serviceAccount:service-105792947502@gcp-sa-aiplatform.iam.
gserviceaccount.com
  role: roles/aiplatform.serviceAgent
- members:
  - serviceAccount:build-sa@riccardo-blog-test-v1.iam.
gserviceaccount.com
  - serviceAccount:service-105792947502@gcp-sa-cloudbuild.iam.
gserviceaccount.com
  role: roles/artifactregistry.admin
- members:
  - serviceAccount:105792947502-compute@developer.
gserviceaccount.com
  - serviceAccount:105792947502@cloudbuild.gserviceaccount.com
  - serviceAccount:tf-gke-jump-app-cluste-0stn@riccardo-blog-
test-v1.iam.gserviceaccount.com
  - serviceAccount:tf-gke-jump-app-cluste-jsy0@riccardo-blog-
test-v1.iam.gserviceaccount.com
  - serviceAccount:tf-gke-jump-app-cluste-tn6a@riccardo-blog-
test-v1.iam.gserviceaccount.com
  role: roles/artifactregistry.reader
```

Now that you've seen the roles, and the principles that have been granted those roles, it's time to see how to find out what repositories are available.

Listing the Artifact Registry repositories available in a project

You can see what repositories are available in your project using the Google Cloud console or the command line. This example uses the command line:

```
gcloud artifacts repositories list --project=$PROJECT_ID \
--location=us-central1
```

Here's the output from that example:

```
Listing items under project $PROJECT_ID, location us-central1.
ARTIFACT_REGISTRY

REPOSITORY: cicd-plat
FORMAT: DOCKER
MODE: STANDARD_REPOSITORY
DESCRIPTION:
LOCATION: us-central1
LABELS:
ENCRYPTION: Google-managed key
```

```
CREATE_TIME: 2022-07-14T23:13:35
UPDATE_TIME: 2022-07-15T00:32:50
SIZE (MB): 212.020

REPOSITORY: continuous-delivery-container-repo
FORMAT: DOCKER
MODE: STANDARD_REPOSITORY
DESCRIPTION: Docker repository example
LOCATION: us-central1
LABELS:
ENCRYPTION: Google-managed key
CREATE_TIME: 2023-07-17T01:35:40
UPDATE_TIME: 2023-07-17T01:35:40
SIZE (MB): 0

REPOSITORY: pop-stats
FORMAT: DOCKER
MODE: STANDARD_REPOSITORY
DESCRIPTION:
LOCATION: us-central1
LABELS:
ENCRYPTION: Google-managed key
CREATE_TIME: 2023-06-06T20:16:07
UPDATE_TIME: 2023-07-14T20:38:23
SIZE (MB): 341.835

REPOSITORY: scdbook-repo
FORMAT: DOCKER
MODE: STANDARD_REPOSITORY
DESCRIPTION: Docker repository for Securing Continuous Delivery Book
LOCATION: us-central1
LABELS:
ENCRYPTION: Google-managed key
CREATE_TIME: 2023-06-08T18:38:28
UPDATE_TIME: 2023-06-09T01:05:51
SIZE (MB): 113.648
```

You've seen which repositories are available in your projects. Next, we'll go ahead and upload a container to the repository.

Uploading a Docker container to Artifact Registry

For this example, we create a sample Dockerfile. Then, we upload the Dockerfile to the repository we created earlier in this chapter, in the *Creating an Artifact Registry Repository to store your image* section:

1. From a shell (Terminal, Cloud Shell, etc.), run the following command to authenticate to Google Cloud:

```
gcloud auth login
```

Then, follow the instructions to finish authenticating.

2. Next, run the following command to create a Docker configuration file with a `credHelper` entry:

```
gcloud auth configure-docker us-central1-docker.pkg.dev
```

3. Run the following command to create the Docker container image:

```
docker build -t hello-example .
```

Here is the output from that command:

```
user@workstation-oss:~/Securing-Continuous-Delivery-on-Google-Cloud-/ch7/docker-example$ docker build -t hello-example .
[+] Building 0.4s (13/13) FINISHED                                                                    docker:default
 => [internal] load build definition from dockerfile                                                            0.0s
 => => transferring dockerfile: 762B                                                                            0.0s
 => [internal] load .dockerignore                                                                               0.0s
 => => transferring context: 2B                                                                                 0.0s
 => [internal] load metadata for docker.io/library/golang:latest                                                0.1s
 => [1/8] FROM docker.io/library/golang:latest@sha256:5f5d61dcb58900bc57b230431b6367c900f9982b583adcabf9fa93fd0aa5544a  0.0s
 => [internal] load build context                                                                               0.0s
 => => transferring context: 1.04kB                                                                             0.0s
 => CACHED [2/8] RUN mkdir /app                                                                                  0.0s
 => CACHED [3/8] WORKDIR /app                                                                                    0.0s
 => CACHED [4/8] COPY go.mod .                                                                                   0.0s
 => CACHED [5/8] COPY go.sum .                                                                                   0.0s
 => CACHED [6/8] RUN go mod download                                                                            0.0s
 => CACHED [7/8] COPY . .                                                                                        0.0s
 => CACHED [8/8] RUN go build -o main                                                                            0.0s
 => exporting to image                                                                                          0.0s
 => => exporting layers                                                                                         0.0s
 => => writing image sha256:f15f10da2282d8473cab1c705ab74254127b45e1a9a24fd6ce28c4dbd6163467                    0.0s
 => => naming to docker.io/library/hello-example                                                                0.0s
user@workstation-oss:~/Securing-Continuous-Delivery-on-Google-Cloud-/ch7/docker-example$
```

Figure 6.3 – The output from the docker build command

4. Run this command to add a tag to the image:

```
docker tag hello-example us-central1-docker.pkg.dev/$PROJECT_ID/
continuous-delivery-container-repo/hello-example:latest
```

5. Run the `docker push` command to push the tagged image to the repository:

```
docker push us-central1-docker.pkg.dev/$PROJECT_ID/continuous-
delivery-container-repo/hello-example:latest
```

Here is the output from that command:

```
user@workstation-oss:~/Securing-Continuous-Delivery-on-Google-Cloud-/ch7/docker-example$ docker push us-central1-docker.pkg.dev/$PRO
JECT_ID/continuous-delivery-container-repo/hello-example:latest
The push refers to repository [us-central1-docker.pkg.dev/riccardo-blog-test-v1/continuous-delivery-container-repo/hello-example]
a265663c80fe: Pushed
54f25f4cd0d8: Layer already exists
ca090c4df8f2: Pushed
9d8ac47a5db1: Pushed
5359587912ac: Pushed
5f70bf18a086: Layer already exists
f4afb9d7ab58: Pushed
1cccecff33e6: Pushed
82428a5ce14c: Pushed
86ef0710f694: Pushed
5bb1de08f5af: Pushed
0dfa23fffa41: Pushed
aa904f36746c: Pushed
latest: digest: sha256:50e8e16bd232aa168e083dd608cd834d51638487bff0b602770e052e831e106f size: 3045
```

Figure 6.4 – The output from the docker push command

Now that you've uploaded a container to Artifact Registry, you can see it by listing the images in the repository, as explained in the next section.

Listing container images in the repository

You can list images in the repository using either the command line or the Google Cloud console. To use the command line to see the image you just pushed to the repository, run the following command:

```
gcloud artifacts docker images list \
us-central1-docker.pkg.dev/$PROJECT_ID/continuous-delivery-container-
repo
```

Here's the output from that command:

```
user@workstation-oss:~/Securing-Continuous-Delivery-on-Google-Cloud-/ch7/docker-example$ gcloud artifacts docker images list us-cent
ral1-docker.pkg.dev/$PROJECT_ID/continuous-delivery-container-repo
Listing items under project riccardo-blog-test-v1, location us-central1, repository continuous-delivery-container-repo.

IMAGE                                                                                                       DIGEST
                                       CREATE_TIME        UPDATE_TIME
us-central1-docker.pkg.dev/riccardo-blog-test-v1/continuous-delivery-container-repo/hello-example  sha256:50e8e16bd232aa168e083dd608
cd834d51638487bff0b602770e052e831e106f  2024-01-23T03:29:25  2024-01-23T03:29:25
```

Figure 6.5 – The output from the docker images list command

Now, let's see how to list images in the repository using the Google Cloud console. Follow the following steps to use the Google Cloud console to view a list of images in your repository:

1. From the main menu, select **Artifact Registry** | **Repositories**. The list of repositories is shown, including the one you created in this chapter.

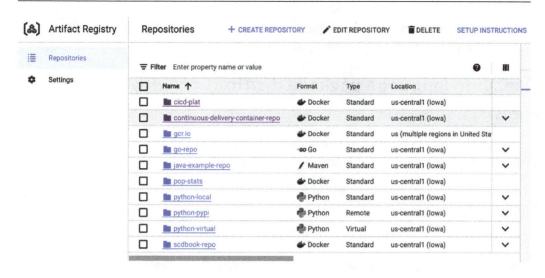

Figure 6.6 – The list of Artifact Registry repositories

> **Important note**
> The other repositories listed, if any, will be different in your project.

2. Click on the repository to open it up. The repository is shown:

Figure 6.7 – The list of image digests in the repository

Now that you've uploaded a container image and seen it listed in your repository, it's time to try pulling the image from the repository.

Pulling a container image/package

Pulling an image from the repository downloads it to your local machine. So, run the following command:

```
docker pull REGION-docker.pkg.dev/PROJECT/REPO/IMAGE:TAG
```

Docker downloads the image to the machine on which you run this command.

Now that you've seen how to manage container images using Artifact Registry, let's take a look at how to use Artifact Registry to manage language packages.

Managing language package distribution with Artifact Registry

You can use Artifact Registry to manage language packages, just as you can use it to manage container images. In this section, you'll do the following:

1. Create a repository for Python packages
2. Upload a package
3. View the packages in the repository

Artifact Registry is designed to be a universal package-management application, supporting multiple package types. Knowing how to manage more than one type can be advantageous. Our first package type shows how Artifact Registry supports Python applications. Our second package type shows Go language packages. This highlights some of the similarities and differences in how different programming languages are supported using Artifact Registry.

First, let's create the repository.

Creating a repository for a Python package from the demo app

The first thing we need to do is to create the repository in which to put our Python package.

Run the following command to create a standard (local) Python repository:

```
gcloud artifacts repositories create python-local \
    --repository-format=python \
    --location=us-central1 \
    --description="local python packages"
```

Here are the results:

```
user@workstation-oss:~$ gcloud artifacts repositories create python-local \
> --repository-format=python \
> --location=us-central1 \
> --description="local python packages"
Create request issued for: [python-local]
Waiting for operation [projects/riccardo-blog-test-v1/locations/us-central1/operations/db5f07ba-2fdb-435f-8f43-651896166720] to complete...done.

Created repository [python-local].
user@workstation-oss:~$
```

Figure 6.8 – The output from the repositories create command

Now that you've created the repository, let's upload the package.

Uploading a Python package to the repository

To upload a Python package to a repository, you'll need to do the following:

1. **Install support files**: Multiple support packages are required before you can upload packages to a Python repository. These support files provide for authentication using a keyring, and Twine for uploading the files to the repository.

   Run the following commands to prepare your Python environment:

   ```
   python3 -m venv venv
   source venv/bin/activate
   python3 -m pip install --upgrade pip
   pip install twine keyrings.google-artifactregistry-auth
   ```

2. **Install Twine**: Run the following command to install Twine:

   ```
   pip3 install twine
   ```

3. **Upload the Python package**: Run the following command to upload your Python package to the repository:

   ```
   twine upload --repository-url \
   https://us-central1-python.pkg. dev/$PROJECT_ID/python-local
   dist/*
   ```

   The output is shown in the following figure:

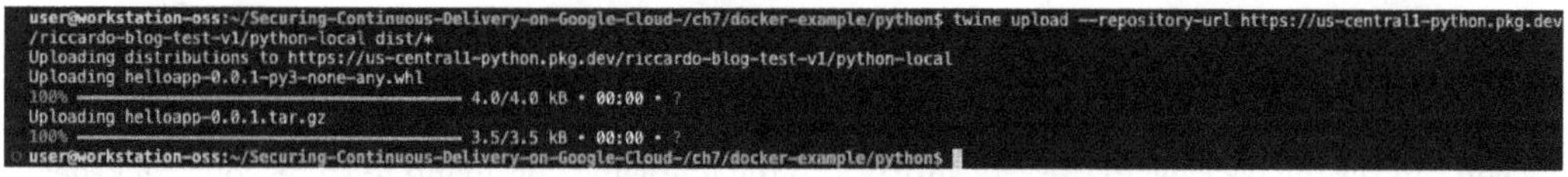

Figure 6.9 – The output from the twine upload command

> **Important note**
>
> Some users may find it more convenient to define multiple repositories in the `.pypirc` file and then refer to those repositories with friendlier names instead of the full URL path.

For example, the `.pypirc` file would change the `upload` command. If you decide to update your `.pypirc` file, be sure to replace the provided repository name and URLs with the name and URL path for your repositories.

> **Important note**
>
> Instead of a URL, the repository name, `python-local`, is used. Developers can use the names given in the `.pypirc` file when referencing Python repositories. `-verbose` is optional and is used to give you a view of the actions taking place when the command executes as well as stating the file path of the `.pypirc` file called.

The alternate `upload` command is as follows:

```
python3 -m twine upload --repository python-local  dist/* --verbose
```

Your `.pypirc` file should contain the following:

```
[distutils]
index-servers =
python-pypi
python-virtual
python-local

[python-pypi]
repository = https://us-central1-python.pkg.dev//python-pypi/

[python-virtual]
repository = https://us-central1-python.pkg.dev/riccardo-blog-test-v1/
python-virtual

[python-local]
repository = https://us-central1-python.pkg.dev/riccardo-blog-test-v1/
python-local
```

Next, we'll look at a list of packages in the repository, showing your uploaded package.

Viewing packages in the standard Python repository

Now you can see the package in the repository. Run the following command to show your package:

```
gcloud artifacts files list \
  --project=$PROJECT_ID \
  --repository=python-local \
  --location=us-central1
```

Here is the output from this command:

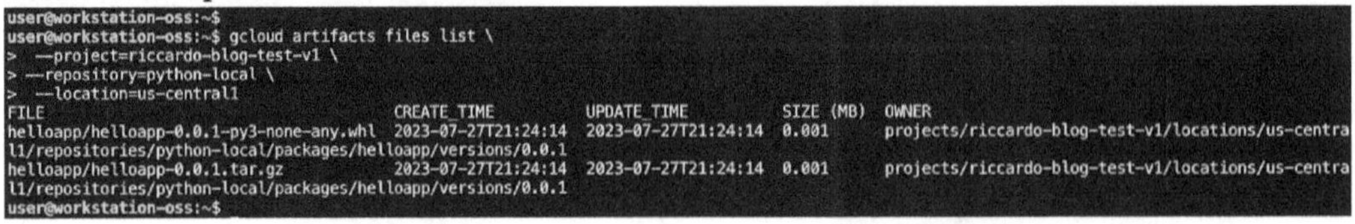

Figure 6.10 – The output from the artifacts list command

Next, you can create another repository; this one for Go packages.

Creating a repo for Go packages from the demo app

Go is a popular programming language. This example shows the diversity of repository types that Artifact Registry supports.

Follow these steps to create a repository for Go packages:

1. Run the following command to install the support files you need for a Go repository:

    ```
    gcloud components install package-go-module
    ```

2. Run the following command to create the repository:

    ```
    gcloud artifacts repositories create go-repo \
    --repository-format=go \
    --location=us-central1 \
    --description=example-go-repository
    ```

    Here is the result of this command:

Figure 6.11 – The output from the repositories create command

You've learned how to create repositories in Artifact Registry, how to upload container images to that repository and view them there, and how to pull images from there. Next, you will learn how to use virtual repositories and remote repositories.

Using virtual and remote repositories

An Artifact Registry remote repository lets you create a repository as a proxy for an external repository, such as Docker Hub. In this way, you can keep the external repository, but it's as if it were an Artifact Registry repository.

A virtual repository lets you create a single repository from one or more upstream repositories, including standard or remote Artifact Registry repositories. This makes it easier for you to have multiple repositories but use them as if they were one.

> **Important note**
> Both remote and virtual repository types are read-only. Packages can be uploaded to standard repositories.

Not all package types support the same features. Earlier, we created a standard Python repository. That repository will serve as a component of the remote and virtual repositories. This section uses Python, as it demonstrates remote and virtual repository types. The `Pypi` Python package repository is used as the upstream repository.

This section includes exercises for doing the following:

- Create a remote repository for Python

- Populate the remote repository with cached files

- List the packages in that repository

- Create a virtual repository using two different repos

- List the files in the virtual repository

To begin, we'll create a remote repository.

Creating a remote repository for Python

Run the following command to create your Python repository:

```
gcloud artifacts repositories create python-pypi \
--project=$PROJECT_ID \
--repository-format=python \
--location=us-central1 \
--description="remote python repo" \
--mode=remote-repository \
--remote-repo-config-desc="remote repo is PYPI" \
--remote-python-repo=PYPI
```

Here is the result of this command:

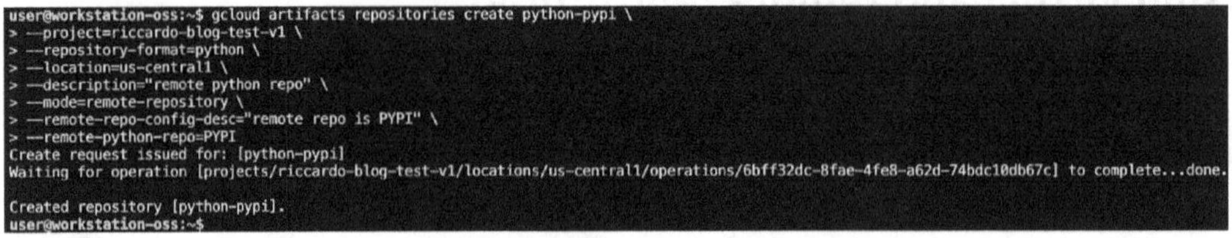

Figure 6.12 – The output from the repositories create command

Now, you have a remote repository. Let's list the packages in it.

Listing the packages in the remote Python repo

A sample Python application is available in the ch6 folder in the GitHub repository. You can use this app with the Python examples if you'd like to package an application.

You can view the repository content using either the command line or the Google Cloud console. The following command shows how to do it using the command line:

```
gcloud artifacts files list \
  --project=$PROJECT_ID \
  --repository=python-pypi \
  --location=us-central1
```

The following is the output from this command:

```
user@workstation-oss-demo:~/demos$ gcloud artifacts files list --project=$PROJECT_ID --repository=python-local --location=us-central1
FILE                                                                                          CREATE_TIME          UPDATE_
TIME        SIZE (MB)  OWNER
blinker/blinker-1.6.2-py3-none-any.whl                                                        2023-08-09T16:48:05  2023-08
-09T16:48:05  0.013      projects/riccardo-blog-test-v1/locations/us-central1/repositories/python-local/packages/blinker/versions/1.6.2
click/click-8.1.6-py3-none-any.whl                                                            2023-08-09T16:48:05  2023-08
-09T16:48:05  0.093      projects/riccardo-blog-test-v1/locations/us-central1/repositories/python-local/packages/click/versions/8.1.6
cpu-load-generator/cpu_load_generator-1.2.0-py3-none-any.whl                                  2023-08-09T16:48:05  2023-08
-09T16:48:05  0.007      projects/riccardo-blog-test-v1/locations/us-central1/repositories/python-local/packages/cpu-load-generator/versions/1.2.0
flask/Flask-2.3.2-py3-none-any.whl                                                            2023-08-09T16:48:04  2023-08
```

Figure 6.13 – The output from the artifacts list command

Now that you've created a remote repository and viewed the packages in it, it's time to create a virtual repository.

Creating a virtual repository from two different Python repositories

Virtual repositories allow you to access multiple repositories using a single repository name. To do so, you'll first create a policy file, and then run the command to create the virtual repository. Follow these steps to create your virtual repository:

1. Create a file called policies.json, and add the following content:

    ```
    [{
    "id" : "upstream1",
    "repository" : "projects/$PROJECT_ID/locations/us-central1/
    repositories/python-local",
    "priority" : 100
    }, {
    "id" : "upstream2",
    "repository" : "projects/$PROJECT_ID/locations/us-central1/
    repositories/python-pypi",
    "priority" : 80
    }]
    ```

    This content identifies the two repositories to be used by the virtual repository.

2. Run the `repositories create` command:

```
gcloud artifacts repositories create python-virtual \
    --project=$PROJECT_ID \
    --repository-format=python \
    --mode=virtual-repository \
    --location=us-central1 \
    --description="virtual python repository" \
    --upstream-policy-file=policies.json
```

The following is the output from this command:

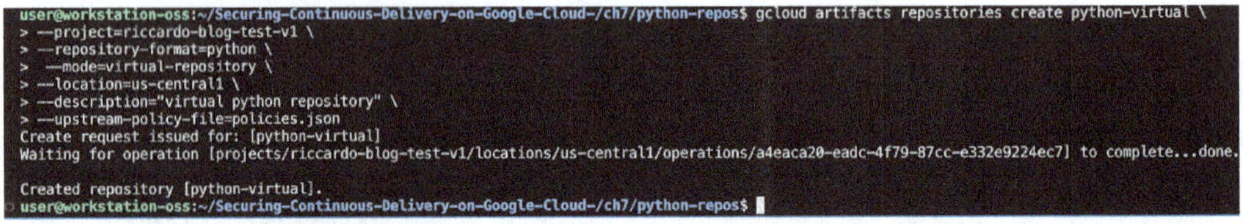

Figure 6.14 – The output from the repositories create command for virtual repo

Now that you've seen how to create virtual and remote repositories, let's learn how to use Artifact Registry to scan for security vulnerabilities.

Using vulnerability scanning to detect threats

Artifact Registry provides vulnerability scanning in the **Artifact Analysis** service, to help detect security vulnerabilities and protect your containers from threats.

In this section, you'll run an **on-demand scan**, and then view the results in the Google Cloud console. Automatic scanning is also available but is not discussed in this chapter.

Running an on-demand scan of your container image

You can run on-demand scans synchronously or asynchronously. Scans can take a considerable amount of time, so asynchronous can be a better choice in some cases.

There are two parts to the on-demand scan. There's the scan and then there's the retrieval and viewing of results. In this exercise, the Docker container uploaded into Artifact Registry earlier will be used for an on-demand scan.

Run the following command to perform a vulnerability scan on our container image:

```
gcloud artifacts docker images scan \
us-central1-docker.pkg.dev/$PROJECT_ID/\
continuous-delivery-container-repo/hello-example \
--remote --location=us
```

The following is the output from this command:

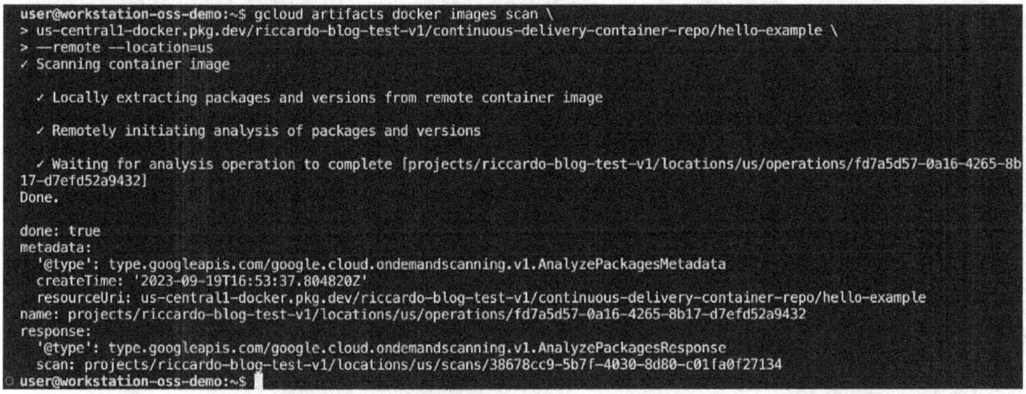

Figure 6.15 – The output from the docker images scan command

Now that you've scanned your image for vulnerabilities, let's view the results.

Seeing the results of the on-demand scan

Because the number of items reported by a vulnerability scan could easily exceed your computer's ability to display them all in the command terminal, the output of the command is sent to a text file called scan-results.txt, which you can open in your favorite text editor or viewer.

Run the following command to generate a text file listing all the vulnerabilities found in your scan:

```
gcloud artifacts docker images list-vulnerabilities \
projects/$PROJECT_ID/riccardo-blog-test-v1/locations/\
us/scans/7ef40c24-79ce-4fe3-b0f8-c7d3ae316ea3 \
>scan-results.txt
```

The following picture shows the output from this command in a text file:

```
artifact-demo >  ≣ scan-results.txt
  1   ───
  2   createTime: '2023-07-28T06:37:05.233300Z'
  3   kind: VULNERABILITY
  4   name: projects/riccardo-blog-test-v1/locations/us/occurrences/007bbc68-f262-493b-9580-12fcc7a964fd
  5   noteName: projects/goog-vulnz/notes/CVE-2023-29007
  6   resourceUri: us-central1-docker.pkg.dev/riccardo-blog-test-v1/continuous-delivery-container-repo/hello-example
  7   updateTime: '2023-07-28T06:37:05.233300Z'
  8   vulnerability:
  9     cvssScore: 7.8
 10     cvssv3:
 11       attackComplexity: ATTACK_COMPLEXITY_LOW
 12       attackVector: ATTACK_VECTOR_LOCAL
 13       availabilityImpact: IMPACT_HIGH
 14       baseScore: 7.8
 15       confidentialityImpact: IMPACT_HIGH
 16       exploitabilityScore: 1.8
 17       impactScore: 5.9
 18       integrityImpact: IMPACT_HIGH
 19       privilegesRequired: PRIVILEGES_REQUIRED_NONE
 20       scope: SCOPE_UNCHANGED
 21       userInteraction: USER_INTERACTION_REQUIRED
 22     effectiveSeverity: LOW
 23     longDescription: Git is a revision control system. Prior to versions 2.30.9, 2.31.8,
 24       2.32.7, 2.33.8, 2.34.8, 2.35.8, 2.36.6, 2.37.7, 2.38.5, 2.39.3, and 2.40.1, a
 25       specially crafted `.gitmodules` file with submodule URLs that are longer than
 26       1024 characters can used to exploit a bug in `config.c::git_config_copy_or_rename_section_in_file()`.
 27       This bug can be used to inject arbitrary configuration into a user's `$GIT_DIR/config`
 28       when attempting to remove the configuration section associated with that submodule.
 29       When the attacker injects configuration values which specify executables to run
 30       (such as `core.pager`, `core.editor`, `core.sshCommand`, etc.) this can lead to
 31       a remote code execution. A fix A fix is available in versions 2.30.9, 2.31.8,
 32       2.32.7, 2.33.8, 2.34.8, 2.35.8, 2.36.6, 2.37.7, 2.38.5, 2.39.3, and 2.40.1. As
```

Figure 6.16 – A partial list of the vulnerabilities saved to the output file

You've used the command line to see your container's vulnerabilities. Next, you'll see how to view vulnerabilities using the Google Cloud console.

Viewing scan results in the Google Cloud Console

To see the results from your vulnerability scan in the Google Cloud console, perform the following steps:

1. From the Google Cloud console main menu, select **Artifact Registry | Repositories**.
2. Select the repository from the list of repositories that is shown.

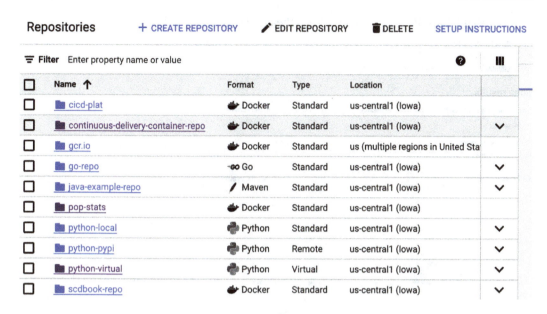

Figure 6.17 – The list of Artifact Registry repositories

3. From the list of repositories, select the repository containing your image, and then select that container image.

   The **Digests** page for that image is displayed.

Figure 6.18 – Digest for our example image

4. Click on that number to open up the list of vulnerabilities.

The **VULNERABILITIES** column shows the number of vulnerabilities found.

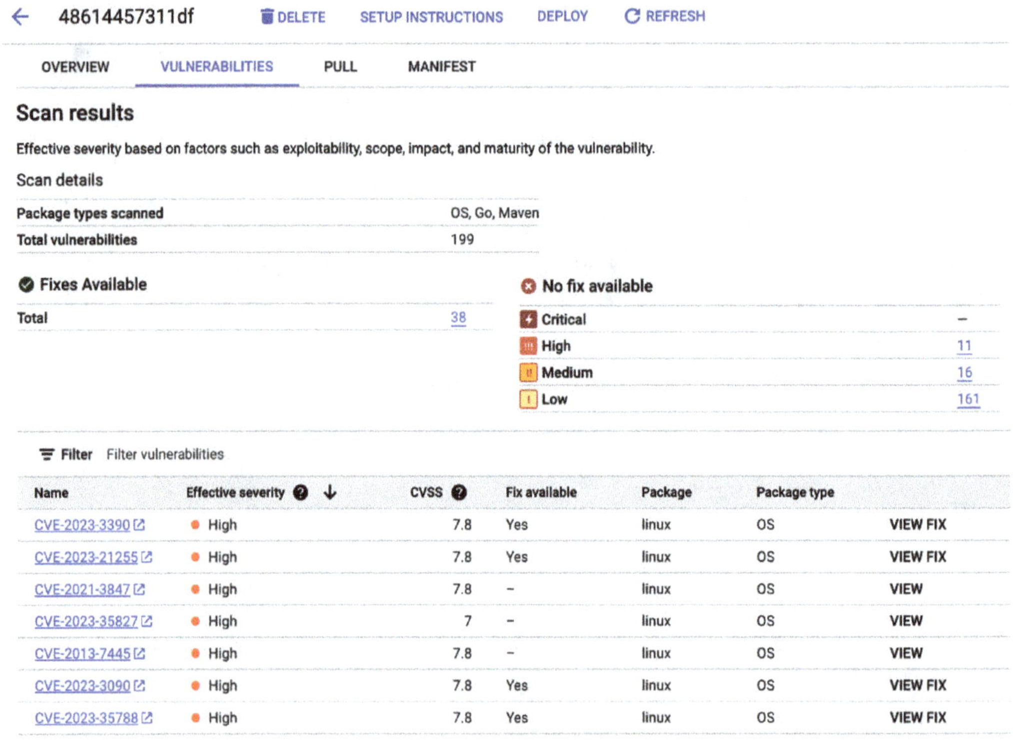

Figure 6.19 – Results of the vulnerability scan shown in the Google Cloud console

The preceding sections showed you how to enable and use vulnerability scanning – an important part of ensuring the security of your applications stored on Artifact Registry.

Summary

Artifact Registry is an important part of your software delivery toolchain.

This chapter showed how to manage container images and language packages, use virtual and remote repositories, and scan for vulnerabilities using Artifact Registry. This knowledge will help you, going forward, to use Artifact Registry as part of your source-to-prod toolchain.

In the next chapter, you'll learn about Google Cloud runtime environments, **GKE**, **Cloud Run**, and **GKE Enterprise**.

References

To learn more about the topics that were covered in this chapter, take a look at the following resources:

- Google Cloud. (2023, December 12). How to set up a private registry with no secrets on AWS for Anthos clusters. `https://cloud.google.com/anthos/clusters/docs/multi-cloud/aws/how-to/private-registry`.

- Google Cloud. (2021, November). Use a private image registry | Anthos clusters on Azure. `https://cloud.google.com/anthos/docs/azure/private-registry`, `https://cloud.google.com/anthos/docs/azure/private-registry`.

Part 3:
Deploy and Run
Your Application

In *Part 3*, you'll learn about the Google Cloud runtime environments Google Kubernetes Engine (GKE) and Cloud Run. You can deploy your application to both of these Google Cloud runtimes, including in hybrid and multi-cloud environments. You'll then learn how to use Cloud Deploy to manage your application deployment progression across different stages. You'll also learn how to protect GKE and Cloud Run with Binary Authorization, so you can restrict them to only execute applications you trust.

This part has the following chapters:

- *Chapter 7, Exploring Runtimes – GKE, GKE Enterprise, and Cloud Run*
- *Chapter 8, Automating Sofware Delivery Using Cloud Deploy*
- *Chapter 9, Securing Your Runtimes with Binary Authorization*

7

Exploring Runtimes – GKE, GKE Enterprise, and Cloud Run

At the end of the source-to-production pipeline is the **runtime**. The runtime is the machine where your application runs. The runtimes covered in this chapter are used for **container-based applications**.

In this chapter, we describe the main Google Cloud execution environments where you can deploy your applications using **Continuous Delivery tooling**, including **Google Kubernetes Engine (GKE)**, **Cloud Run**, and **GKE Enterprise** (hosted on-premises or on other hyperscale clouds). In this chapter, we cover the following topics:

- Understanding containers
- Understanding Google Kubernetes Engine
- Understanding Cloud Run

Understanding containers

Containers have become popular because they allow code to be packaged to easily run on a developer's workstation and a multi-node cluster in the cloud. Think of a standard shipping container. It's designed to hold a variety of goods and can be transported seamlessly by trucks, ships, and trains. Similarly, a software container holds an application and its supporting files, allowing it to run reliably on different computers (servers, laptops, the cloud, etc.). A container has everything your application needs to run:

- **The code**: The actual instructions that make your application work
- **Runtime environment**: The software that understands and executes your code (such as Python, Java, or Node.js)
- **Libraries and tools**: The *helpers* your code relies on to do specific tasks
- **Settings**: The configurations that tell your application how to behave

Container portability makes it possible for an application to go from a developer's laptop to Cloud Run, and then on to GKE should the need arise. By packaging an application's code and dependencies, containers simplify the process of sharing application code.

Cloud Build helps you build your code into a container-based application. **Artifact Registry** lets you store the container you've built and access it from your pipeline. **Google Cloud Deploy** takes a container and deploys it to one of the runtime environments described in this chapter. These products are all part of the toolchain that gets you from code to a running application on Google Cloud.

Moreover, Google Cloud capabilities are designed to integrate with GKE and Cloud Run. Logs are available in Cloud Logging and Cloud Monitoring. Identity and Access Management accounts and permissions are provided by Google Cloud IAM. GKE and Cloud Run are first-class citizens with Google Cloud, allowing for integration in ways that simplify management, because the same skills are spread against the broader Google Cloud ecosystem.

Understanding Google Kubernetes Engine

Google Kubernetes Engine (GKE) is a Google-managed service for running Kubernetes. You can use GKE to deploy, manage, and scale containerized applications on Google Cloud. GKE runs Kubernetes on clustered **Compute Engine instances**.

GKE is built on the open source **Kubernetes** container orchestration platform. GKE uses Kubernetes commands to manage workloads. Kubernetes itself is based on technology used within Google for deploying, administering, managing, and monitoring applications. This internal Google system—called **Borg**—is often pointed to as the inspiration for Kubernetes. This means that organizations other than Google can benefit from years of experience scheduling containers to power major systems such as Search and YouTube.

The following sections talk about GKE, why it's important, its components, and two modes of operation for GKE clusters. This information will help you decide whether or not to deploy your applications to GKE, and which operation mode to use.

What's the big deal about GKE?

GKE is managed by Kubernetes with additional services to make working with Kubernetes easier for Google Cloud users. These features not only reduce the complexity of Kubernetes but also provide a faster path to value.

Native Kubernetes developed a reputation for being somewhat difficult to set up and complex to manage. GKE simplifies these aspects of Kubernetes so that teams can focus more on the applications themselves and less on the infrastructure. GKE provides features such as node management, service mesh (for microservices management), and auto-upgrade capabilities for clusters and nodes. GKE also gives teams the ability to control the level of stability and feature availability in their Kubernetes clusters by setting the release channel to stable, regular, or rapid.

Each GKE release channel level corresponds to the level of risk accepted. The rapid channel provides features the fastest, however, there's a higher chance of encountering issues. This setting is recommended for test and other non-production systems when users want to stay on the bleeding edge. The regular channel is the default and is a good balance of new features and stability. The stable channel prioritizes stability over bleeding-edge features. GKE makes container orchestration easier. Because Kubernetes is a container-based system, workloads must be packaged as container images before being deployed onto a GKE cluster. You can do this using one of the popular container-creation tools, such as **Docker** or **buildpacks**. Containers can be built by developers and tested on their local machines before sending them to be used elsewhere. *Containers are lightweight packages of your application code together with dependencies such as specific versions of programming language runtimes and libraries required to run your software services* (*Google, 2024*). The containerized applications are then, typically, stored in an artifact repository such as **Google Artifact Registry** or **JFrog Artifactory**.

Here are some of those features:

- GKE provides an autopilot cluster configuration capability, which dramatically simplifies creating and managing a functional Kubernetes cluster.
- GKE lets you upgrade the version of the control plane and node pool manually or automatically.
- Logging is integrated with Google operations management tooling.
- GKE supports using private nodes, which cannot be accessed by the public internet.
- You can manage multiple GKE clusters as fleets, with a consistent set of configurations across the clusters. This is helpful for enterprises that want to manage large numbers of Kubernetes clusters on Google Cloud.

That's a little bit about what GKE can do. Next, we'll take a quick look at some of its limits.

GKE limitations

The following table shows the limitations of GKE as of the time of writing:

Attributes	GKE Standard	GKE Autopilot
Nodes per cluster	15,000	5,000
Nodes per node pool	1,000	N/A
Nodes in a zone	1,000 when using group-based instances, otherwise no node limit	N/A
Pods per node	256	32
Pods per cluster	200,000	25,000
Containers per cluster	400,000	25,000

Table 7.1 – Limitations of GKE

Next, we discuss the two cluster operation modes.

GKE cluster modes

GKE supports two cluster modes:

- **Autopilot**: Autopilot simplifies node and cluster management for users. Autopilot uses clusters and nodes that are pre-configured and optimized for production workloads. In fact, Google manages the cluster and node infrastructure.

- **Standard**: Standard provides customers with full control over clusters and nodes. This mode gives customers as much flexibility as possible over available resources.

Google recommends using Autopilot unless there are specific requirements that can only be achieved when using Standard. GKE Standard allows customers to manipulate nodes, unlike Autopilot. GKE Standard allows SSH access to nodes, customized node configuration, and the ability to install software on the nodes.

Let's talk about GKE components now.

GKE components

The architecture of a GKE cluster includes a **control plane** and **nodes**. Nodes are the machines (Compute Engine instances) that run your application. Together, the control plane and nodes make up the **Kubernetes cluster orchestration system**.

When you create a GKE cluster, you can choose GKE Standard mode or GKE Autopilot. With Standard mode, GKE manages the control plane and other parts of the system while you manage the nodes. With Autopilot, GKE manages the whole infrastructure, control plane, nodes, and system components.

The following diagram shows the parts of a GKE cluster and how they work together to deliver your applications to your users.

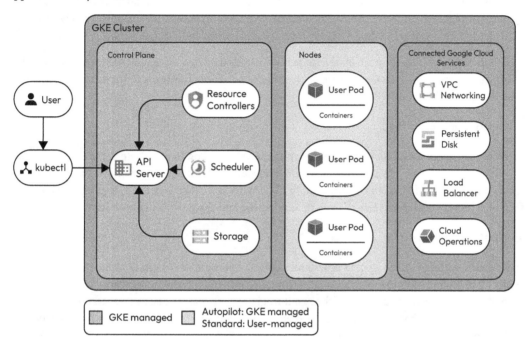

Figure 7.1 – Architecture of a GKE cluster

The control plane includes the Kubernetes API server, scheduler, and resource controllers. GKE manages the control plane for you during the entire life of the cluster. You can even have GKE automatically upgrade the version of Kubernetes running on the control plane.

This brings us to autoscaling, which you'll see in the following subsection.

Autoscaling

Every time a program runs, it consumes resources: compute, memory, and storage. Before public-cloud computing, increasing any of these resources required a technician to open the computer and add or replace parts. Cloud computing makes it possible to increase available resources on demand, or to release unneeded resources. This ability is sometimes called an **accordion model**.

Autoscaling uses the flexibility of cloud computing, to help applications consume or release resources based on a set of predefined conditions. Two common autoscaling methods are horizontal autoscaling (scaling out and in) and vertical autoscaling (scaling up and down). Expanding and contracting resources based on demand provides operators and application owners with improved reliability and cost optimization over traditional enterprise bare-metal hardware. These separate types of scaling can be used independently, or you can use them together, in multidimensional autoscaling. Systems engineers configure autoscaling to occur before resources are exhausted and customers receive errors. GKE supports both types of autoscaling (in both GKE Standard and GKE Autopilot).

When both forms of workloads are used together, workloads use the optimal amount of resources both horizontally (number of Pods) and vertically (resources per Pod). This leads to the best performance at the lowest possible cost.

Horizontal autoscaling

Horizontal autoscaling (*scaling in and out*) copies the primary Pod to distribute the user load across more Pods. If a Pod were a house, then additional houses would be added, forming a row of houses. This technique is the more common one used in Kubernetes and other systems, as adding more copies of a Pod is less disruptive and less risky than altering the Pod that's servicing user connections.

Vertical autoscaling

Vertical autoscaling (*scaling up and down*) increases the amount of resources available on the Pod. Think of it as adding more floors to an existing building. As with a home renovation, there is a higher risk of disrupted functionality. Also, although it might appear that a node has added more RAM or CPU to the Pod, what happens is that GKE creates a new Pod with the new sizes, and then starts the application container on the new Pod.

You've learned about GKE, what it consists of, and how you can use it. Next, we'll look at GKE Enterprise.

Understanding GKE Enterprise

GKE Enterprise is a superset of GKE. GKE Enterprise has all the features of GKE, in addition to some features suited to helping customers manage GKE clusters at scale. Standard Kubernetes is fine for managing a small number of clusters. GKE Enterprise is for large-scale Kubernetes deployments. GKE Enterprise provides a single console enabling streamlined configuration and enhanced security features.

The management capabilities of GKE Enterprise stretch across public cloud and on-premises environments. Groups of clusters are called fleets, which can include clusters from multiple projects.

Identity management

Fleets provide two mechanisms for authentication across clusters: **Connect Gateway** and **GKE Identity Service**. Connect Gateway can be selected by those who wish to use Google Cloud as the identity provider. For those who want to use a different identity provider, GKE Identity Service can be used.

An example of when GKE Enterprise would be used is in situations where a large company has multiple data centers as well as computing at the edge. Imagine a retail chain that has edge computing needs in each store along with headquarters' compute, and even a website and mobile app.

GKE Enterprise is a modern application platform from Google Cloud that helps you manage, govern, and operate containerized workloads, at enterprise scale, on fleets of clusters. A **fleet** is a logical grouping of Kubernetes clusters to be managed together.

GKE clusters can be hosted on any of the following:

- On Google Cloud
- Outside of Google Cloud:
  - On-premises
  - On another public cloud, such as AWS or Azure

GKE Enterprise provides the following tools to standardize Kubernetes configurations and security across clusters, wherever they are:

- **Config Management**: A set of tools that lets operators share their configurations automatically and enforce security policies on GKE on Google Cloud, GKE on-premises, and GKE on other cloud providers
- **Policy Controller**: A tool that helps you apply and enforce policies for your Kubernetes clusters
- **Service mesh**: A set of tools to manage traffic among an application's microservices, including service-to-service communication
- **Connect gateway**: An interface to connect to and run commands against a fleet of registered clusters on Google Cloud, on-premises, or on other public clouds.

GKE Enterprise on on-premises clusters

GKE Enterprise lets customers use Google Cloud to manage their on-premises **bare-metal clusters** or on-premises **VMware clusters**, and workloads running on those clusters. By extending the control plane to these additional resources, organizations can consolidate the management of on-premises resources through cloud-based management tools.

The following sections describe the types of GKE Enterprise on-premises clusters.

GKE Enterprise on VMware

GKE Enterprise clusters on VMware let you create and manage Kubernetes clusters on premises in a GKE-like way, using the Google Cloud console. The following diagram shows how the components of GKE on VMware work together to deliver services to your users.

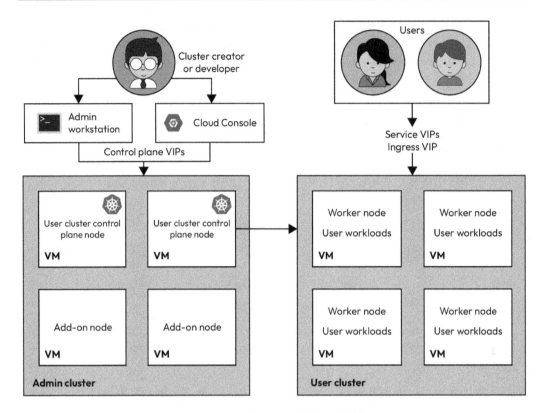

Figure 7.2 – Architecture of GKE on VMware

As shown in this diagram, users interact with workloads running on worker nodes on the user cluster, which are administered from control-plane instances running on the admin cluster, accessed from an admin workstation, or using the Google Cloud console.

GKE Enterprise on bare metal

You can use GKE clusters on bare metal to create and manage Kubernetes clusters on hardware in your own on-premises data center while using Google Cloud features.

You have direct control over application scale, security, and network latency because you're using your own hardware and network, but you can manage your containerized applications using GKE.

The following diagram shows how the components of GKE Enterprise on bare metal work together to deliver services to your users.

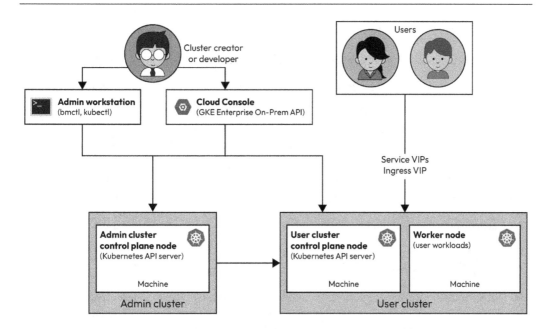

Figure 7.3 – Architecture of GKE on bare metal

As shown in this diagram, users interact with application workloads running on worker nodes, which are controlled using the user cluster control plane. That control plane is in turn controlled from the admin cluster, accessed from an admin workstation or using the Google Cloud console.

GKE Enterprise can even extend to non-Google public clouds.

Limitations of GKE Enterprise on bare metal

The following table shows the limitations of GKE Enterprise on bare metal. Google recommends keeping the number of Pods per cluster at 15,000 or fewer.

Pods per node	Nodes per cluster	Pods per Cluster
110	136	14,960
100	150	15,000
75	200	15,000

Table 7.2 – Limitations of GKE on bare metal

And finally, let's look at GKE Enterprise for AWS and Azure.

GKE Enterprise clusters on AWS and Azure

GKE Enterprise can be configured for use on non-Google public clouds.

You can use the Google Cloud console to manage your Kubernetes clusters on AWS and Azure. And with Connect Gateway, you can use your Google Cloud identity to authenticate to these clusters.

While GKE Enterprise builds on top of GKE, the choice between the two often comes down to the scale and location(s) of the clusters to be controlled. Often, a handful of clusters can be managed with GKE Standard or Autopilot. When the number of clusters grows beyond the bounds of GKE, then Enterprise capabilities should be used to deploy, configure, and secure clusters at scale on Google Cloud, on-premises, or on other public clouds.

You've learned about the GKE and GKE Enterprise features. Read on to find out about Cloud Run.

Understanding Cloud Run

Cloud Run gives developers a way to run containerized applications on Google Cloud without having to manage virtual machines, clusters, or Kubernetes. Cloud Run is a managed service that runs customer containers on Google's scalable infrastructure. Cloud Run is typically viewed as simple enough for a single developer to team up with a few infrastructure personnel to get running.

Cloud Run services have a stable HTTPS URL. Cloud Run-hosted services are triggered by HTTPS requests. Anything that sends HTTPS requests can be a trigger. HTTPS requests can come from multiple sources, including some that may not immediately come to mind, such as Eventarc, Pub/Sub, and Workflows.

Here are some of the features:

- **Serverless execution**: Focus purely on code. Cloud Run handles server provisioning, scaling, and infrastructure management.

- **HTTP request-driven**: Cloud Run services are triggered by HTTP requests, making them ideal for web applications, APIs, and event-driven architectures.

- **Automatic scaling** (including to zero): Handles scaling up to meet traffic demands and scaling down to zero when there's no traffic, optimizing resource usage.

- **Pay-per-use pricing**: You only pay for the exact compute time your containers use.

- **Build from source**: Cloud Run can automatically build container images directly from your source code.

- **Revision management**: Manages multiple revisions of your service, allowing for easy rollbacks and traffic splitting.

Cloud Run comes in two flavors:

- **Cloud Run services**: Used for permanent containers that respond to HTTP requests
- **Cloud Run jobs**: Used for containers that are meant to be executed and then terminated

---

What about the session state?

You may have heard that Cloud Run is for stateless applications. That's understandable because Cloud Run containers are ephemeral; however, that's not the end of the story. There is a way to run stateful workloads on Cloud Run. Stateful applications are applications that save state locally. Stateful applications tend to also store session state in memory. Cloud Run can be used for stateful applications by storing information about the state external to the Cloud Run service. This can be achieved by storing session state and other data external to Cloud Run. New containers spun up from autoscaling connect to the same external location. Session state that would normally be stored in the server's memory can be stored in Redis. Google Cloud has a managed version of Redis called Memorystore. Cloud Run can also be connected to persistent storage via Cloud Run volume mounts and Filestore. Cloud Run also easily connects to Cloud SQL databases.

We'll first discuss Cloud Run services.

Cloud Run services

Cloud Run services make it easy to host your application, supporting **HTTPS endpoints**, **Transport Layer Security (TLS)**, **Websockets**, and **gRPC** (which are **Remote Procedure Calls**, from Google). Cloud Run can run on a private network or a public, internet-accessible network.

Cloud Run supports any programming language you choose. If you can build a container image for your application, you can run it on Cloud Run. Cloud Run can also build the container for you using best practices for that language if you supply non-containerized code, as the source, written in any of the following languages:

- .NET Core
- Go
- Java
- Kotlin
- Node.js
- PHP
- Python
- Ruby

A single Google Cloud project can host multiple Cloud Run services in many regions. Services automatically expose unique endpoints and independently scale their infrastructure to accommodate varying request volumes. Services can even scale to zero when no requests are received. Alternatively, a minimum number of instances can be configured if the application needs less latency than that associated when scaling from zero. Services are replicated across multiple zones within a region for redundancy and failover. The amount of traffic sent to a revision can be configured to values that work best for the customer. Some or all of the traffic can be sent to a new revision. Controlling the amount of traffic sent to each revision provides the ability to use a new revision (N+1) alongside the current version (N). The new revision can receive little traffic at first, then receive more as confidence in it working without errors grows.

It's also easy to deploy complex applications because Cloud Run integrates with other Google Cloud services, such as the following:

- Cloud SQL databases
- Cloud Storage
- Google Cloud Load Balancing

Cloud Run supports standalone applications as well as applications that are part of larger systems.

The following diagram shows how serverless computing works in Google Cloud.

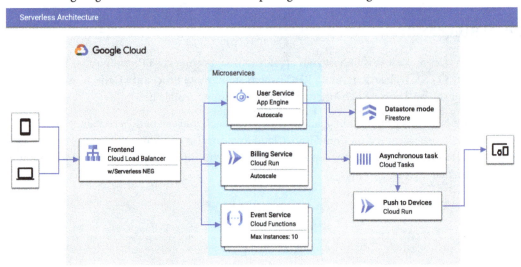

Figure 7.4 – Google Cloud serverless architecture

Cloud Run services have many popular uses, such as the website frontend, APIs, microservices, and the processing of messages in a streaming data pipeline.

In the preceding diagram, Cloud Run lives alongside Cloud Functions and App Engine for Google's serverless offerings. Now, let's talk about Cloud Run jobs.

Cloud Run jobs

In addition to its standard operation, Cloud Run can also be run as a job. Cloud Run jobs are specifically designed for running tasks that are expected to execute and then terminate. It's particularly well-suited for scheduled tasks.

Similar to Cloud Run services, Cloud Run jobs can be built from containers or source-based deployment.

One of the key advantages of using cloud services such as Cloud Run is the pay-for-what-you-use model. Cloud Run takes this concept to a new level by allowing for a minimum of 0 instances and the ability to scale up to 1,000 instances without the need to manually adjust default quota amounts. The number of containers is automatically adjusted based on the number of requests, ensuring efficient resource utilization.

Cloud Run integrations

Cloud Run seamlessly integrates with various tools in Google Cloud. These integrations enables developers to create applications with a comprehensive range of features, simplifying the development process and enhancing the overall functionality of their solutions. The following table explains them briefly:

Capability	Description
Logging and error reporting	Logs are sent to Cloud Logging where they can be examined for errors along with other Google Cloud services
Service identity	Each revision is equipped with a dedicated service account that it utilizes when accessing APIs, thereby facilitating the tracking of actions performed.
Continuous delivery	Cloud Run has deep integrations with Cloud Build, Artifact Registry, and Cloud Deploy. Cloud Run leverages Cloud Build to enable continuous deployment from a source code repository such as GitHub.
Private networking	Through Serverless VPC Access, Cloud Run can gain access to resources and connect to target VPCs without utilizing the public internet.
Google Cloud APIs	Uses IAM to authenticate against other Google Cloud APIs such as AI and Machine Learning APIs, such as the Cloud Vision API, Speech-to-Text API, AutoML Natural Language API, and Cloud Translation API.

Table 7.3 – Cloud Run integrations with Google Cloud tools

As we now know about the integration features, let's move on to some limitations.

Cloud Run limitations

As with all technologies, there are limits. Here are the limitations of Cloud Run:

CPU – maximum number of vCPU	8
Memory – maximum memory size, in GiB	32
Storage – maximum writable, in-memory filesystem, limited by instance memory, in GiB	32
Container instance – inbound requests per second to an HTTP/1 container port (doesn't apply to HTTP/2 container ports)	800
Container instance – outbound connections per second	700

Table 7.4 – Limitations of Cloud Run services

With this knowledge in place, in the next two sections, we will look at Cloud Run pricing and how to choose between GKE and Cloud Run.

Cloud Run pricing

In Cloud Run, billing occurs when an instance is starting, processing requests, or shutting down gracefully. If you configure a minimum number of instances, they will incur an *idle* billing rate when not actively handling requests.

Choosing between GKE and Cloud Run

How a team chooses between GKE and Cloud Run is a common question and often mirrors the question of whether or not it's best to use Kubernetes or serverless.

The right choice depends on your application's needs and your priorities. Go with Kubernetes (GKE) in the following situations:

- **You have large, complex applications**: You need to manage many interconnected microservices that require fine-grained control over how they talk to each other.

- **Control is essential**: You want to customize every aspect of your deployment – networking, how your app scales, resource usage, and so on.

- **You need to manage databases or other stateful parts**: Your application needs to store data persistently.

- **Your team knows Kubernetes**: You're comfortable with the added complexity to get the flexibility it offers.

Go with Cloud Run in the following situations:

- **Simplicity is key**: You want to focus on your code, not managing servers or clusters.

- **Your app is stateless**: It doesn't need to store data persistently within the container itself.

- **Scaling matters most**: Your traffic is unpredictable, and you want your app to automatically scale up to handle demand and down to zero when not in use.

- **You want to pay per use**: Paying only for the exact resources you consume is a priority.

> **Tip**
> Start with Cloud Run if you're unsure. It's easier to adopt, and you can always move parts of your application to Kubernetes later if complexity demands it. Cloud Run is also great for creating proof-of-concept applications when looking to share a vision of what is to be delivered.

The choice between GKE and Cloud Run does not have to be seen as an either/or decision. Many successful setups use GKE for core infrastructure and Cloud Run for specific services.

Summary

The runtime environment is the last stop for your source-to-production workflow, so knowing what runtimes are available for you to deploy your applications to is important for many of your organization's software development decisions.

Google Cloud offers numerous runtime environments. In this chapter, you learned about GKE and Cloud Run.

In *Chapter 8*, we create some GKE clusters and deploy them.

References

To learn more about the topics covered in this chapter, please refer to the following resources:

- Choose a GKE mode of operation: `https://cloud.google.com/kubernetes-engine/docs/concepts/choose-cluster-mode`

- Google (2024, February 2). Build applications with Buildpacks. Retrieved from `https://cloud.google.com/docs/buildpacks/build-application`

- Google (2024, February 5). Configuring minimum instances. Cloud Run Documentation: `https://cloud.google.com/run/docs/configuring/min-instances`

- Google (2024, February 5). What is Cloud Run? Cloud Run Documentation. Retrieved from `https://cloud.google.com/run/docs/overview/what-is-cloud-run`

- Google (2024, February 6). What are containers? Google Cloud Learn. Retrieved from `https://cloud.google.com/learn/what-are-containers`

8

Automating Software Delivery Using Cloud Deploy

In this chapter, we introduce **Cloud Deploy**, a service you can use to automate how your application is delivered to a series of runtime environments, known as **targets**. With Cloud Deploy, you can define delivery pipelines to deploy container images to GKE and Cloud Run targets in a predetermined sequence.

In this chapter, you'll learn about the Cloud Deploy architecture, the resources that Cloud Deploy creates for you, and the service's capabilities. We'll also show you how to create the software delivery pipeline that guides your application delivery to those target environments.

What you'll learn in this chapter will help you understand the end-to-end software delivery toolchain in Google Cloud (Cloud Code to Cloud Build to Artifact Registry to Cloud Deploy to your runtime). This toolchain will be presented in more detail in *Chapter 10*.

This chapter includes the following sections:

- Exploring the Cloud Deploy architecture
- Understanding Cloud Deploy target types
- Using the Kubernetes manifest and Kustomization
- Using a Skaffold configuration
- Preparing your project
- Creating a delivery pipeline
- Creating a release
- Verifying your deployment
- Using a deployment strategy

Technical requirements

To perform the tasks in this chapter, you need a **Google Cloud project**, with billing or a free trial enabled. You can reuse the project you've been using throughout this book.

In this case, you will need the following, in addition to the APIs you enabled in previous chapters:

- The Cloud Deploy API
- The `gcloud` command-line tool, installed on your machine
- You can also use Cloud Shell, which has `gcloud` installed
- You need the two GKE clusters you created in *Chapter 2*:
  - `qa-cluster`
  - `prod-cluster`

The code that will be used in this chapter is available in the `ch8` folder of this book's GitHub repository: `https://github.com/PacktPublishing/Secure-Continuous-Delivery-on-Google-Cloud`.

Exploring the Cloud Deploy architecture

This section describes how Cloud Deploy fits in with the software delivery ecosystem, as well as its components, including what resources the service manages.

Cloud Deploy among software delivery tools

You use Cloud Deploy near the end of your source-to-prod software delivery process. Downstream from Cloud Deploy are the runtime environment, any monitoring tools you use, and your users.

Upstream from Cloud Deploy are the many tools and methods available to you for creating, building, and testing your software. Cloud Deploy supports almost any **continuous integration** (**CI**) or build tooling you use. Cloud Deploy has no restrictions regarding where you store your artifacts (such as your container image). It's up to the runtime to retrieve that artifact:

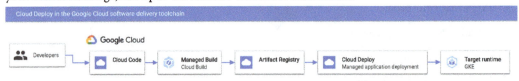

Figure 8.1 – Cloud Deploy among Google Cloud's software delivery tools

In this diagram, a software developer uses Cloud Code to write, and locally test, code. Cloud Build builds the application, which is stored in Artifact Registry. Then, Cloud Deploy pulls the container image from Artifact Registry and deploys it to, in this case, GKE. Thus, this diagram shows Cloud Deploy as part of the Google Cloud software-delivery toolchain.

In addition to the other Google Cloud products you use to write, build, store, and deploy your applications, Cloud Deploy requires the following tools:

- **Cloud Storage**: Cloud Deploy stores rendered manifests and other resources in Cloud Storage. You don't need to do anything to set this up, but charges may apply.

- **Skaffold**: Cloud Deploy uses Skaffold for render and deploy operations, and it's included with Cloud Deploy.

- **Pub/Sub (optional)**: Cloud Deploy publishes notifications to Pub/Sub for some events, such as when an operation is run against any core resource, or when approval is needed. You can subscribe to any notification type, and you can use those notifications to automate your processes around Cloud Deploy.

With that, we've looked at how Cloud Deploy fits into the software delivery toolchain. Next, we'll look at how the components of Cloud Deploy fit with each other.

The Cloud Deploy resource model

The following is a list of the Cloud Deploy resources that are used to deliver your application to a runtime environment:

- **Delivery pipeline:** The delivery pipeline defines the progression sequence or the order in which the targets receive the deployed application.

- **Target:** Targets represent the specific runtime environments you're deploying to. If you're going to deploy to a given GKE cluster, you must create a target for that cluster, include the cluster information in the cluster config, and reference it from the correct position in the pipeline's progression.

- **Release**: A release is an attempt to deliver your application to all the targets in your delivery pipeline progression. Under normal circumstances, when you create a release, Cloud Deploy deploys the application automatically into the first target. After that, you can promote it to each of the remaining targets, in sequence. All of this is done within a single release.

- **Rollout**: A rollout associates a release with a target. For each target in the release, there is one rollout. So if you have three targets in your delivery pipeline, there are three rollouts for each release.

    Within a rollout, there are the following constructs:

    - **Phase**: Rollouts consist of phases, which are logical subdivisions of what happens during a rollout. All rollouts have a stable phase, and for deployment strategies, such as canary, there can be other phases.

- **Jobs**: A given phase runs one or more jobs. A job is a task that Cloud Deploy performs during a given phase. For example, the **stable** phase includes a **deploy job** and a **verify job** (which might be disabled).

- **Job runs**: This is an attempt at a job. You can retry jobs, and each attempt is a job run.

These are the resources that Cloud Deploy creates and manages to execute your delivery pipeline. But there is another component that's critical to how Cloud Deploy works: the execution environment.

The Cloud Deploy execution environment

Cloud Deploy operations run inside an **execution environment**. This execution environment consists of the following values:

- **Worker pool**: Cloud Deploy runs in the default **Cloud Build worker pool**. The Cloud Build worker pool is a collection of workers that execute your Cloud Build builds, with each build running in its own worker. You can use this default pool, without having to do anything to set it up, or you can configure a private worker pool in Cloud Build and specify that private pool in the Cloud Deploy execution environment.

- **Execution service account**: This is the Google Cloud service account that is used for Cloud Deploy and Cloud Build operations. Cloud Deploy uses the default Compute Engine service account unless you select a different service account.

- **Storage location**: This is the Cloud Storage bucket where Cloud Deploy stores your rendered manifests.

- **Cloud Build timeout**: This is the maximum amount of time Cloud Build will take on any of the operations it performs for Cloud Deploy.

You can change any of these values for a custom execution environment. All of these options are set in the target configuration. See the Cloud Deploy documentation for more information on how to change these.

For the exercises in this chapter, you can continue to use the default execution environment.

Now that you've learned how Cloud Deploy fits in with your CI/CD toolchain, and know a little bit about the components of Cloud Deploy, including the execution environment, let's look at what happens when a delivery pipeline runs.

What happens when a delivery pipeline executes?

The following process describes what happens when you start a Cloud Deploy delivery pipeline:

1. You invoke a delivery pipeline by creating a release.

   Creating a release is described later in this chapter.

2. Cloud Deploy creates a rollout, which associates a release with the intended target.

3. Skaffold renders the manifest (including the Cloud Run service config).

    Skaffold substitutes values for the placeholders that were in the un-rendered manifest.

> **Important note**
>
> Cloud Deploy also supports *deploy parameters*, which are extra placeholders you can include in your manifest, and which are substituted at deploy time.

4. The rendered manifest is applied to the target runtime, thus deploying the application.

    The release is now waiting to be promoted.

5. You promote the release to the next target, either using the Google Cloud console or from the command line.

6. Cloud Deploy creates a new rollout, and Skaffold renders the manifest again for the new targets.

7. The rendered manifest is applied to the new target.

    If that was the last target in your delivery pipeline progression, the application is now fully deployed. Otherwise, the steps are repeated, starting with promoting the release.

8. If you have enabled a canary deployment strategy for any target, the rollout for that target is executed according to the configured canary.

    The canary deployment strategy is described later in this chapter, in the *Configuring the delivery pipeline for a canary deployment* section.

9. If you have deployment verification enabled for any target, that verification is performed after the application is deployed on that target.

    Deployment verification is described later in this chapter, in the *Verifying your deployment* section.

Next, let's take a look at Cloud Deploy target types.

Understanding Cloud Deploy target types

A target is a Cloud Deploy construct, and each target represents a specific runtime instance where you are deploying your application. A target *type* represents a type of runtime environment that Cloud Deploy supports. The following are the target types that Cloud Deploy supports:

- **Google Kubernetes Engine (GKE)** clusters

- Cloud Run services

- GKE Enterprise user clusters

These are the same runtime environments that we discussed in *Chapter 7*.

Cloud Deploy supports all three of these runtimes, but there are some rules to follow regarding target types:

- Within a delivery pipeline, all targets must be of the same type.

  For example, you can't deploy to a GKE cluster and a Cloud Run service using the same delivery pipeline.

- If you're using parallel deployment, all child targets for a given multi-target must be of the same type (though they can be in different locations).

Now that we've discussed target types, let's learn about the declarative resources that help to define what's being deployed – the Kubernetes manifest and Kustomization.

Using the Kubernetes manifest and Kustomization

Cloud Deploy uses Skaffold to render your manifest (or service definition, for **Cloud Run**) and deploy it to the target runtime. In *Chapter 2*, you learned about Skaffold (and the skaffold.yaml configuration file), and you learned about using **Kustomize** with Skaffold profiles to tailor your configuration for each target.

This chapter uses a Kubernetes manifest and **Kustomization** (a configuration file for Kustomize), which is available in this book's GitHub repository: https://github.com/PacktPublishing/Secure-Continuous-Delivery-on-Google-Cloud/tree/main/ch8.

You can get the manifest from this book's repository, but here's a look at what's in the file:

```
# Copyright 2021 Google LLC
#
# Licensed under the Apache License, Version 2.0 (the "License");
# you may not use this file except in compliance with the License.
# You may obtain a copy of the License at
#
#      http://www.apache.org/licenses/LICENSE-2.0
#
# Unless required by applicable law or agreed to in writing, software
# distributed under the License is distributed on an "AS IS" BASIS,
# WITHOUT WARRANTIES OR CONDITIONS OF ANY KIND, either express or
implied.
# See the License for the specific language governing permissions and
# limitations under the License.

apiVersion: v1
kind: Service
metadata:
  name: scdongcp-app
```

```
    labels:
      app: scdongcp-app
spec:
  ports:
  - name: http
    port: 80
    targetPort: 8081
  selector:
    app: scdongcp-app
  type: LoadBalancer
---
apiVersion: apps/v1
kind: Deployment
metadata:
  name: scdongcp-app
  labels:
    app: scdongcp-app
spec:
  replicas: 4
  selector:
    matchLabels:
      app: scdongcp-app
  template:
    metadata:
      labels:
        app: scdongcp-app
    spec:
      containers:
      - name: scdongcp-app
        image: scdongcp-app
        ports:
        - containerPort: 8081
          name: http
```

This manifest defines a Kubernetes **deployment** and a Kubernetes **service**. The deployment identifies the container image to deploy, as well as the port for accessing it, the number of replicas, and metadata. The service defines a load balancer for that container. The Kustomization, not shown here but available in this book's GitHub repository, provides target-specific overlays for your separate environments.

In addition to the Kubernetes manifest and Kustomizations, you can configure Skaffold to specify render and deploy operations. This configuration is described in the next section.

Using a Skaffold configuration

Cloud Deploy requires that you have at least a minimal Skaffold configuration. Cloud Deploy uses Skaffold to render your manifest (or service definition, for Cloud Run) and apply that manifest to deploy your application.

As with the Kubernetes manifest, you can find the Skaffold configuration (`skaffold.yaml`) in the same GitHub repository folder: `https://github.com/PacktPublishing/Secure-Continuous-Delivery-on-Google-Cloud/tree/main/ch8`.

This is what the `skaffold.yaml` looks like:

```
# Copyright 2021 Google LLC
#
# Licensed under the Apache License, Version 2.0 (the "License");
# you may not use this file except in compliance with the License.
# You may obtain a copy of the License at
#
#       http://www.apache.org/licenses/LICENSE-2.0
#
# Unless required by applicable law or agreed to in writing, software
# distributed under the License is distributed on an "AS IS" BASIS,
# WITHOUT WARRANTIES OR CONDITIONS OF ANY KIND, either express or
implied.
# See the License for the specific language governing permissions and
# limitations under the License.

apiVersion: skaffold/v4beta3
kind: Config
build:
  artifacts:
    - image: scdongcp-app
      docker:
        dockerfile: Dockerfile
manifests:
  kustomize:
    paths:
      - kubernetes/dev
profiles:
  - name: qa
    manifests:
      kustomize:
        paths:
          - kubernetes/qa
  - name: prod
```

```
    manifests:
      kustomize:
        paths:
          - kubernetes/prod
```

This configuration defines the container image to build. It includes separate profiles for the different targets and points to the Kustomize overlays that define what is to be deployed.

With that, you learned a little bit about how Cloud Deploy works. Now, it's time to try it out. We'll start by granting the **Identity and Access Management** (**IAM**) roles and permissions you need to perform the tasks in the rest of this chapter.

Preparing your project

Before you can create a delivery pipeline, targets, and a release, you need to enable some APIs in Google Cloud and grant the necessary IAM roles and permissions.

Enabling the API

In *Chapter 2*, you enabled most of the APIs you need to use Cloud Deploy. Besides those APIs, you need to enable the Cloud Deploy API.

The following command assumes you still have your current Google Cloud project configured as the default project on your command line. Run this command to enable the Compute Engine API and the Cloud Deploy API:

```
gcloud services enable clouddeploy.googleapis.com \
   && gcloud services enable compute.googleapis.com
```

With these APIs enabled, you can now create your GKE clusters, as described in the next section.

Creating the GKE clusters

In this chapter, you will create two Cloud Deploy targets, each of which points to a GKE cluster that you will deploy to. Before you can do that, you need to create the two clusters. The command assumes that you have the GKE API enabled and that you have $PROJECT_ID defined in your environment.

Run the following command to create two GKE "autopilot" clusters, named qa-cluster and prod-cluster:

```
gcloud container clusters create-auto qa-cluster \
      --project=$PROJECT_ID \
      --region=us-central1 \
   && gcloud container clusters create-auto prod-cluster \
```

```
    --project=$PROJECT_ID \
    --region=us-central1
```

Granting the necessary permissions

To create the delivery pipeline and targets, as well as create a release and promote it to `prod`, you need some IAM roles and permissions. Cloud Deploy uses the Compute Engine default service account by default. The commands in this section grant these roles and permissions to this default service account, for the project you're using.

As always, be sure to replace `PROJECT_ID` in these commands with the name of the Google Cloud project you're using. It doesn't matter where you run these IAM commands, so long as it's on a machine with access to the Google Cloud SDK (`gcloud`).

To add the `clouddeploy.jobRunner` role, run the following command:

```
gcloud projects add-iam-policy-binding PROJECT_ID \
    --member=serviceAccount:$(gcloud projects describe PROJECT_ID \
    --format="value(projectNumber)")-compute@developer.
gserviceaccount.com \
    --role="roles/clouddeploy.jobRunner"
```

To add the Kubernetes developer permission, run the following command:

```
gcloud projects add-iam-policy-binding PROJECT_ID \
    --member=serviceAccount:$(gcloud projects describe PROJECT_ID \
    --format="value(projectNumber)")-compute@developer.
gserviceaccount.com \
    --role="roles/container.developer"
```

To add the `serviceAccountUser` role, run the following command:

```
gcloud iam service-accounts add-iam-policy-binding $(gcloud projects
describe PROJECT_ID \
    --format="value(projectNumber)")-compute@developer.
gserviceaccount.com \
    --member=serviceAccount:$(gcloud projects describe PROJECT_ID \
    --format="value(projectNumber)")-compute@developer.
gserviceaccount.com \
    --role="roles/iam.serviceAccountUser" \
    --project=PROJECT_ID
```

Now that you have the necessary IAM roles and permissions, you can start creating your delivery pipeline.

Creating a delivery pipeline

The delivery pipeline defines the order in which your application is delivered to your targets.

Consider a simple sequence of two targets:

- qa: This target represents the runtime environment where you deploy your finished application as you test it to ensure it's ready to release

- prod: This target represents your final production runtime, where your thoroughly tested application is made available to your users

Of course, you can call these anything you want, but these names reflect a typical set of environments and the order in which you deploy them. The delivery pipeline that you create defines this sequence so that Cloud Deploy can deliver your application to the right runtimes in the right order.

The delivery pipeline is defined in a file called clouddeploy.yaml. You can find this file in the same folder from the cloned repository where you found the skaffold.yaml file and the Kubernetes manifests. The name clouddeploy.yaml is used by convention, but you can call the file anything you want. Also, you can define the targets in the same file as the pipeline, which is what we're doing here, or you can create the targets in separate files. Using separate files makes it easier to reuse targets with different pipelines.

The sections that follow describe key concepts for delivery pipelines (the progression and targets), as well as how to register the delivery pipeline and targets to create them as Cloud Deploy resources.

Understanding the progression

The delivery pipeline progression is a list of the targets in the sequence in which you want to deploy them. As such, the progression is the essential element of the pipeline. The following clouddeploy.yaml configuration file shows the pipeline progression (stages) near the top of the file:

```
apiVersion: deploy.cloud.google.com/v1
kind: DeliveryPipeline
metadata:
  name: packt-deploy-pipeline
description: main application pipeline for Packt sample
serialPipeline:
  stages:
  - targetId: qa
    profiles: [qa]
  - targetId: prod
    profiles: [prod]
---
```

The progression is defined under `serialPipeline.stages`. Notice that there are two `targetId` values: qa and prod. Those are the two pipeline stages, and they refer to the names of the two targets shown in the next section.

Understanding targets

A target is a Cloud Deploy resource that represents the specific runtime environment where you'll deploy your application. For example, if you have a GKE cluster you want to use for quality assurance testing, you can define a qa target that points to that cluster.

The rest of the `clouddeploy.yaml` file, after the progression definition, defines the two targets we're using for this chapter. The configuration for the two targets is shown here:

```
apiVersion: deploy.cloud.google.com/v1
kind: Target
metadata:
  name: qa
description: qa cluster
gke:
  cluster: projects/PROJECT_ID/locations/us-central1/clusters/qa-
cluster
---

apiVersion: deploy.cloud.google.com/v1
kind: Target
metadata:
  name: prod
description: production cluster
gke:
  cluster: projects/PROJECT_ID/locations/us-central1/clusters/prod-
cluster
```

Notice the two clusters that were identified for the two targets: qa-cluster and prod-cluster. *Chapter 2* contains instructions for creating those, and those instructions are repeated in this chapter, under *Preparing your project*.

The value for the `cluster:` property includes the PROJECT_ID placeholder. For this delivery pipeline to work, you need to replace that with the name of your project.

With that, you've learned about Cloud Deploy targets and saw how they're configured. But the pipeline and targets don't exist as Cloud Deploy resources yet. We'll register them next so that we can create those resources.

Registering the delivery pipeline and targets

To register the delivery pipeline and the three targets in Cloud Deploy, run the following command from the ch8 directory in this book's GitHub repository:

```
gcloud deploy apply --file=clouddeploy.yaml --region=us-central1
--project=PROJECT_ID
```

Remember to replace PROJECT_ID with your project name.

Cloud Deploy generates the delivery pipeline and target resources based on the configuration you supplied in clouddeploy.yaml.

Now, you can navigate to https://console.cloud.google.com/deploy, the main Cloud Deploy page in the Google Cloud console, where you will see your pipeline listed:

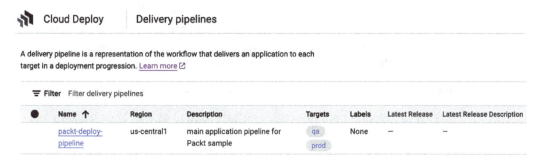

Figure 8.2 – Cloud Deploy's Delivery pipelines page

You've created your delivery pipeline and targets, and you've configured the skaffold.yaml file and manifest or service definition. Next, we'll create a release so that we can start executing the pipeline.

Creating a release

In Cloud Deploy, a **release** is a resource that represents a set of changes to be deployed (updated software, configuration, or both) and an attempt to deploy them to your targets. This section describes how to create a release, and what happens when you do.

Here's the process in brief:

1. You invoke a release from the command line, specifying the name of the delivery pipeline you created previously.

    You run this command from the directory that contains your skaffold.yaml file and manifest. This also assumes that your container image is built and is available in the location specified in your manifest or on the command line.

You can also pass values to your manifest, either by passing them when you create the release or by placing them in the delivery pipeline or targets. Deploy parameters aren't included in this chapter, but you can find out more about them in the Google Cloud documentation.

2. Cloud Deploy renders your manifest (for GKE and GKE Enterprise) or service definition (for Cloud Run) and stores it in a Cloud Storage bucket.

3. Cloud Deploy creates a rollout resource for each target.

    The rollout associates the release with the target, and at its simplest, it consists of just a `stable` phase. It becomes more complicated if you're using deployment verification or a deployment strategy.

4. The rollout results in the manifest or service definition being applied to the first target-specific runtime.

5. For each subsequent target, you have to promote the release to the next target.

    It doesn't have to be you, specifically, but someone with the proper IAM permissions can do so. You can do this from the command line or by clicking the **Promote** button in the **Cloud Deploy pipeline visualization** in the Google Cloud console.

6. This continues until your application is deployed in the last target in your progression.

That's the basic process for creating a release and seeing it through to its end. Now, let's try it out. Follow these steps to create and promote a release:

1. Run the following command from the same directory where you saved the `clouddeploy.yaml` file:

    ```
    gcloud deploy releases create packt-deploy-release-001 \
    --project=PROJECT_ID \
    --region=us-central1 \
    --delivery-pipeline=packt-deploy-pipeline \
    --image="scdongcp-app=us-central1-docker.pkg.dev/$PROJECT_ID/
    scdbook-repo/scdongcp-app:$TAG"
    ```

    `$TAG` will be the image tag for this container, from *Chapter 2*.

    Cloud Deploy creates a `.tar` archive of the contents of this directory, so be sure not to run this command from your home directory.

    Cloud Deploy starts a release, creates a rollout, renders your `skaffold.yaml` file and manifest or service definition, and deploys the container in the first target (qa). All manifests for all targets are rendered as the first rollout is being processed.

In the Google Cloud console, you can see your progress in the delivery pipeline visualization. It can take a few minutes for the rollout to finish:

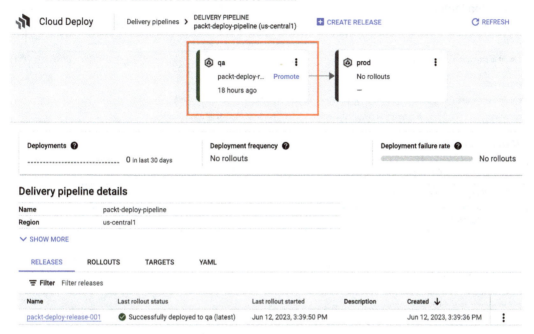

Figure 8.3 – The Cloud Deploy delivery pipeline visualization

Notice the **Promote** link in the first target in the delivery pipeline visualization:

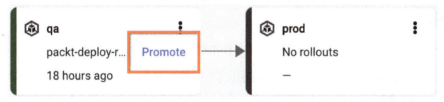

Figure 8.4 – The pipeline visualization, showing the Promote button

2.   Click the **Promote** link to deploy the container into the next target (prod).

The **Promote** dialog will be displayed:

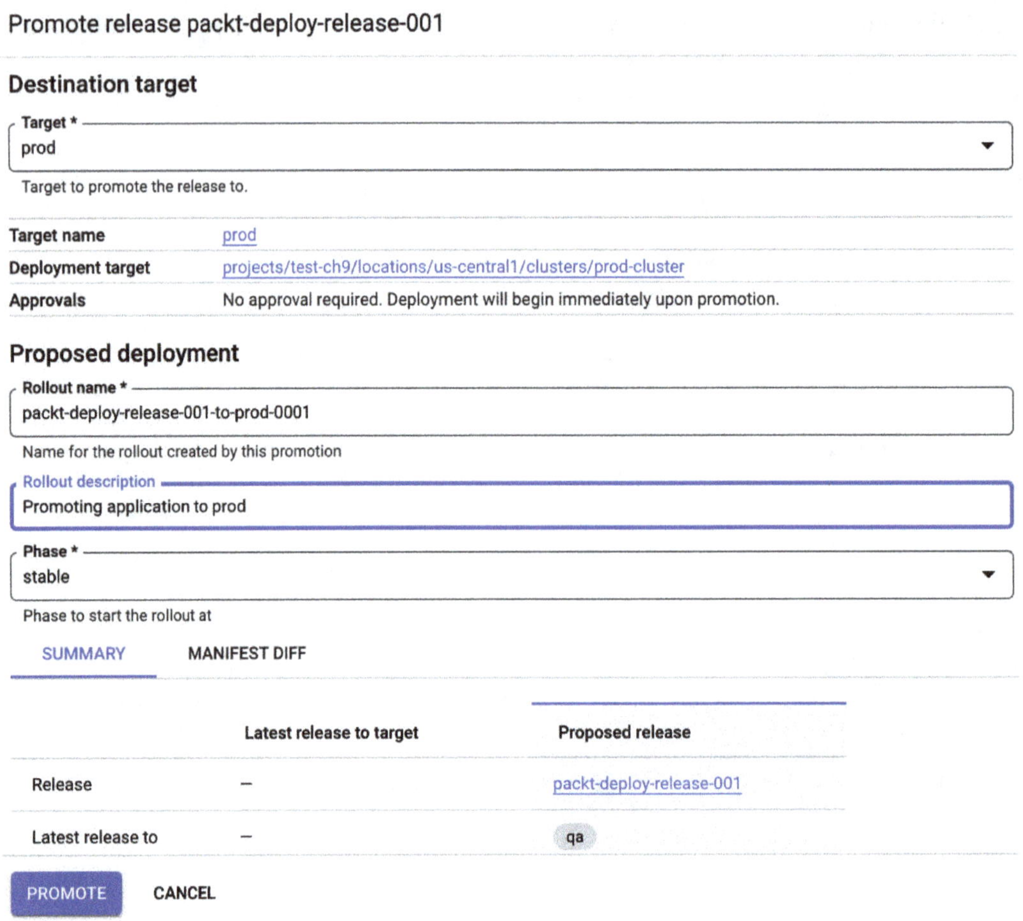

Promote release packt-deploy-release-001

Destination target

Target *

prod ▾

Target to promote the release to.

Target name	prod
Deployment target	projects/test-ch9/locations/us-central1/clusters/prod-cluster
Approvals	No approval required. Deployment will begin immediately upon promotion.

Proposed deployment

Rollout name *

packt-deploy-release-001-to-prod-0001

Name for the rollout created by this promotion

Rollout description

Promoting application to prod

Phase *

stable ▾

Phase to start the rollout at

SUMMARY   MANIFEST DIFF

	Latest release to target	Proposed release
Release	—	packt-deploy-release-001
Latest release to	—	qa

PROMOTE   CANCEL

Figure 8.5 – The Promote dialog

You can also promote it from the command line by using `glcoud deploy releases promote`. See the Cloud Deploy documentation for more information about this command. Another rollout will be created, and the application will be deployed into `prod`.

3. Click **PROMOTE** to deploy the application to `prod`.

4. Wait for the rollout to finish.

After a while, in the delivery pipeline visualization, you will see that the application was deployed successfully (hopefully) in your production environment:

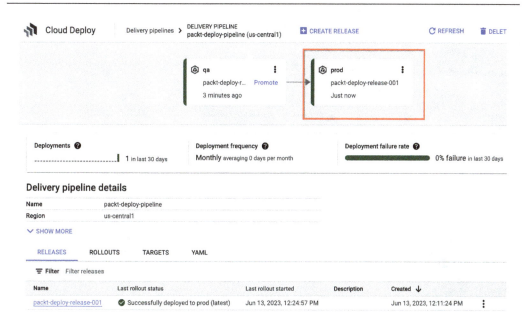

Figure 8.6 – Delivery pipeline visualization showing a successful deployment to prod

With that, you've used a Cloud Deploy delivery pipeline to deploy your application to a series of three targets. Next, let's look at the release using the Cloud Deploy release inspector.

Examining a release

You can view information about releases and rollouts using the Cloud Deploy release inspector. The information you can view includes the following:

- Release metadata

- Rollout details

- Approval status

- Render logs and deployment logs

- Rollout phases (`Canary`, `Stable`) and jobs (`Deploy`, `Verify`)

- Rendered artifacts (manifests, `skaffold.yaml`)

Follow these steps to use the Cloud Deploy release inspector to view information about your release and rollouts:

1. From Cloud Deploy's main page, `https://cloud.google.com/deploy`, select the delivery pipeline we created (**packt-deploy-pipeline**).

    The pipeline visualization will be shown.

2. Click the **SHOW MORE** link under **Delivery pipeline details** to reveal information about the pipeline:

Figure 8.7 – Delivery pipeline details

3. On the **RELEASES** tab, click the name of the release we created (**packt-deploy-release-001**). The **Release details** page will appear.

4. Click the **SHOW MORE** link under **Release details** to show information about the release:

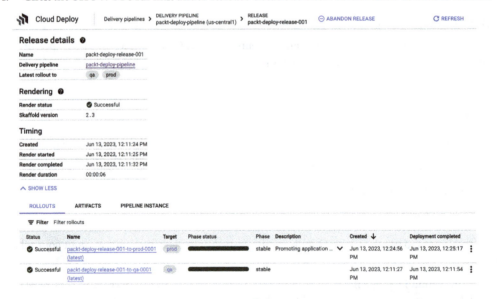

Figure 8.8 – Release details, expanded

5. On the **ROLLOUTS** tab, click the name of either rollout.

The rollout details will be shown:

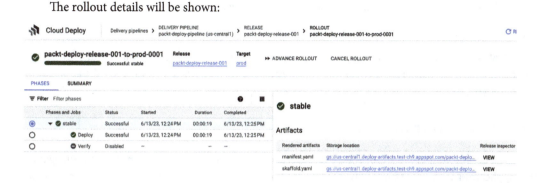

Figure 8.9 – Rollout details

The **PHASES** tab (selected by default) shows the rollout phases and the jobs for this rollout.

For each phase or job that you select, the panel on the right shows the details for that job. For jobs, you can also choose to retry (if the rollout failed), ignore failures, or terminate the job.

6. With the **PHASES** tab selected, select a phase – in this case, **stable** – and click on any of the links under **Artifacts**.

    There will be a link for your rendered **manifest.yaml** and a link for your rendered **skaffold.yaml**.

    Clicking either of these will open that object in Cloud Storage. You can download and view the rendered files from here.

7. Back on the rollout details page, click on the **SUMMARY** tab to view the metadata for the rollout, approval status, and a link to render logs:

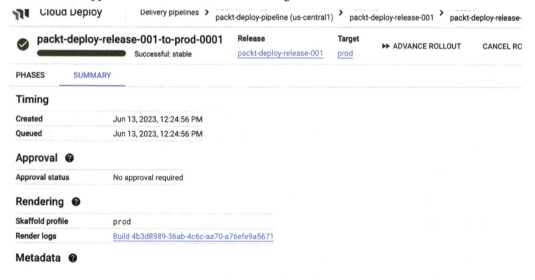

Figure 8.10 – Rollout metadata and other details

8.   To view render logs, click the link next to **Render logs**, under **Rendering**.

The Cloud Build render logs will be shown.

With that, you've learned how to view details from your release, including rollout details, rendering and deployment logs, and rendered configuration files. Next, you'll learn how to verify the application you deployed.

Verifying your deployment

After you deploy your application, you can run an arbitrary container that contains tests to run against that application so that you can verify it's running properly. Deployment verification uses the Skaffold `skaffold verify` command. You can learn more about this command, and other Skaffold commands, by reading the documentation at `https://skaffold.dev/docs/`.

Typically, the container you run will contain a script for testing your deployed application. However, the contents of this container are up to you. Cloud Deploy considers verification to be successful if your container's exit code is 0. A non-zero exit code indicates failure.

Follow these steps to verify your deployment:

1.   Edit your `clouddeploy.yaml` file to enable verification for one pipeline stage. To do so, add a `strategy` stanza. We'll do this for the qa stage:

```
stages:
- targetId: qa
  profiles: [qa]
  strategy:
    standard:
       verify: true
- targetId: prod
  profiles: [qa]
```

This enables verification for the qa stage.

2.   Re-register your delivery pipeline and targets by using the following command:

```
gcloud deploy apply --file=clouddeploy.yaml --region=us-central1
--project=PROJECT_ID
```

As always, replace PROJECT_ID with the name of the project you're using.

3.   Edit your `skaffold.yaml` file and add a `verify` stanza.

Add this stanza at the end of the file, at the top level of the schema (flush left):

```
verify:
- name: verify-endpoint-test
  container:
```

```
name: alpine-wget
image: alpine:3.15.4
command: ["/bin/sh"]
args: ["-c", "wget http://www.google.com"]
```

You can learn more about Skaffold's verification capability by reading the Skaffold documentation at `https://skaffold.dev/docs/verify/`.

4. Create another release:

```
gcloud deploy releases create packt-deploy-release-002 \
--project=PROJECT_ID \
--region=us-central1 \
--delivery-pipeline=packt-deploy-pipeline \
--images=scdongcp-app=us-central1-docker.pkg.dev/$PROJECT_ID/
scdbook-repo/scdongcp-app:$TAG
```

With verification enabled in the delivery pipeline, and configured in `skaffold.yaml`, the identified verification container runs after deployment. Because we configured verification on the qa stage, it only runs there, not in `prod`. By default, the container, and the script it contains, run in the default or configured Cloud Deploy execution environment.

5. After the rollout to qa finishes, click the **ROLLOUTS** tab under **Delivery pipeline details** and click the latest rollout:

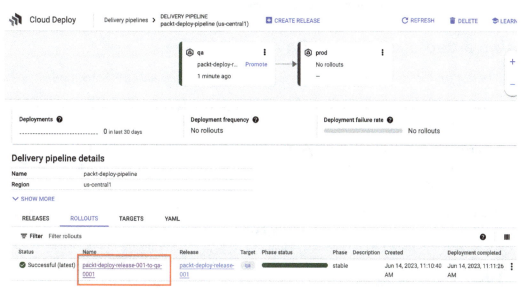

Figure 8.11 – Delivery pipeline details, showing the rollout

6. On the rollout details page, select the **Verify** job, and view the results of the verification:

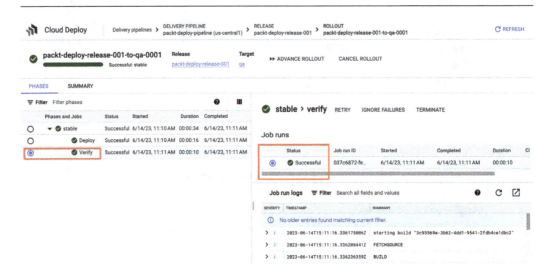

Figure 8.12 – Rollout details page, showing a successful "Verify" job run

The verification job succeeds if the command in the container (configured in Skaffold) returns with an exit code of 0. Any non-zero exit code results in verification failure.

In this section, you used the deployment-verification feature to ensure your deployed application's integrity. Now, let's try a deployment strategy: a canary deployment.

Using a deployment strategy

Cloud Deploy supports two *deployment strategies* for GKE, Cloud Run, and GKE Enterprise:

- **Standard**: This is the default strategy. It deploys the new or changed application into the target runtime, fully replacing any previous version.

- **Canary**: This strategy incrementally deploys the changed application into the target runtime, gradually replacing the old version with the new one by configured percentages. This can be by the percentage of traffic or by the percentage of GKE pods.

In this section, we'll configure and run a simple canary that replaces the old version with the new, first by 50%, then fully. The manifest we created at the beginning of this chapter specifies four replicas. The first phase of this canary will split them so that two replicas are running the old version and two are running the new version. Then, the last phase (which is always the stable phase) will deploy the new version to all four replicas.

Configuring the delivery pipeline for a canary deployment

Follow these steps to configure the prod stage of your delivery pipeline so that it uses a canary deployment strategy:

1. Open your skaffold.yaml file for editing.

2. Remove the configuration for deployment verification (the verify stanza) since we're not going to need that anymore:

    ```
    apiVersion: skaffold/v4beta2
    kind: Config
    metadata:
      name: single
    build:
      artifacts:
      - image: scdongcp-app
        docker:
          dockerfile: Dockerfile
    manifests:
      rawYaml:
      - kubernetes/deployment.yaml
    ```

3. Open your clouddeploy.yaml file for editing.

4. In the delivery pipeline progression, remove the verify stanza from the qa stage, as follows:

    ```
    apiVersion: deploy.cloud.google.com/v1
    kind: DeliveryPipeline
    metadata:
      name: packt-deploy-pipeline
    description: main application pipeline for Packt sample
    serialPipeline:
      stages:
      - targetId: qa
        profiles: [qa]
      - targetId: prod
        profiles: [prod]
    ```

5. Add a strategy stanza to the prod stage, as follows:

    ```
      - targetId: prod
        profiles: [prod]
        strategy:
          canary:
            runtimeConfig:
              kubernetes:
    ```

```
            serviceNetworking:
               service: "scdongcp-app"
               deployment: "scdongcp-app"
         canaryDeployment:
            percentages: [50]
            verify: false
   ---
```

The `percentages` property is set to `50`, which means a 50% canary stage. The final stage is always `stable`, which represents 100% deployed, so we don't need to include `100` here.

For simplicity, we are not enabling deployment verification at this stage.

Your delivery pipeline will now look like this:

```
apiVersion: deploy.cloud.google.com/v1
kind: DeliveryPipeline
metadata:
  name: packt-deploy-pipeline
description: main application pipeline for Packt sample
serialPipeline:
  stages:
  - targetId: qa
    profiles: [qa]
  - targetId: prod
    profiles: [prod]
    strategy:
      canary:
        runtimeConfig:
          kubernetes:
            serviceNetworking:
              service: "scdongcp-app"
              deployment: "scdongcp-app"
        canaryDeployment:
          percentages: [50]
          verify: false
```

This definition shows the progression (stages) as well as the canary strategy.

Your targets will now look like this:

```
apiVersion: deploy.cloud.google.com/v1
kind: Target
metadata:
  name: qa
```

```
description: qa cluster
gke:
  cluster: projects/PROJECT_ID/locations/us-central1/clusters/qa_
cluster
---

apiVersion: deploy.cloud.google.com/v1
kind: Target
metadata:
  name: prod
description: production cluster
gke:
  cluster: projects/PROJECT_ID/locations/us-central1/clusters/prod_
cluster
```

This configuration shows two targets, qa and prod, pointing to two separate GKE clusters.

Now that you've configured the delivery pipeline and targets to run a 50%-to-stable canary deployment, let's create a release and observe the canary deployment in action.

Running the canary deployment

Follow these steps to run your canary deployment:

1. Re-register your delivery pipeline and targets:

    ```
    gcloud deploy apply --file=clouddeploy.yaml --region=us-central1
    --project=PROJECT_ID
    ```

    As always, replace PROJECT_ID with the name of the project you're using.

2. Create a new release by using the following command:

    ```
    gcloud deploy releases create packt-deploy-release-003 \
    --project=PROJECT_ID \
    --region=us-central1 \
    --delivery-pipeline=packt-deploy-pipeline
    ```

    The release will be automatically deployed into the first target, qa. This target uses a standard deployment strategy – not canary.

3. When the release is successfully deployed into qa, click **Promote** in the delivery pipeline visualization, and click **Promote** again in the **Promote release** dialog.

    The rollout will be created for the prod target. This rollout has two phases – canary-50 and stable. Each of these two phases has two jobs, Deploy and Verify, where Verify is disabled.

We disabled deployment verification for this stage for simplicity, to show just the canary phases, but in a real-world situation, a canary deployment is a good opportunity for deployment verification: partially deploy, then run tests to verify that your application is working properly, then run the next canary phase until your application is fully deployed in the target runtime.

The pipeline visualization will show that the release is in the `canary-50` stage:

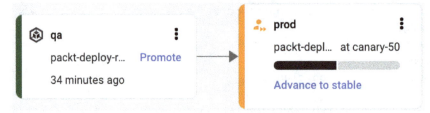

Figure 8.13 – Delivery pipeline visualization showing the current rollout in the prod target

4. Watch the delivery pipeline visualization to see when the `canary-50` phase is complete, then click **Advance to stable**.

    The `stable` phase will begin:

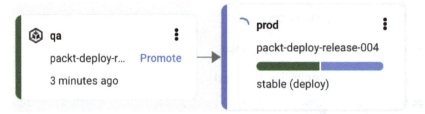

Figure 8.14 – Delivery pipeline visualization showing the deployment to prod in progress

When it's finished, your application will be fully deployed:

Figure 8.15 – Delivery pipeline visualization showing a successful deployment to all targets

With that, you've successfully run a canary deployment strategy.

Summary

In this chapter, you created a Cloud Deploy delivery pipeline to deliver your application to a series of runtime environments. You also tried deploying to multiple target runtimes at the same time, and you ran a verification script against your deployed application. Finally, you performed a canary deployment strategy.

You now understand how to use Cloud Deploy to reliably deliver your applications to target runtimes.

In the next chapter, you'll learn how to use binary authorization to ensure that only trusted container images are deployed to your GKE or Cloud Run environment.

9

Securing Your Runtimes
with Binary Authorization

In the previous chapter, you learned how to use Cloud Deploy to automate your software delivery process. In this chapter, we'll describe Binary Authorization, a Google Cloud service that helps ensure you're only deploying verified authorized container images to Google Cloud runtimes, further strengthening the security of your software products.

This chapter includes the following sections:

- Understanding Binary Authorization concepts
- Setting up Binary Authorization
- Setting up attestations
- Configuring Binary Authorization policies

Technical requirements

Before proceeding with this chapter, enable the following two APIs if they're not already enabled:

- Binary Authorization
- **Customer-managed encryption keys (CMEK)**

You can enable both of these from the API Library, in the **Google Cloud console**.

Additionally, be sure to install the **Google Cloud CLI**, if it's not already installed, and select a Google Cloud project.

Understanding Binary Authorization concepts

Binary Authorization is a part of the secure software supply chain. The service ensures that only authorized container images are executed on container-based runtimes such as **Google Kubernetes Engine (GKE)**, **GKE Enterprise**, and **Cloud Run**. Based on the **Kritis** specification, which is part of the **Grafeas open source project**, the service uses policies that are enforced when someone deploys a container onto a runtime.

Containers can come from many places, such as public DockerHub. When using containers from public repositories, it's possible to introduce malware or unknown elements. A secure software supply chain should validate that it knows the source of containers running in their environments. Enterprises should use Binary Authorization on Google Cloud for several compelling reasons to enhance their software supply chain security:

- **Enforce trust and verification**:

  - **Control over deployments**: Binary Authorization acts as a gatekeeper, ensuring that only images that have been digitally signed by trusted authorities (for example, your development team, build systems, and so on) can be deployed. This safeguards against unauthorized or potentially malicious code slipping into your production environments.

  - **Attestations for compliance**: Binary Authorization can verify that images meet specific criteria before deployment by using attestations. These attestations may demonstrate that the images were built with a secure build process, passed vulnerability scans, or adhered to company policies.

- **Reduce risk and improve the security posture**:

  - **Mitigate supply chain attacks**: Binary Authorization reduces the chances of software supply chain attacks, where malicious actors might try to inject tampered code into your pipeline.

  - **Early vulnerability detection**: By integrating vulnerability scanning into your attestations, you can catch potential security flaws before they reach production.

  - **Proactive security**: Binary Authorization moves security to the left – into the development process. This ensures security isn't an afterthought, but rather a key feature of your development life cycle.

- **Regulatory compliance and auditability**:

  - **Stricter controls**: Many industries have regulations around software integrity and secure development practices. Binary Authorization helps you demonstrate compliance.

  - **Stronger audit trails**: Logs and attestations used within Binary Authorization provide a clear trail of who approved what image and when, simplifying audits and incident investigations.

- **Streamline secure container deployment**:

  - **Policy-driven**: Binary Authorization allows you to define clear policies governing the conditions under which images can be deployed. This enforces standardization and consistency across your environments.

  - **Flexibility**: You can implement policies for different stages of your deployment pipeline (for example, development, staging, and production), ensuring the right level of control at each point.

In summary, Binary Authorization on Google Cloud provides enterprises with a robust mechanism to verify the origin and integrity of software throughout their supply chain, leading to a more secure, compliant, and auditable environment.

Binary Authorization supports the following runtime environments:

- GKE
- GKE Enterprise
- Cloud Run

Binary Authorization is part of a container management architecture that includes Artifact Registry and Artifact Analysis. Artifact Analysis provides vulnerability information that Binary Authorization uses to secure deployments. Separately, Artifact Analysis stores trusted metadata used for authorization.

At deployment time, Binary Authorization ensures that only trusted container images are deployed on GKE or Cloud Run. You can require images to be signed by trusted authorities during development, and then enforce signature validation when deploying. Thus, you gain tighter control over your container environment by ensuring that only verified images are integrated into the build-and-release process.

Binary authorization is often deployed as part of a defense-in-depth strategy. Developers who interact with the pipeline by checking the code into the source control repository and/or merging branches might never come into contact with Binary Authorization. Unless developers have access to the runtime environment, Binary Authorization tends to go unnoticed by developers.

Another option is the ability to allow container images stored in a repository that has been explicitly stated in an allow list. Binary authorization includes a pre-defined policy that exempts images from Google-provided system image paths.

The following table lists and describes the features that are available in Binary Authorization:

Feature	Description
Policy creation	Define policies at the project and cluster levels based on the security requirements of your organization.
Policy verification and enforcement	By verifying signatures from vulnerability scanning tools, you can help ensure that your images aren't vulnerable to known security risks. This can help protect your applications and data from attack.
Cloud Security Command Center integration	By viewing policy violations in the Security Command Center, you can gain insights into how your policies are enforced and identify potential security risks. You can also explore events, such as failed deploy attempts due to policy restrictions or breakglass activities, to understand how your policies are being used and to identify any potential security concerns.
Audit logging	By tracking policy violations and failed deployment attempts, you can gain insights into how your policies are being enforced and identify potential security risks. This can help you protect your GCP resources from unauthorized access and malicious attacks.
Cloud KMS support	By using an asymmetric key pair to sign images and verify signatures, you can ensure that the images haven't been tampered with. This helps protect the integrity of your images and the data that they contain.
Open source support for Kubernetes	Signature verification can be enforced using **Kritis Signer**. Kritis is an open source tool you can use for binary authorization attestations. Those attestations are based on security vulnerabilities.
Dry run support	By testing changes to your policy and using Cloud Audit Logs, you can identify any potential problems with a change before it is deployed to production. This can help prevent disruptions to your services and protect your data from unauthorized access.
Breakglass support	Use breakglass to deploy images. even when they fail to meet the binary authorization policy.
Integration with third-party solutions	You can use Binary Authorization with a variety of tools from vendors other than Google.
Continuous validation	Checking container images regularly helps ensure that your organization's systems and data are protected from security risks.

Table 9.1 – List of features in Binary Authorization

Now that you know a few things about Binary Authorization, let's set it up in a Google Cloud project.

Setting up Binary Authorization

Binary Authorization evaluates containerized workloads. It requires the container to be signed using a compliant key. We can sign the container images using either a Google-managed key or one created with Google's CMEK. Also, the image must comply with a customer-defined policy.

This exercise will walk you through the steps of setting up the environment and then signing the container.

Here is an overview of the process:

1. Environment preparation:

   I.   Create a key with CMEK.

   II.   Create a Binary Authorization policy.

   III. Enable the policy.

2. Container preparation:

   I.   Create a container.

   II.   Sign the container.

   III. Deploy the container.

Let's get started.

Creating a CMEK

Encryption keys are fundamental to the security of your applications and the systems you use to deliver those applications. CMEKs give you control over the keys you use to keep your customers' data secure.

Binary Authorization uses either a customer-managed key or a Google-managed key. CMEKs are created and managed by the customer using Cloud KMS. Greater control and flexibility are often cited as a reason for using CMEK. Neither key type is more secure than the other. The preference comes down to who can access the data based on the keys. Enterprises and other customers like the fact that Google cannot decrypt data.

Follow the steps in this section to create a key ring and generate the key. This key will be used later as part of the attestation process. Before you can create a key, you need to create a key ring, if you don't already have one.

If you don't already have a key ring, follow these steps to create one:

1. From the main Google Cloud console menu, select **Security | Key Management** and click + **CREATE KEY RING**.

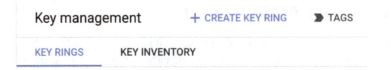

Figure 9.1 – The Key management dialog

2. Provide a name for the key ring and select a region.

    Choose **Multi-region** and then select **global (Global)** from the drop-down menu.

    Key rings group keys together to keep them organized. In the next step, you'll create keys that are in this key ring. Learn more ☑

Project name

chapter10

┌─ Key ring name * ──┐
│ binauthz-ring   ❓ │
└──┘

Location type ❓

○ Region
   Lower latency within a single region

◉ Multi-region
   Highest availability across largest area

┌─ Multi-region * ───┐
│ global (Global)   ▼   ❓ │
└──┘

EKM is not available in this location See available regions ☑

[**CREATE**]   [CANCEL]

Figure 9.2 – The key ring creation dialog

3. Select **CREATE**.

    You will be automatically taken to the **Create key** page.

Now that you've created a key ring, you'll need to create the key itself.

Creating a key

The **Create key** page will appear after you create the key ring. If that doesn't happen, manually launch the **Create key** page by selecting **Security| Key management | Select the key ring | CREATE KEY**.

Follow these steps to create your key:

1. Provide a name for the key.

2. Select **Software** under **Protection Level** and click **CONTINUE**.

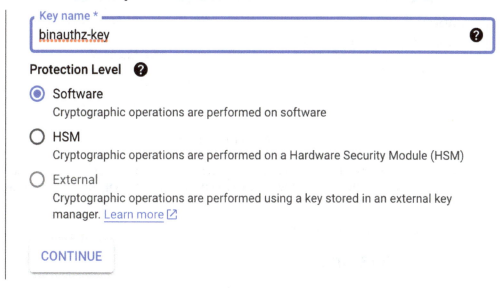

A cryptographic key is a resource that is used for encrypting and decrypting data or for producing and verifying digital signatures. A key can have multiple versions.
Learn more �

● **Name and protection level**

> Key name *
> binauthz-key   ❓

Protection Level ❓

◉ Software
   Cryptographic operations are performed on software

○ HSM
   Cryptographic operations are performed on a Hardware Security Module (HSM)

○ External
   Cryptographic operations are performed using a key stored in an external key
   manager. Learn more �

CONTINUE

Figure 9.3 – The key creation dialog

3. Under **Key material**, select **Generated key**, then click **CONTINUE**.

- ## Key material

  ● **Generated key**
  The key material will be generated for you. Learn more ⤴

  ○ **Imported key**
  Import your key material into GCP. Learn more ⤴

  CONTINUE

- ## Purpose and algorithm

  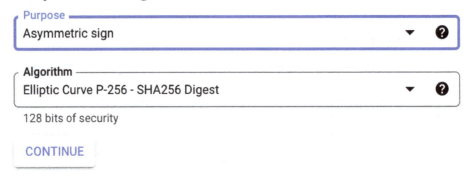

  Purpose

  Asymmetric sign ▾ ❓

  Algorithm

  Elliptic Curve P-256 - SHA256 Digest ▾ ❓

  128 bits of security

  CONTINUE

Figure 9.4 – The key creation dialog, continued

As shown in the lower part of the preceding screenshot, under **Purpose and algorithm**, select **Asymmetric sign** for **Purpose** and **Elliptic Curve P-256 - SHA256 Digest** for **Algorithm**, then click **CONTINUE**.

4.   Under **Versions**, click **CONTINUE**.

- ## Versions

  Key rotation

  Automatic key rotation is not available for asymmetric keys

  CONTINUE

Figure 9.5 – The key creation dialog, continued

5.   Under **Additional settings,** choose the number of days before this key is destroyed, then click **CREATE**.

Figure 9.6 – Finishing creating the key

> **Important note**
>
> It's a good practice to rotate keys frequently. We've entered 30 here to simplify this demonstration. Shorter durations are better for production environments.

Now that the key has been created, we're ready to set up Binary Authorization on GKE.

Setting up Binary Authorization on GKE

You can configure Binary Authorization using the Google Cloud console or the Google Cloud CLI. You can also perform some setup steps by using the **Binary Authorization REST API**.

To set up Binary Authorization on a GKE cluster, perform the following steps:

1. Create a GKE cluster with Binary Authorization enabled, or enable it on an existing cluster.

2. Edit the cluster by selecting the cluster you wish to edit.

Figure 9.7 – List of clusters on GKE's main page

3. In the **Security** section, click the edit icon next to **Binary authorization** and select **Enable**.

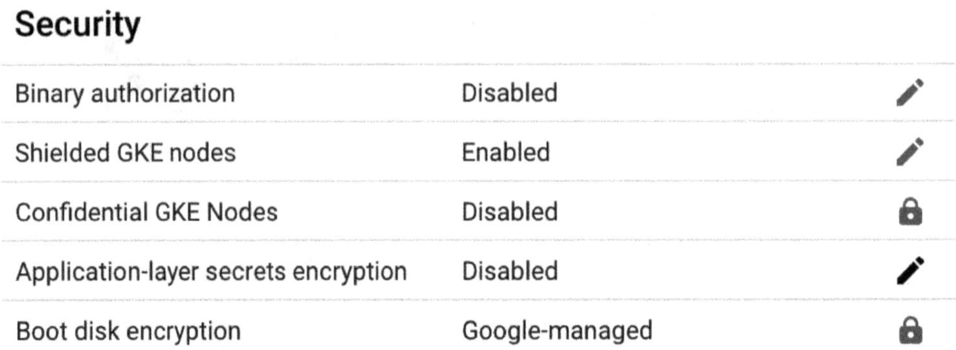

Security

Binary authorization	Disabled	✏️
Shielded GKE nodes	Enabled	✏️
Confidential GKE Nodes	Disabled	🔒
Application-layer secrets encryption	Disabled	✏️
Boot disk encryption	Google-managed	🔒

Figure 9.8 – Turning security settings on for your new or existing cluster

With that, you have enabled Binary Authorization on a GKE cluster. Binary Authorization can also be configured for Cloud Run serverless workloads, as described in the following section.

Setting up Binary Authorization on Cloud Run

You can set a Binary Authorization policy on Cloud Run services and jobs. In this chapter, we're only concerned with services.

For a Cloud Run service, Cloud Run checks the policy with each deployment. The revision is either deployed or stopped based on the status of the policy check.

The breakglass feature can be used to deploy a revision, even if it fails the policy check.

Earlier, we discussed the two types of encryption keys – Google-managed keys and Customer CMEKs. CMEK was used in the GKE example. This Cloud Run example will use Google-managed keys as an alternative.

> **Important note**
> When the Binary Authorization policy changes, it only applies to new revisions.

To set up Binary Authorization for Cloud Run, perform the following steps:

1. From the **Cloud Run** page in the Google Cloud console, select **+ CREATE SERVICE**.

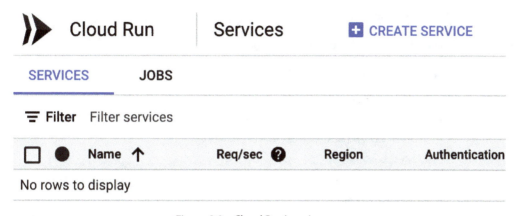

Figure 9.9 – Cloud Run's main page

2. Choose **SELECT** to pick the container image you created in *Chapter 2, Using Skaffold for Development, Build, and Deploy*.

A service exposes a unique endpoint and automatically scales the underlying infrastructure to handle incoming requests. Service name and region cannot be changed later.

🔘 Deploy one revision from an existing container image

Container image URL   SELECT

TEST WITH A SAMPLE CONTAINER

Should listen for HTTP requests on $PORT and not rely on local state. How to build a container? ⧉

Figure 9.10 – Cloud Run's service creation dialog

3. In the **Select container image** side panel, drill down until you find the image you created in *Chapter 2*, then choose it and click **SELECT**.

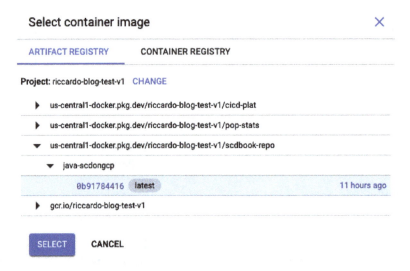

Figure 9.11 – Cloud Run's service creation dialog | Select container image

4.   Under **Authentication**, select **Allow unauthenticated invocations**.

Authentication * ❷

◉ Allow unauthenticated invocations
Check this if you are creating a public API or website.

○ Require authentication
Manage authorized users with Cloud IAM.

Figure 9.12 – Authentication options for the Cloud Run service

5.   Expand **CONTAINER, NETWORKING**, and **SECURITY**, select the **SECURITY** tab, and
enable **Verify container deployment with Binary Authorization**.

Container, Networking, Security

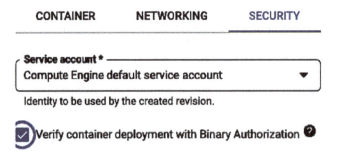

Figure 9.13 – Cloud Run networking security for the container

6. With the **Google-managed encryption key** selected, click **CREATE**.

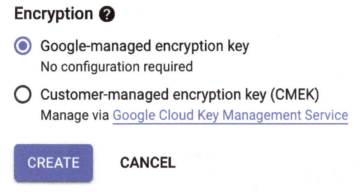

Figure 9.14 – Encryption choices for container security

7. After the creation process completes, click the link provided by Cloud Run to verify the container deployment.

Figure 9.15 – Cloud Run service URL

You should see that your application is running:

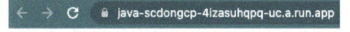

scd-on-gcp app updated in target: local !!

Figure 9.16 – Results of running the app in Cloud Run

With that, we've seen how to enable Binary Authorization for GKE and Cloud Run. We'll build on this in upcoming sections. Next, we'll take a look at Binary Authorization for GKE Enterprise.

Using Binary Authorization on GKE on other public clouds

Binary Authorization is also available for GKE on non-Google Cloud platforms. For non-Google Cloud platforms, Binary Authorization uses an app that runs on non-Google Kubernetes clusters. This app uses an authentication webhook. The request is forwarded to Google Cloud, where the request is validated by the Binary Authorization enforcer, which then returns an *accept* or *reject* based on policy compliance.

The following diagram shows how Binary Authorization on Google Cloud interacts with a non-GKE-compatible Kubernetes cluster:

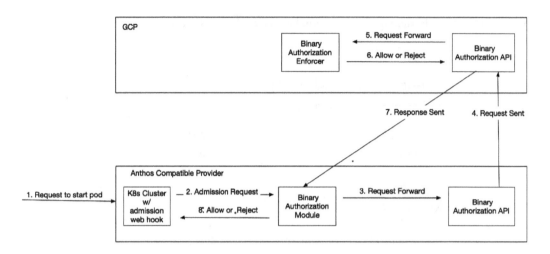

Figure 9.17 – Architecture of Binary Authorization for GKE Enterprise

> **Important note**
>
> Installation of GKE Enterprise on non-Google Cloud platforms isn't covered here. To learn more about installing GKE Enterprise, see the official Google Cloud documentation: `https://cloud.google.com/binary-authorization/docs/setting-up-on-prem`.

Now that we've learned how to set up Binary Authorization on GKE, Cloud Run, and GKE Enterprise, let's take a look at attestations.

Setting up attestations

An **attestation** is a digital document that certifies a container image. During deployment, Binary Authorization verifies the attestation using the attestor's public key before allowing the image to be deployed. An attestation is created after an image is built using a private key.

Creating an attestation

Follow these steps to create an attestation:

1. Copy the resource name of the key you created earlier:

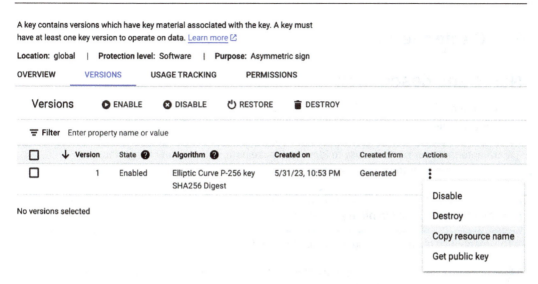

A key contains versions which have key material associated with the key. A key must have at least one key version to operate on data. Learn more

Location: global | Protection level: Software | Purpose: Asymmetric sign

OVERVIEW   VERSIONS   USAGE TRACKING   PERMISSIONS

Figure 9.18 – Getting the resource name of the key

2. Select **Security | Binary Authorization** and under **Binary Authorization setup**, select **CREATE ATTESTORS**:

Figure 9.19 – Using Binary Authorization setup to start creating an attestor

3. Provide **Name and description** values for the attestor. There is also a built-in attestor called **built-by-cloud-build** attestor. This attestor does as you'd expect – it can be used to ensure that only images are built using Cloud Build, such as in a CI/CD pipeline:

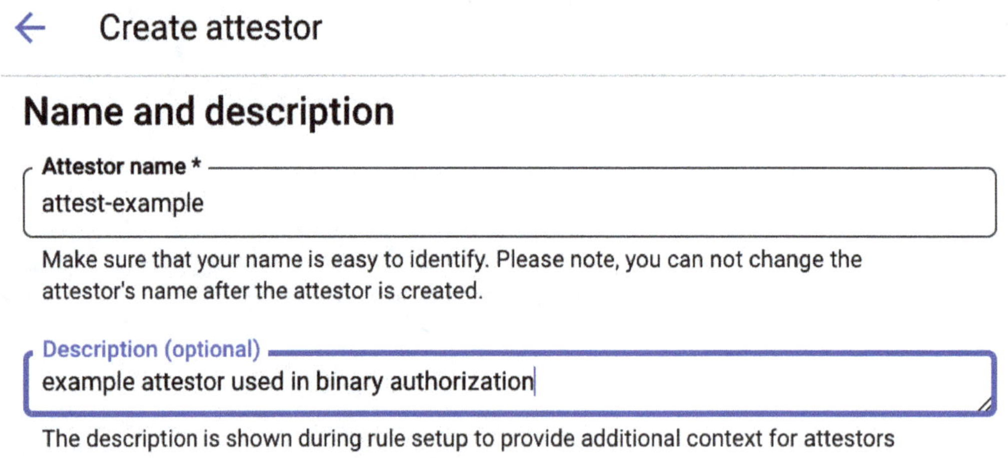

←   Create attestor

Name and description

Attestor name *

attest-example

Make sure that your name is easy to identify. Please note, you can not change the attestor's name after the attestor is created.

Description (optional)

example attestor used in binary authorization

The description is shown during rule setup to provide additional context for attestors

Figure 9.20 – The Create attestor dialog

4.   Select **ADD A PKIX PUBLIC KEY**:

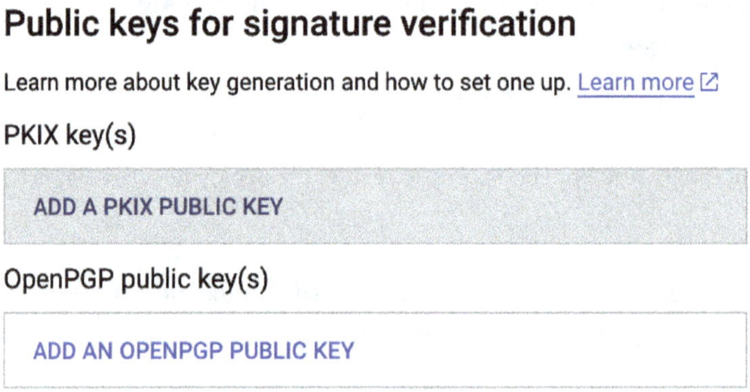

Public keys for signature verification

Learn more about key generation and how to set one up. Learn more ☐

PKIX key(s)

ADD A PKIX PUBLIC KEY

OpenPGP public key(s)

ADD AN OPENPGP PUBLIC KEY

Figure 9.21 – Attestor creation flow

5.   Select **IMPORT FROM CLOUD KMS**:

Public keys for signature verification

Learn more about key generation and how to set one up. Learn more ⧉

PKIX key(s)

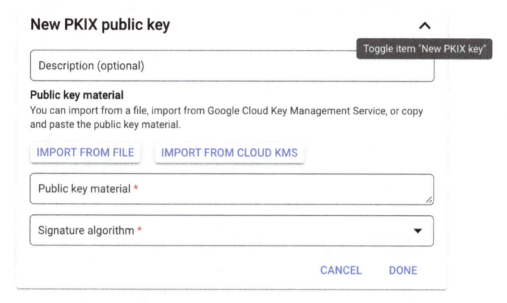

Figure 9.22 – The Public keys for signature verification dialog

6. Paste the resource name of the key you copied earlier into the **Key version resource ID** box and click **SUBMIT**.

Import from Cloud KMS

You can import from Google Cloud Key Management Service by copy and pasting the key version resource ID here. The public key material will be imported and copied into the attestor.

Key version resource ID *
cations/global/keyRings/binauthz-ring/cryptoKeys/binauthz-key/cryptoKeyVersions/1

Example format: "projects/project-name/locations/global/keyRings/key-ring-name/
cryptoKeys/key-name/cryptoKeyVersions/1"
The prefix "//cloudkms.googleapis.com/v1/" will be appended to your key.

CANCEL   **SUBMIT**

Figure 9.23 – The Public key import dialog showing the resource name you copied

7. Click **DONE**:

PKIX key(s)

Figure 9.24 – The Create public key dialog

8. Under **Advanced Settings**, click **CREATE**:

Figure 9.25 – Public key advanced settings

9. Use the following command to verify that the attestor exists:

```
gcloud container binauthz attestors list
```

The output will look like this:

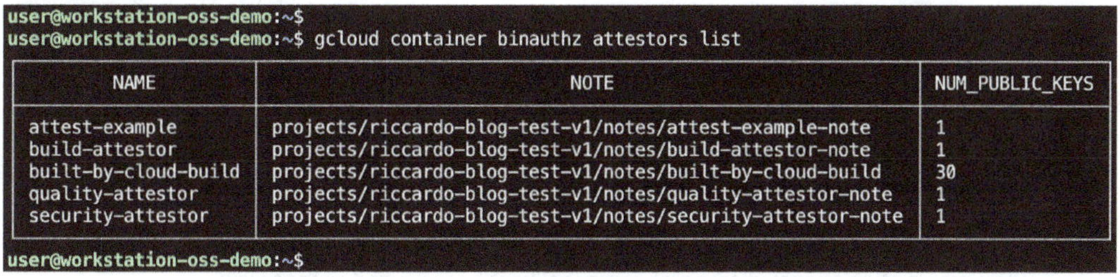

```
user@workstation-oss-demo:~$
user@workstation-oss-demo:~$ gcloud container binauthz attestors list
     NAME                              NOTE                                    NUM_PUBLIC_KEYS
 attest-example       projects/riccardo-blog-test-v1/notes/attest-example-note    1
 build-attestor       projects/riccardo-blog-test-v1/notes/build-attestor-note    1
 built-by-cloud-build projects/riccardo-blog-test-v1/notes/built-by-cloud-build   30
 quality-attestor     projects/riccardo-blog-test-v1/notes/quality-attestor-note  1
 security-attestor    projects/riccardo-blog-test-v1/notes/security-attestor-note 1
user@workstation-oss-demo:~$
```

Figure 9.26 – Output from the command to list attestors

Now that you've created an attestation, you can configure your Binary Authorization policy.

Configuring Binary Authorization policies

A Binary Authorization policy is a set of rules for determining whether an image can be deployed on a platform. You can define this policy using one of two methods:

- The Google Cloud console
- gcloud commands

The following procedure describes how to do this using the Google Cloud console.

Creating the policy

Follow these steps to configure a Binary Authorization policy:

1. From the Google Cloud Console's main menu, select **Security | Binary Authorization**.
2. Select **EDIT POLICY**.

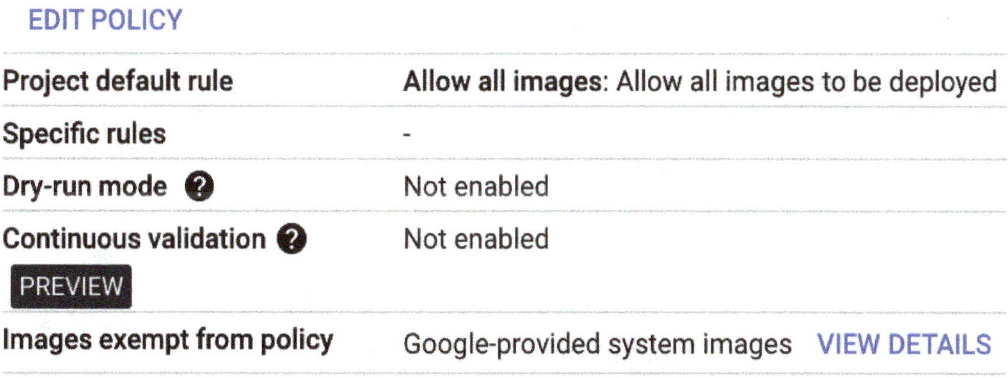

EDIT POLICY

Project default rule	**Allow all images**: Allow all images to be deployed
Specific rules	-
Dry-run mode ❓	Not enabled
Continuous validation ❓ PREVIEW	Not enabled
Images exempt from policy	Google-provided system images VIEW DETAILS

Figure 9.27 – The EDIT POLICY dialog

3.   Select **Require attestations** and enter the name of the attestor you created in the previous section.

Default rule

The default rule determines whether container images are allowed to be deployed unless the rule is overridden by specific rules or exempt images. Learn more

○   **Allow all images**: Allow all images to be deployed

○   **Disallow all images**: Blocks all images from deployment

◉   **Require attestations**: Allow only images that have been verified by the following attestors

Figure 9.28 – Choosing the default rule for the policy – Require attestations

4.   Select **ADD ATTESTORS**.

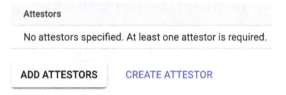

Figure 9.29 – The Attestors dialog

The **Add attestors** dialog will be displayed. The following screenshot shows the dialog with a project name and attestor name provided:

Figure 9.30 – The Add attestors dialog

5.   Select **ADD 1 ATTESTOR**.

You can skip **Additional settings for GKE and GKE Enterprise**:

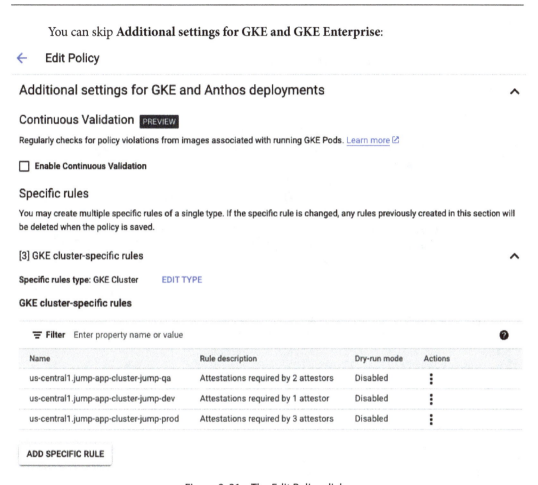

Figure 9. 31 – The Edit Policy dialog

6.   Select **SAVE POLICY**.

Google system image exemption

☑ Trust all Google-provided system images.   VIEW DETAILS

SAVE POLICY   **CANCEL**

Figure 9.32 – Saving the policy

Now that you've created a policy and added an attestor, the next step is to apply an attestation to the image.

Applying an attestation to the image

Follow these steps to apply an attestation to the container image you created in *Chapter 2*:

1. Execute the following command, substituting your values for the variables:

```
gcloud beta container binauthz attestations sign-and-create \
    --project="${ATTESTATION_PROJECT_ID}" \
    --artifact-url="${IMAGE_TO_ATTEST}" \
    --attestor="${ATTESTOR_NAME}" \
    --attestor-project="${ATTESTOR_PROJECT_ID}" \
    --keyversion-project="${KMS_KEY_PROJECT_ID}" \
    --keyversion-location="${KMS_KEY_LOCATION}" \
    --keyversion-keyring="${KMS_KEYRING_NAME}" \
    --keyversion-key="${KMS_KEY_NAME}" \
    --keyversion="${KMS_KEY_VERSION}"
```

2. View the attestations on the image, substituting the values in your environment for the variables:

```
gcloud container binauthz attestations list\
    --project="${ATTESTATION_PROJECT_ID}"\
    --attestor="projects/${ATTESTOR_PROJECT_ID}/
attestors/${ATTESTOR_NAME}"\
    --artifact-url="${IMAGE_TO_ATTEST}"
```

Here's an example of the output after running the preceding command:

```
---
attestation:
  serializedPayload: ewogICJjcml0aWNhbCI6IHsKICAgICJpZGVudG-
10eSI6IHsKICAgICAgImZvY2tlci1yZWdlcmVuY2UiOiAidXMtY2VudHJhb-
DEtZG9ja2VyLnBrZy5kZXYvcmljY2FyZG8tYmxvZy10ZXN0LXYxL3NjZGJvb-
2stcmVwby9qYXZhLXNjZG9uZ2NwIgogICAgfSwKICAgICJpbWFnZSI6IHsKI-
CAgICAgImRvY2tlci1tYW5pZmVzdC1kaWdlc3QiOiAic2hhMjU2OjBiOTE3OD-
Q0MTZiMzRkZjg0ZDliZTViMjM0ZmJlYjAxMTczOTMyN2QxZTc5MzY2MWNiMT-
dhYzQ5MmNmNTc2YTUiCiAgICB9LAogICAgInR5cGUiOiAiR29vZ2xlIGNsb-
3VkIGJpbmF1dGgiIGNvbnRhaW5lciBzaWduYXR1cmUiCiAgfQp9Cg==
  signatures:
  - publicKeyId: //cloudkms.googleapis.com/v1/projects/riccardo-
blog-test-v1/locations/global/keyRings/binauthz-ring/cryptoKeys/
binauthz-key/cryptoKeyVersions/1
    signature: MEUCIESmYJ4sFGxcksYczh8L4R3G3lVr1BLkgE0PlbM9n3n-
kAiEAv9PqJmhdgnbR1mbB2dfzn0_vwMIhe62gr8px3Z1PxvI=
createTime: '2023-06-09T01:37:00.474633Z'
kind: ATTESTATION
name: projects/riccardo-blog-test-v1/occurrences/1921869e-b3bf-
4f77-a402-5f990e4354ea
noteName: projects/riccardo-blog-test-v1/notes/attest-exam-
ple-note
```

```
resourceUri: us-central1-docker.pkg.dev/riccardo-blog-test-v1/
scdbook-repo/java-scdongcp@sha256:0b91784416b34df84d9be5b234f-
beb011739327d1e793661cb17ac492cf576a5
updateTime: '2023-06-09T01:37:00.474633Z'
```

The preceding output shows what's returned from the `gcloud container binauthz attestations list` command. It includes information about the attestation on the container image.

Summary

Multiple attack vectors can compromise a software supply chain. Binary Authorization is a powerful tool for defending your supply chain against bad actors because it helps ensure that only the images you've allowed via a policy are deployed onto modern container-based runtimes.

In this chapter, you learned how to configure Binary Authorization for three different Google Cloud runtimes, as well as how to create policies, attestations, and attestors to ensure that your container images are safe to deploy.

In the next chapter, we'll show you an end-to-end software delivery pipeline, thus bringing together the source-to-prod process for securely delivering your application to a Google Cloud runtime.

Part 4: Hands-On Secure Pipeline Delivery and Looking Forward

In *Part 4*, we will guide you to create an end-to-end software-delivery pipeline, representing a real production environment, with multiple actors involved, using all the services you learned about in the previous parts of this book. We will also show you some examples of integrating these tools with other services that you might have. Moreover, we provide some additional best practices and insights on possible future trends.

This part has the following chapters:

- *Chapter 10, Demonstrating an End-to-End Software Delivery Pipeline*
- *Chapter 11, Integrating with Your Organization's Workflows*
- *Chapter 12, Diving into Best Practices and Trends in Continuous Delivery*

10

Demonstrating an End-to-End Software Delivery Pipeline

In this chapter, we will use all the Google Cloud tools that we've described in the book to build an end-to-end pipeline, from code to production, given an example application.

You'll update your app in Cloud Code, commit your changes to trigger a build in Cloud Build, scan for vulnerabilities using Artifact Registry, and use Cloud Deploy to deploy your app in a QA GKE cluster, where integration and usability tests can be performed, and then deploy it using a canary deployment strategy to a production GKE cluster.

Performing the steps in this chapter gives you a chance to practice the complete software delivery flow in Google Cloud.

To avoid confusion, note that this chapter uses the terms **pipeline** and **software delivery pipeline** to refer to the components and processes that make up your end-to-end delivery journey. But in a Cloud Deploy context, a **delivery pipeline** is a specific Cloud Deploy resource that defines your sequence of targets.

This chapter covers the following topics:

- Software delivery pipeline overview
- Building your pipeline
- Running your pipeline

Technical requirements

To perform the tasks in this chapter, you need the assets described here. The instructions in this chapter assume you are reusing these assets as created in previous chapters:

- A Google Cloud project, with billing or free trial enabled.

  The project must have all the Google Cloud APIs that you used in previous chapters enabled.

- An Artifact Registry repository.

- A personal GitHub account.

  You will connect this account to Cloud Build to configure automatic build execution. If you cannot provide that, you can use other supported repositories, but the steps might be different from those described in the chapter.

- You need to have the following installed:

  - The Google Cloud CLI

  - Git

  - kubectl

  - Skaffold

  - Docker

The code used in this chapter is available in the folder named `ch10` of the book repository at the following URL: `https://github.com/PacktPublishing/Secure-Continuous-Delivery-on-Google-Cloud`

To start, let's learn about the overall software delivery pipeline.

Software delivery pipeline overview

Following the instructions in this chapter, you will create and execute an end-to-end software delivery pipeline. The end-to-end process includes creating all the necessary resources, updating code, triggering a build, deploying to staging, and promoting to production.

Our pipeline process is as follows:

1. A developer creates a feature branch from an application repository.

2. The developer changes code using Cloud Code on Cloud Workstations (or using Cloud Shell Editor).

   The change is continuously deployed in the developer's Minikube cluster, running as part of Cloud Code.

3. After the developer tests the changes locally, they open a pull request to the `main` branch.

4. The QA team comments on the pull request.

   This comment invokes a Cloud Build trigger, which builds a container using Skaffold, then scans the image for vulnerabilities and checks the found vulnerabilities against a security policy.

5. Because the original artifact has vulnerabilities not allowed by the policy, the build process fails.

6. The developer updates the artifact and commits the change to the pull request.

7. A member of the security team reviews the change and comments on the pull request to retry the build, which now succeeds because the vulnerability has been patched.

8. The build completes, resulting in the creation of a release in Cloud Deploy.

9. The release is rolled out in a QA GKE cluster, where the QA team runs user acceptance tests.

10. After the tests are completed, the QA team merges the pull request, triggering the promotion of the release to a production GKE cluster.

11. The Cloud Deploy `prod` target requires approval, so an approval request is triggered.

12. The product manager for the application checks the rollout and approves it, and the app is released in production using a canary deployment strategy.

13. After checking the canary release, the app release team advances the rollout to 100%, fully deploying the application.

There are many roles mentioned in the process. You will play all of them as you go through the exercises in this chapter.

To simulate this process efficiently, you will use a single GitHub account and repository in which, as a developer, you will work on a feature branch and then open a pull request to the `main` branch, managed by the QA team. In a real-world scenario, the multiple roles would use multiple GitHub accounts, and developers would probably fork the main repository into their own accounts.

The following diagram shows the pipeline from a high level:

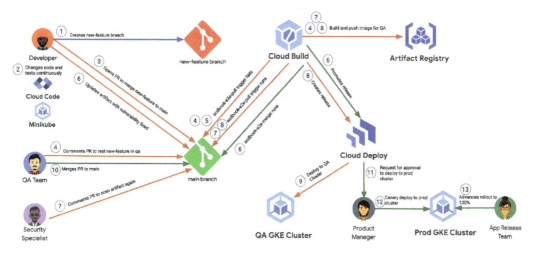

Figure 10.1 – The source-to-production pipeline

Our first step in this end-to-end journey is to build the components of the software delivery pipeline, including the following:

- Source code repository
- Required IAM roles
- The GKE clusters to deploy to
- GKE gateway resources
- The Cloud Deploy delivery pipeline
- Security policies
- Connection between Cloud Build and the source code repository
- Cloud Build triggers
- An initializing release in Cloud Deploy

Next, let's get started by creating these components.

Building your software delivery pipeline

Follow the instructions in this section to create the building blocks of your end-to-end software delivery pipeline.

Since the steps in the *Running your pipeline* section require Cloud Code, we advise you to run all the tasks in this section and the following one from a Cloud Workstations instance (or Cloud Shell Editor) that has all the needed tools already installed.

Before performing all the tasks in this section, use the following command to authenticate to Google Cloud, set your project, and then export your project ID and project number:

```
export PROJECT_ID=$(gcloud config get-value project)
export PROJECT_NUMBER=$(gcloud projects list \
--filter="${PROJECT_ID}" \
--format=»value(PROJECT_NUMBER)»)
```

With your Google Cloud project ready to go, let's start with the first component of our software delivery pipeline, the source code repository.

Creating your source code repository

To create an end-to-end software delivery pipeline, you need your own repository, connected to Cloud Build triggers, as you did in *Chapter 5*.

To create one, run the following steps from the `ch10` folder (`https://github.com/PacktPublishing/Secure-Continuous-Delivery-on-Google-Cloud/tree/main/ch10`):

1. Create a new repository in your GitHub account. Call it `scdbook-e2e`.

2. Export your GitHub account name to the `GIT_ACCOUNT` variable using the following command:

   ```
   export GIT_ACCOUNT=yourgithubaccount
   ```

3. Run the following two commands to locally clone the book repository and change to the local repository folder:

   ```
   git clone
   cd Secure-Continuous-Delivery-on-Google-Cloud-/
   ```

4. Run the following commands, from the root folder of your local repository, to copy the content of the `ch10` folder as the content of your new repository, and initialize the new repository:

   ```
   cp -r ch5 ../scdbook-ch5
   cd ../scdbook-e2e
   git init
   git add .
   git commit -m "first commit"
   git branch -M main
   git remote add origin https://github.com/$GIT_ACCOUNT/scdbook-e2e.git
   git push -u origin main
   ```

   You might need to authenticate to your GitHub account.

You've now created the repository that you'll connect to Cloud Build, so updating this repository will trigger a build and deploy.

In the next section, we'll make sure our service accounts have the necessary **Identity and Access Management (IAM)** roles.

Configuring the required IAM roles

To run the pipeline, you need to assign some roles to some service accounts so that the different services involved can interact among them.

Run the following command to assign the needed roles on Cloud Deploy, Container Analysis, and KMS (needed to manage releases and produce and sign attestations) to the Cloud Build service account:

```
gcloud projects add-iam-policy-binding $PROJECT_ID --member
serviceAccount:$PROJECT_NUMBER@cloudbuild.gserviceaccount.com --role
roles/clouddeploy.releaser
gcloud iam service-accounts add-iam-policy-binding
$PROJECT_NUMBER-compute@developer.gserviceaccount.com
--member=serviceAccount:$PROJECT_NUMBER@cloudbuild.gserviceaccount.
com    --role=roles/iam.serviceAccountUser
gcloud projects add-iam-policy-binding $PROJECT_ID --member
serviceAccount:$PROJECT_NUMBER@cloudbuild.gserviceaccount.com --role
roles/containeranalysis.notes.editor
gcloud projects add-iam-policy-binding $PROJECT_ID --member
serviceAccount:$PROJECT_NUMBER@cloudbuild.gserviceaccount.com --role
roles/containeranalysis.notes.occurrences.viewer
gcloud projects add-iam-policy-binding $PROJECT_ID --member
serviceAccount:$PROJECT_NUMBER@cloudbuild.gserviceaccount.com --role
roles/containeranalysis.occurrences.editor
gcloud projects add-iam-policy-binding $PROJECT_ID --member
serviceAccount:$PROJECT_NUMBER@cloudbuild.gserviceaccount.com --role
roles/cloudkms.signer
```

With these roles in place, your service accounts now have the permissions they need in order to run the pipeline.

Next, you'll create the GKE clusters onto which you'll deploy your application.

Creating two GKE clusters

Run the following command to create two GKE clusters to deploy to, one as the QA environment and one for production, with Binary Authorization enabled:

```
gcloud container clusters create qa-cluster \
    --zone=us-central1-b \
    --gateway-api=standard \
    --binauthz-evaluation-mode=PROJECT_SINGLETON_POLICY_ENFORCE \
    --async \
    && gcloud container clusters create prod-cluster \
    --zone=us-central1-b \
    --gateway-api=standard \
    --binauthz-evaluation-mode=PROJECT_SINGLETON_POLICY_ENFORCE \
    --async
```

Run the following command to check that your clusters have been provisioned:

```
gcloud container clusters list
```

As soon as your clusters have `STATUS RUNNING`, run the following command to get the credentials and create `kubeconfig` contexts for your clusters:

```
gcloud container clusters get-credentials qa-cluster --zone
us-central1-b --project $PROJECT_ID
gcloud container clusters get-credentials prod-cluster --zone
us-central1-b --project $PROJECT_ID
```

Now, run the following command to get the `kubeconfig` contexts:

```
kubectl config get-contexts
```

The contexts for the clusters you just created are named using the `gke_$PROJECT_ID_us-central1-b_qa-cluster` and `gke_$PROJECT_ID_us-central1-b_prod-cluster` formats.

Next, we'll create GKE gateway resources, so that traffic is correctly apportioned during the Cloud Deploy canary deployment.

Creating GKE gateway resources

To split traffic across two versions of the application, as part of a Cloud Deploy canary deployment strategy, we rely on the Kubernetes Gateway API and, specifically, the GKE controller implementation, using the `gke-17-regional-external-managed` gateway class driving a Google Cloud regional external application load balancer.

Follow these steps to create the resources you need to use the preceding configuration:

1. Create a proxy-only subnet in your VPC with the following command:

    ```
    gcloud compute networks subnets create gtw-subnet \
        --purpose=REGIONAL_MANAGED_PROXY \
        --role=ACTIVE \
        --region=us-central1 \
        --network=default \
        --range=10.127.0.0/23
    ```

2. Create two static IP addresses for your gateways, using the following command:

    ```
    gcloud compute addresses create qa-gtw-ip \
        --region=us-central1 \
        --network-tier=STANDARD
    gcloud compute addresses create prod-gtw-ip \
        --region=us-central1 \
        --network-tier=STANDARD
    ```

3. Run the following command to create a gateway resource on both clusters, so you can use the Gateway API HTTPRoute resource weight-based traffic splitting to perform a canary release:

```
kubectl --context=gke_${PROJECT_ID}_us-central1-b_qa-cluster
apply -f qa-gateway.yaml
kubectl --context=gke_${PROJECT_ID}_us-central1-b_prod-cluster
apply -f prod-gateway.yaml
```

With gateway resources in place, let's create the Cloud Deploy delivery pipeline.

Creating your Cloud Deploy delivery pipeline

Perform the following steps to create the Cloud Deploy delivery pipeline that will deploy your application to two targets:

1. Examine the delivery-pipeline.yaml manifest file at the root of your repository.

    The manifest creates a Cloud Deploy delivery pipeline with two stages: qa and prod. These stages map to the two GKE clusters you created: qa-cluster and prod-cluster. In the prod stage, we configure Cloud Deploy to use a canary deployment strategy, with the Kubernetes Gateway API, using an HTTPRoute resource to do traffic splitting. The configuration is shown here:

    ```
    strategy:
        canary:
          runtimeConfig:
            kubernetes:
              gatewayServiceMesh:
                httpRoute: "scdongcp-route"
                service: "scdongcp-app"
                deployment: "scdongcp-app"
                routeUpdateWaitTime: 60s
          canaryDeployment:
            percentages: [50]
            verify: false
    ```

    This configuration directs 50% of the traffic to the canary release. In a real-world scenario, a canary release would probably use a smaller traffic percentage, but we put it at 50% here so you can easily experiment with the canary from a single client.

    Because the HTTPRoute resource programs the load balancer to split traffic across versions, the routeUpdateWaitTime parameter allows time to propagate configuration changes across the load balancer infrastructure.

2. Use the following command to edit this manifest to change the $PROJECT_ID variable to the project ID of your project:

    ```
    sed -i "s/yourproject/$PROJECT_ID/g" delivery-pipeline.yaml
    ```

3. Use the following command to commit and push this update to your remote repository:

```
git add .
git commit -m "ready to run"
git push -u origin main
```

4. Now run the following command to apply the manifest to create your delivery pipeline resource:

```
gcloud deploy apply --file=delivery-pipeline.yaml   --region=us-
central1 --project=$PROJECT_ID
```

With the delivery pipeline defined, we'll now set up security policies.

Configuring security policies for your pipeline

In your pipeline, you will use Kritis Signer to check the output of a vulnerability scan done on the image at every build and create a signed attestation only if the image satisfies a configured policy. Kritis Signer is an open source tool that can trigger artifact analysis vulnerability scanning and create Binary Authorization attestations. You will also configure Binary Authorization on the two target clusters to allow only the deployment of images signed by Kritis Signer.

In the following sections, you'll configure security policies by creating a Kritis Signer custom builder and attestor and then set up the Binary Authorization policy. These go together to enable the security policy that Binary Authorization will use at runtime.

Creating a Kritis Signer custom builder

Follow these steps to create a Kritis Signer custom builder:

1. Run the following commands to change directories outside of your repository folder, clone the Kritis repository, and move into the local directory:

```
cd ..
git clone https://github.com/grafeas/kritis.git
cd kritis
```

2. Run the following command to build the Kritis Signer custom builder and push it to your Artifact Registry repository:

```
gcloud builds submit . \
   --config deploy/kritis-signer/cloudbuild.yaml
```

With the custom builder in place, we can now create an attestor.

Creating an attestor for Kritis

Create an attestor for Kritis, following the instructions from *Chapter 9*, and reusing the key and keyring you created in that chapter. Name the attestor `vuln-scanner` and leave the option to generate a Container Analysis note selected.

Configuring your Binary Authorization policy

Configure a Binary Authorization policy, following the instructions from *Chapter 9*, requiring the attestation from the `vuln-scanner` attestor you previously created for Kritis Signer.

With your security policies in place, your next steps are to connect your repository and create Cloud Build triggers that will invoke your pipeline.

Connecting your source code repository to Cloud Build

Link your newly created repository to Cloud Build following the instructions in *Chapter 5*. You can reuse the same host connection. And that's all you need to do to connect the repository and Cloud Build.

Creating two Cloud Build triggers for your repository

To execute our end-to-end pipeline, we need to create two Cloud Build triggers, both in the `us-central1` region and connected to the source code repository we just created. Create and enable both triggers following the instructions in *Chapter 5*. Configure the triggers as described in the following sections.

The scdbook-e2e-pull trigger

The `scdbook-e2e-pull` trigger is invoked by a pull request, which in this case requires comment control (as shown in the following figure).

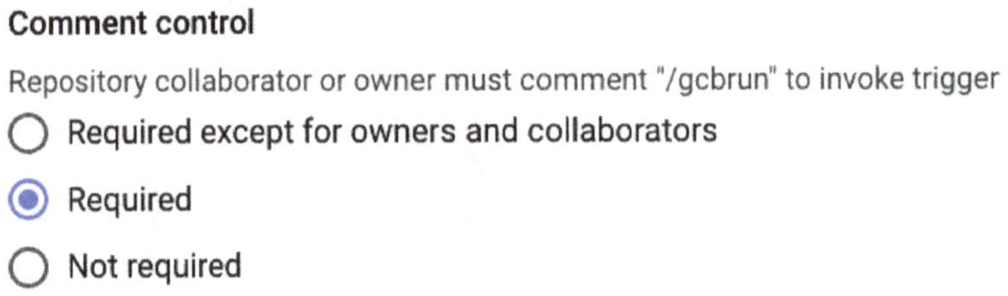

Comment control

Repository collaborator or owner must comment "/gcbrun" to invoke trigger

○ Required except for owners and collaborators

◉ Required

○ Not required

Figure 10.2 – Adding comment control to a trigger

Use the `build-qa.yaml` build config, which is shown here:

```
steps:
- name: gcr.io/k8s-skaffold/skaffold
  entrypoint: /bin/bash
  args:
```

```
    - -c
    - |
      skaffold build --interactive=false --file-output=/workspace/
artifacts.json --default-repo=us-central1-docker.pkg.dev/$PROJECT_ID/
scdbook-repo --push=true
      docker image inspect us-central1-docker.pkg.dev/$PROJECT_ID/
scdbook-repo/scdongcp-app:${SHORT_SHA} --format '{{index .RepoDigests
0}}' > image-digest.txt &&
      cat image-digest.txt
  id: skaffold-build
- name: gcr.io/$PROJECT_ID/kritis-signer
  entrypoint: /bin/bash
  args:
  - -c
  - |
    /kritis/signer \
    -v=10 \
    -alsologtostderr \
    -image=$(/bin/cat image-digest.txt) \
    -policy=vulnz-signing-policy.yaml \
    -kms_key_name=${_KMS_KEY_NAME} \
    -kms_digest_alg=${_KMS_DIGEST_ALG} \
    -note_name=${_NOTE_NAME}
  waitFor: ['skaffold-build']
  id: vuln-scanner
- name: gcr.io/google.com/cloudsdktool/cloud-sdk
  entrypoint: gcloud
  args:
    [
      "deploy", "releases", "create", "scdongcp-rel",
      "--delivery-pipeline", "scd-on-gcp-pipeline",
      "--region", "us-central1",
      "--annotations", "commitId=${REVISION_ID}",
      "--build-artifacts", "/workspace/artifacts.json"
    ]
  waitFor: ['vuln-scanner']
images:
- us-central1-docker.pkg.dev/$PROJECT_ID/scdbook-repo/scdongcp-
app:${SHORT_SHA}
options:
  requestedVerifyOption: VERIFIED
```

This build config does the following:

1. Builds a container image from the code in the repository using Skaffold and the included `skaffold.yaml` file

2. Scans the image for vulnerabilities with `kritis-signer` and checks the output against the `vulnz-signing-policy.yaml` Kritis policy that allows a maximum fixable vulnerability of severity `HIGH` and a maximum unfixable vulnerability of severity `MEDIUM`

> **Important note**
>
> If the image complies with the policy, Kritis generates and signs an attestation using the key and note you set up, so that Binary Authorization allows the image to be deployed. Otherwise, the build fails.

3. Creates the `scdongcp-rel` release in Cloud Deploy and rolls it out to the `qa` target

This trigger is executed when a developer creates a pull request to the `main` repository to merge their code, and the QA team includes the `/gcbrun` string as a comment. The goal is to build the image, scan it to assess its security posture, and, if the image complies with the security policy, deploy it on the QA cluster so it's available for usability testing.

With the pull request trigger in place, next, we'll create a merge trigger.

The scdbook-e2e-merge trigger

The `scdbook-e2e-merge` trigger is invoked by a push to the `main` branch. This trigger uses the `release-prod.yaml` build config, shown here:

```
steps:
- name: gcr.io/google.com/cloudsdktool/cloud-sdk
  entrypoint: gcloud
  args:
    [
        "deploy", "releases", "promote", "--delivery-pipeline",
        "scd-on-gcp-pipeline", "--release", "scdongcp-rel",
        "--region", "us-central1"
    ]
```

This config promotes the previous release to the `prod` stage.

This trigger runs when the QA team, after running the usability tests and the security scan, merges the pull request to the main repository.

In the `scdbook-e2e-merge` trigger, configure the following three user-defined substitution variables (as you learned in *Chapter 5*, which are needed by the Kritis Signer:

- `_KMS_KEY_NAME = projects/$PROJECT_ID/locations/global/keyRings/binauthz-ring/cryptoKeys/binauthz-key/cryptoKeyVersions/1`

   This assumes your keyring is called `binauthz-ring` and your key is `binauthz-key`, as instructed in *Chapter 9*, in the *Creating a CMEK* section. These values are also configured in the `createrelease.sh` script in the book repository. If you have changed these values, modify the value shown previously.

- `_KMS_DIGEST_ALG = SHA256`

- `_NOTE_NAME = projects/$PROJECT_ID/notes/vuln-scanner-note`

Next, you'll create a release so that your Cloud Deploy delivery pipeline has an existing application deployed to run a canary deployment against.

Creating your initial release

In order to run a canary deployment, we run our pipeline to update an existing application that is already running in our production environment, to create this initial release:

1. Go back to your local copy of the book repository.

2. Run the script:

   ```
   ./createrelease.sh
   ```

3. The script executes a build. You can monitor the execution from the **Cloud Build History** section in the Google Cloud console.

4. After the build completes, go to the **Cloud Deploy** page in the Google Cloud console.

   When your first release is deployed to your qa stage, promote the release to the `stable` phase of the `prod` stage and approve the rollout. When the rollout completes, you should see your first release deployed in both the qa and `prod` stages.

Figure 10.3 – The Cloud Deploy delivery pipeline after the initial release

Your end-to-end secure software delivery pipeline is now in place, including your application already deployed into production so that you have something to canary against. Next, we'll run that pipeline.

Running your pipeline

Follow the instructions in this section to run your end-to-end software delivery pipeline. This procedure has you playing multiple roles, as described in the overview section of this chapter.

In this section, you'll perform the following steps to test your triggers for building and deploying:

1. Update the code.

2. Build the application and scan it for vulnerabilities.

3. Merge the code and deploy the app to production.

Updating your code as a developer

In this section, you will act in the role of developer. You will create a new branch from the main repository, update the code, and open a pull request to submit your changes to the repository.

The following steps are based on a Code OSS-based Cloud Workstations instance. If you were already using one to complete the tasks in the previous section, you can continue as you were doing:

1. If you haven't already done so, click on **Cloud Code - Sign in** in the lower bar to sign in to Google Cloud.

2. Select your Google Cloud project.

3. If you moved to a different machine since you last used Cloud Code, clone your `scdbook-e2e` repository locally. Otherwise, you should already be in that local clone.

4. Create a new branch of the repository with the name `new feature` and check out that branch using the following command:

```
git checkout -b new-feature
```

5. In the editor, click **File | Open Folder…** and open your local repository folder.

Figure 10.4 – Opening the local repository in Cloud Code

6. Click on the project name at the left of the lower bar, then select **Control minikube**.

7. Click **Start**.

   Cloud Code starts a local Minikube cluster.

8. After Minikube has started, click again on the project name at the left of the lower bar and select **Run on Kubernetes**.

9. When prompted, choose the `skaffold.yaml` file, not `skaffold-first.yaml`.

10. Choose the [**default**] Skaffold profile.

11. Answer **Yes** if you're prompted to use the current context pointing to Minikube.

    The Cloud Code Kubernetes Explorer is displayed on the left, showing all the tasks that are executed.

12. When the deployment is completed, click on the **Open** link close to **scdongcp-app**, under **Portforward URLs (1) - service**.

    Cloud Code opens the locally forwarded port of your application in your browser.

13. To update your code, open the `app.go` file in the `scdongcp-app` folder, and change the message in row 25 to `scd-on-gcp app updated in target:` ....

    The new code is immediately built and re-deployed.

14. Refresh the browser window to see your change implemented.

15. Run the following commands in the terminal to commit and push your changes to the `new-feature` branch:

```
git add scdongcp-app/app.go
git commit -m "new feature"
git push origin new-feature
```

16. Open a pull request to merge your code:

    A. In the Git output in the terminal, *Ctrl* + click (or *Cmd* + click) on the `https://github.com/$GIT_ACCOUNT/scdbook-e2e/pull/new/new-feature` URL.

    B. On the GitHub page, click **Create pull request**.

    You will see that the checks fail. The `scdbook-e2e-pull` Cloud Build trigger you created requires a comment to execute.

In the next section, you'll create a comment to invoke the trigger.

Running an automatic build and scan of your artifact

Now you will act the part of a member of the QA team that reviews the proposed code and allows execution of an automated build and scan of the resulting container image. Perform the following steps to invoke the `scdbook-e2e-pull` trigger and then fix a vulnerability:

1. In the **GitHub new feature #1** pull request page, click on **Files changed** and review the proposed changes.

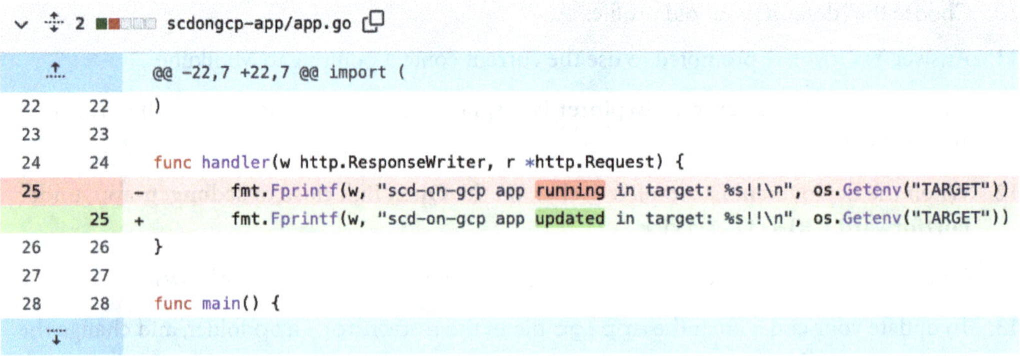

Figure 10.5 – Reviewing changes to the application source file

2. Then go back to the **Conversation** tab in GitHub and add the `/gcbrun` string as a new comment. Then, click **Comment**.

    This allows the `in` trigger to run.

3. From the Google Cloud console main menu, select **Cloud Build | History**.

4. Click on the last build (the one on top).

    You'll see the **Build details** page with **Build Summary** and a line for each step.

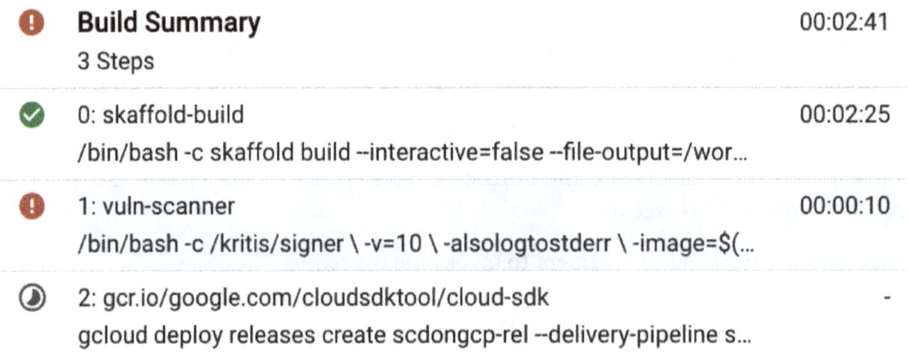

Figure 10.6 – Build steps in Cloud Build history

> **Important note**
>
> The build fails at the `vuln-scanner` task because the image has a critical vulnerability, so it is not compliant with the Kritis policy.

```
14 gcr.io/galloro-demos/kritis-signer:latest
15 I1113 23:19:32.834221        1 main.go:147] Signer mode: check-and-sign.
16 I1113 23:19:32.842917        1 main.go:182] Policy req: {HIGH MEDIUM []}
17 I1113 23:19:33.158213        1 containeranalysis.go:354] Found vulnerabilities after 314.993803ms
18 E1113 23:19:33.346171        1 main.go:208] Image "us-central1-docker.pkg.dev/galloro-demos/scdbook-repo/
   scdongcp-app@sha256:c721fce75a44ec57081a1862d63f11587d4f4f2ecd485d5a1d1955196f5e0a2a" does not pass VulnzSigningPolicy "my-vsp":
19 E1113 23:19:33.347222        1 main.go:209] Found 1 violations in image us-central1-docker.pkg.dev/galloro-demos/scdbook-repo/
   scdongcp-app@sha256:c721fce75a44ec57081a1862d63f11587d4f4f2ecd485d5a1d1955196f5e0a2a:
20 E1113 23:19:33.347248        1 main.go:211] found fixable CVE projects/goog-vulnz/notes/CVE-2021-36159 in us-central1-docker.pkg.dev/galloro-demos/scdbook-repo/
   scdongcp-app@sha256:c721fce75a44ec57081a1862d63f11587d4f4f2ecd485d5a1d1955196f5e0a2a, which has severity CRITICAL exceeding max fixable severity HIGH
```

Figure 10.7 – Vulnerabilities found in the container image

Because your image could not complete the build in this condition, your pull request cannot be merged.

5. Now, acting as a developer, update the Dockerfile inside the `scdongcp-app` folder with the most recent images for `golang-alpine` and `alpine`:

```
FROM golang:1.21-alpine3.18 as builder
COPY app.go .
RUN go env -w GO111MODULE=auto
RUN go build -o /app .

FROM alpine:3.18
CMD ["./app"]
COPY --from=builder /app .
```

You can copy the content from `refDockerfile` in the same folder (also reported as follows) that uses newer images. If newer critical vulnerabilities are later discovered in these versions, you'll have to update to newer versions.

6. Use the following commands to commit and push your changes:

```
git add scdongcp-app/Dockerfile
git commit -m "Vuln fixed"
git push origin new-feature
```

In this section, we invoked a build, via a trigger, and when the build failed because a vulnerability was found, we fixed that vulnerability. Next, we'll review the changes and then merge the pull request, triggering the next build and deploying into production.

Merging your code and deploying your application to production

Perform the following steps to merge the pull request, resulting in a new build and invocation of the Cloud Deploy delivery pipeline to deploy the app to the targets, including a canary deployment in `prod`:

1. Acting as a member of the security team, go back to the pull request GitHub page and review the updated Dockerfile.

```
∨  ⟂ 5 ■■■■■ scdongcp-app/Dockerfile ⧉

 ↥..         @@ -12,10 +12,11 @@
  12    12     # See the License for the specific language governing permissions and
  13    13     # limitations under the License.
  14    14
  15         − FROM golang:1.12.9-alpine3.10 as builder
        15  + FROM golang:1.21-alpine3.18 as builder
  16    16     COPY app.go .
        17  + RUN go env -w GO111MODULE=auto
  17    18     RUN go build -o /app .
  18    19
  19         − FROM alpine:3.10
        20  + FROM alpine:3.18
  20    21     CMD ["./app"]
  21    22     COPY --from=builder /app .
```

Figure 10.8 – Reviewing changes in the Dockerfile

2. Because the update seems to have resolved the issue, retry the build by typing `/gcbrun` again in a new comment in the **Conversation** tab.

3. From the Google Cloud console main menu, select **Cloud Build | History**.

    You should see a new build running; wait for it to finish. The Kritis `vuln-scanner` task should succeed this time and should create, sign, and upload an attestation for the image. The last step should create the `scdongcp-rel` release and roll it out to the `qa` stage.

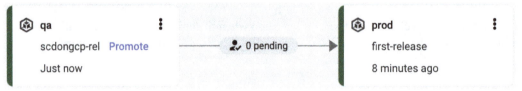

Figure 10.9 – Cloud Deploy delivery pipeline, completed

4. Run the following command to get the QA cluster gateway-assigned IP:

```
kubectl --context=gke_galloro-demos_us-central1-b_qa-cluster get
gtw
```

5. Use your browser to open that address.

    You should see the updated application deployed in the QA stage.

    In a real-world scenario, the QA team would now perform usability tests in this environment. Let's assume that these have been completed successfully and you, now acting as a member of the QA team, want to merge the changed code to the main branch.

6. Go to the GitHub pull request page and click **Merge pull request**, and then select **Confirm merge**.

    A new build now runs, linked to the scdbook-e2e-merge trigger. You can see the execution in Cloud Build history.

    When the build is completed, your release is promoted to the prod stage, but waiting for approval, as you can see in Cloud Deploy:

Figure 10.10 – Cloud Deploy delivery pipeline, requiring approval for promotion

7. Now acting as the application's product manager, who has to approve the promotion to production, click on **Review**.

    You'll see a rollout waiting for approval.

8. Click on **Review** again.

9. On the **Approve rollout to prod** page, click **APPROVE** to finally approve the promotion to prod.

    The rollout to prod starts, in the canary phase. After some time, the rollout stabilizes and is ready to be advanced to the stable phase.

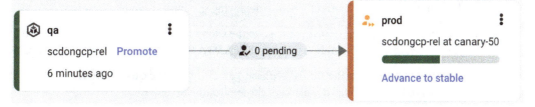

Figure 10.11 – Cloud Deploy delivery pipeline, in the canary phase

But first, let's try to observe how traffic is managed in this phase.

10. Use the following command to get the `prod-cluster` gateway-assigned IP address:

```
kubectl --context=gke_galloro-demos_us-central1-b_prod-cluster
get gtw
```

11. Now, use the following command to generate some requests to the production application endpoint (replacing `x.x.x.x` with your gateway IP address):

```
while true;do curl x.x.x.x;done
```

After some time, you should see responses from both your previous release and the new (canary) release. There could be some errors due to the time needed to propagate the configuration and the fact we kept the wait time relatively low. In a real-world scenario, we would have waited longer and hopefully gotten no errors.

```
scd-on-gcp app updated in target: prod!!
scd-on-gcp app running in target: prod!!
scd-on-gcp app running in target: prod!!
scd-on-gcp app running in target: prod!!
scd-on-gcp app running in target: prod!!
scd-on-gcp app updated in target: prod!!
scd-on-gcp app updated in target: prod!!
scd-on-gcp app updated in target: prod!!
scd-on-gcp app running in target: prod!!
scd-on-gcp app running in target: prod!!
scd-on-gcp app updated in target: prod!!
scd-on-gcp app running in target: prod!!
scd-on-gcp app running in target: prod!!
scd-on-gcp app updated in target: prod!!
scd-on-gcp app running in target: prod!!
scd-on-gcp app running in target: prod!!
scd-on-gcp app updated in target: prod!!
scd-on-gcp app updated in target: prod!!
scd-on-gcp app running in target: prod!!
scd-on-gcp app updated in target: prod!!
scd-on-gcp app updated in target: prod!!
scd-on-gcp app updated in target: prod!!
scd-on-gcp app updated in target: prod!!
scd-on-gcp app updated in target: prod!!
```

Figure 10.12 – Responses to curl command against the application

The app release team gets metrics and other observability data from the canary to make sure the application is performing correctly before deploying the application to all users.

12. Acting as a member of the app release team, go to the Cloud Deploy page in the Google Cloud console and click **Advance to stable**, and then click **ADVANCE** on the confirmation popup.

After the rollout progresses to the `stable` phase, you can see in the `curl` output that all the requests are served by the updated version of the application.

In this section, we merged a pull request, which triggered a build, and then deployed into the `prod` target, using a canary deployment strategy. After advancing that canary to the stable phase, we now have a fully deployed application.

Summary

You've now put together a complete end-to-end continuous delivery pipeline on Google Cloud, using a trigger to invoke a build after merging code changes and manually fixing a vulnerability.

You also saw how to approve a promotion in a Cloud Deploy delivery pipeline and manually advance a rollout from a canary phase to a stable phase, fully directing all traffic to the application in production.

This is the experience of secure software delivery on Google Cloud.

In the next chapter, we will show how you can integrate Cloud Build and Cloud Deploy with automated testing and third-party tools.

11

Integrating with Your Organization's Workflows

In this chapter, we'll show you how to integrate your software development pipeline with external systems that your organization might use to deliver **continuous integration/continuous delivery (CI/CD)**.

For this chapter, we'll use third-party source code management systems through a **Cloud Build trigger**. After a successful test execution, we'll automate Cloud Deploy promotion and integrate Cloud Deploy approval with third-party workflow management tools using **Cloud Pub/Sub**.

This chapter includes references to third-party tools from non-Google vendors. Examples of third-party tools include source control repositories such as GitHub, GitLab, and BitBucket, and project-management tools such as Jira, ServiceNow, Remedy, and others. You can use these applications along with your CI/CD pipelines to support capabilities such as approval workflows and repository interactions.

Google Cloud's first-party tools provide many of the functions you need for developing, building, testing, and deploying your software, as well as storing artifacts. However, software development doesn't occur in isolation. The third-party tools you'll integrate with your software delivery pipeline in this chapter will allow you to include external repositories, testing tools, and workflow management tools.

This chapter includes the following sections:

- Connecting a Cloud Build trigger to a third-party repository
- Integrating Cloud Deploy with automated testing
- Integrating Cloud Deploy approval with third-party workflow management tools

Technical requirements

To perform the tasks in this chapter, you'll need a Google Cloud project with billing or a free trial enabled. You can reuse the project you've been using throughout this book. In addition to these items, and what you've already enabled in previous chapters, you'll need the following:

- An account on `gitlab.com`
- A repository on `gitlab.com`
- The Google Pub/Sub API enabled

The source code for this chapter is available in this book's GitHub repository at `https://github.com/PacktPublishing/Secure-Continuous-Delivery-on-Google-Cloud`.

For our first look at third-party integration, we'll connect a Cloud Build trigger to a non-Google source code repository: GitLab.

Connecting a Cloud Build trigger to a third-party repository

Other chapters of this book use GitHub as a source code repository. Although GitHub is very popular, there are other top-tier repository providers out there, such as GitLab and BitBucket. This chapter's example uses GitLab to illustrate a different integration than we've used in previous chapters.

To use GitLab as a source repository, there are three main steps:

1. Create a host connection.
2. Create a link to the repository.
3. Create a Cloud Build trigger.

These three steps will be expanded upon in the following sections, starting with connecting to GitLab.

Creating a host connection to GitLab

Follow these steps to create a host connection to GitLab. This procedure assumes you have a GitLab account. These steps create two tokens. The first provides full API access, while the second provides API read-only access:

1. In GitLab, create an **api** personal access token.

    A. Under **User Settings**, click **Access Tokens**.

    B. Under **Personal Access Tokens**, click **Add new token**.

    C. Enter a value for **Token name**.

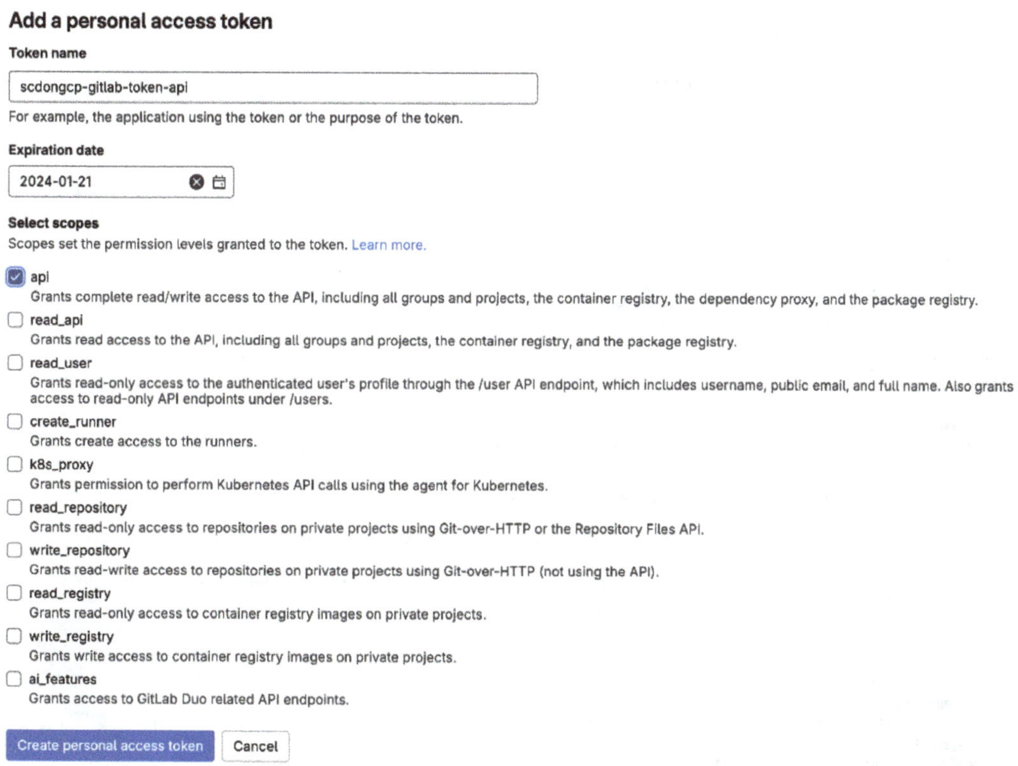

Add a personal access token

Token name

    scdongcp-gitlab-token-api

For example, the application using the token or the purpose of the token.

Expiration date

    2024-01-21   ❌ 🗓

Select scopes

Scopes set the permission levels granted to the token. Learn more.

- ☑ **api**
  Grants complete read/write access to the API, including all groups and projects, the container registry, the dependency proxy, and the package registry.
- ☐ read_api
  Grants read access to the API, including all groups and projects, the container registry, and the package registry.
- ☐ read_user
  Grants read-only access to the authenticated user's profile through the /user API endpoint, which includes username, public email, and full name. Also grants access to read-only API endpoints under /users.
- ☐ create_runner
  Grants create access to the runners.
- ☐ k8s_proxy
  Grants permission to perform Kubernetes API calls using the agent for Kubernetes.
- ☐ read_repository
  Grants read-only access to repositories on private projects using Git-over-HTTP or the Repository Files API.
- ☐ write_repository
  Grants read-write access to repositories on private projects using Git-over-HTTP (not using the API).
- ☐ read_registry
  Grants read-only access to container registry images on private projects.
- ☐ write_registry
  Grants write access to container registry images on private projects.
- ☐ ai_features
  Grants access to GitLab Duo related API endpoints.

[Create personal access token]   [Cancel]

Figure 11.1 – Adding a personal access token

    D. Provide an **Expiration date** value for this token.

    E. Select **api** as the scope.

    F. Click **Create personal access token**.

    G. Copy the new personal access token to a safe location:

Personal Access Tokens

You can generate a personal access token for each application you use that needs access to the GitLab API. You can also use personal access tokens to authenticate against Git over HTTP. They are the only accepted password when you have Two-Factor Authentication (2FA) enabled.

Figure 11.2 – Your GitLab personal access token

2.   In GitLab, create a **read_api** personal access token:

    A.   Provide a name for the token.

    B.   Keep the default for **Expiration date**.

    C.   Select **read_api** as the scope:

User Settings / **Access Tokens**

Personal Access Tokens

Add a personal access token

Token name

    scdongcp-gitlab-token-read

For example, the application using the token or the purpose of the token.

Expiration date

    2024-01-21   ✕ 📅

Select scopes

Scopes set the permission levels granted to the token. Learn more.

☐ api
    Grants complete read/write access to the API, including all groups and projects, the container registry, the dependency proxy, and the package registry.

☑ read_api
    Grants read access to the API, including all groups and projects, the container registry, and the package registry.

☐ read_user
    Grants read-only access to the authenticated user's profile through the /user API endpoint, which includes username, public email, and full name. Also grants access to read-only API endpoints under /users.

☐ create_runner
    Grants create access to the runners.

☐ k8s_proxy
    Grants permission to perform Kubernetes API calls using the agent for Kubernetes.

☐ read_repository
    Grants read-only access to repositories on private projects using Git-over-HTTP or the Repository Files API.

☐ write_repository
    Grants read-write access to repositories on private projects using Git-over-HTTP (not using the API).

☐ read_registry
    Grants read-only access to container registry images on private projects.

☐ write_registry
    Grants write access to container registry images on private projects.

☐ ai_features
    Grants access to GitLab Duo related API endpoints.

    Create personal access token   Cancel

Figure 11.3 – The scope is set to read_api

3. Select **Create personal access token**.

    Copy the new personal access token to a safe location.

4. From the Google Cloud console's main menu, select **Cloud Build | Repositories**:

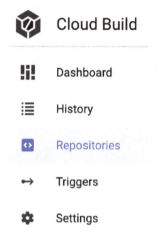

Figure 11.4 – The Cloud Build menu

5. Select the **2ND GEN** tab:

Figure 11.5 – The 2ND GEN tab

6. Click + **CREATE HOST CONNECTION**:

Figure 11.6 – Creating the host connection

7. Select **GitLab** as the provider:

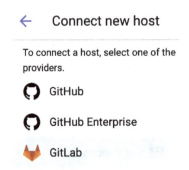

Figure 11.7 – Connecting a new host

8. Select **us-central1 (Iowa)** as the region.

9. Provide a name for the connection. For this example, we're calling it `gitlab-scdongcp-connection`.

10. Paste the appropriate personal access token(s) for full API access and API read-only access.

11. Select **CONNECT**:

Configure Connection

Region *
us-central1 (Iowa)

Name *
gitlab-scdongcp-connection

Host details

GitLab host

◉ GitLab.com

○ Self-managed GitLab Enterprise Edition

Personal access tokens

These personal access tokens will be stored in Secret Manager in this Cloud project. Cloud Build uses the latest version of the secret for authorizing access to GitLab when executing builds.

API access token *
•••••••••••••••••••••••••

Read API access token *
•••••••••••••••••••••••••

By clicking the connect button, you authorize Google Cloud Build to access your GitLab account on your behalf. You may revoke access by deleting active access tokens from your GitLab host at any time.

CONNECT

Figure 11.8 – The Configure Connection dialog

Now that you've created a host connection to a GitLab repository, you can create a link to it from Cloud Build. We'll do this in the next section.

Creating a link to the GitLab repository

Follow these steps to create a link from Cloud Build to your GitLab repository:

1. In the Google Cloud console, select **Cloud Build | Repositories | 2ND GEN**.

2. Select **Link Repository**.

    The **Link repositories** dialog is displayed:

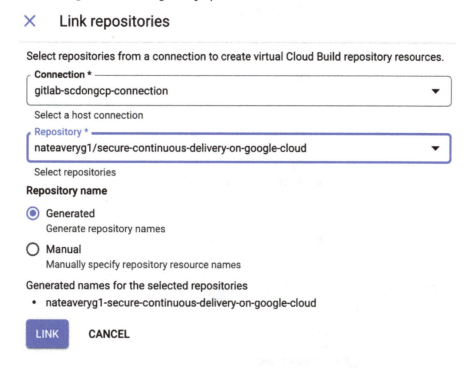

Figure 11.9 – The Link Repositories dialog

3. In the **Connection** dropdown, select the new GitLab connection you created.

4. In the **Repository** dropdown, select the name of the repository you wish to link.

5. For **Repository name**, leave it as is (**Generated**).

6. Click **Link** to finish creating the link.

Now that you've established a connection between Cloud Build and GitLab, you can create a Cloud Build trigger.

Creating a trigger

Follow these steps to create a Cloud Build trigger that starts a build upon manual invocation:

1. From the Google Cloud console's main navigational menu, select **Cloud Build | Triggers**:

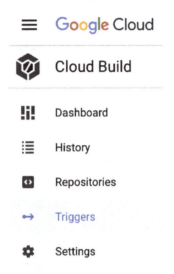

Figure 11.10 – The Cloud Build menu

2. Select **Create Trigger**.
3. Provide a name for the trigger. For this example, I've chosen `gitlab-scdongcp-trigger`.
4. For **Region**, select **us-central1**.
5. For **Event**, select **Manual invocation**.

Event

Repository event that invokes trigger

○ Push to a branch

○ Push new tag

○ Pull request
   Not available for Cloud Source Repositories

Or in response to

◉ Manual invocation

○ Pub/Sub message

○ Webhook event

Figure 11-11 – Choosing an event to invoke the trigger

6. For **Source**, select **2nd Gen**.

7. In the **Repository** drop-down list, select your GitLab repository.

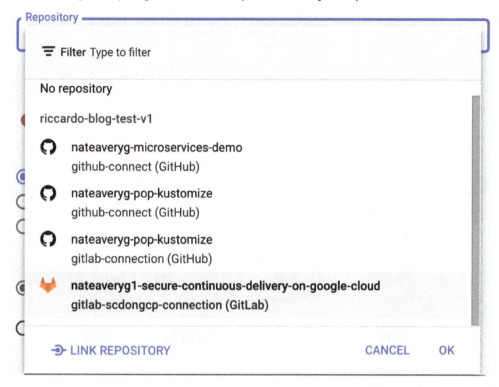

Figure 11.12 – Selecting your GitLab repository

8. Under **Revision**, select **Branch**, and enter main as the value for **Branch name**:

Revision

◉ Branch

○ Tag

Branch name *

main

To clone when trigger is invoked. Regular expressions not accepted

Figure 11.13 – Selecting the branch to clone when the trigger is invoked

9. Under **Configuration**, select **Cloud build configuration**.

10. Under **Location**, select **Repository**:

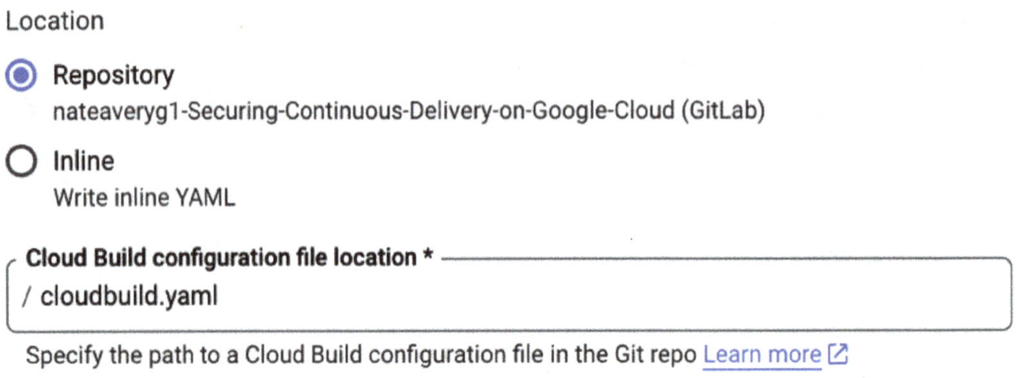

Location

◉ **Repository**
    nateaveryg1-Securing-Continuous-Delivery-on-Google-Cloud (GitLab)

○ **Inline**
    Write inline YAML

Cloud Build configuration file location *
/ cloudbuild.yaml

Specify the path to a Cloud Build configuration file in the Git repo Learn more ↗

Figure 11.14 – Pointing to the Cloud Build configuration file

11. Accept the defaults for the remaining options.

12. Click **Create** to finish creating this trigger.

You now have a Cloud Build trigger on a GitLab repository. For your next integration, you'll tie automated testing in with Cloud Deploy. In the next section, you'll learn how to use Pub/Sub to automate Cloud Deploy promotion after a successful test execution.

Integrating Cloud Deploy with automated testing

Automated testing is an important part of a source-to-prod workflow. You can use deployment verification after any completed deployment to confirm that your deployment works as expected.

In addition to deployment verification, you can use **deploy hooks** to reach out to local or remote resources. Sometimes, you need to connect to a third-party service after deployment has been completed. Post-deploy hooks make that possible. As with verification, post-deploy hooks run from a user-defined container. Unlike verification, deploy hooks are intended for actions that only have an effect when they're run for the first time, for a given release.

In the example in this section, the delivery pipeline uses a post-deploy hook to call an API from the Google **PageSpeed Insights** (**PSI**) tool. PSI assesses your website's user experience across mobile and desktop environments while also providing suggestions to improve performance. This tool is representative of a type of tool that's called in CI/CD pipelines to judge performance. Many organizations use services that fall into a category called application performance monitoring. Examples of application performance monitoring tools can be found at this Slashdot link: `https://slashdot.org/software/application-performance-monitoring-apm/for-google-cloud-platform/`.

The post-deploy action calls a Docker container running Ubuntu. From that container, we run a `curl` command against the PageSpeed API URL, using our website URL as a parameter.

First, we need to update the `skaffold.yaml` and `clouddeploy.yaml` files to specify a post-deploy hook to call the API. `skaffold.yaml` needs a new stanza to define the action and provide it with any additional information, such as any needed parameters. Here's that stanza:

```
- name: postdeploy-action
  containers:
  - name: predeploy-echo
    image: gcr.io/gcp-runtimes/ubuntu_18_0_4
    command: [«curl»]
    args: ["https://www.googleapis.com/pagespeedonline/v5/
runPagespeed?url=<Insert your website URL here>"]
```

Here's the full `skaffold.yaml` file, with that stanza now included:

```
apiVersion: skaffold/v4beta5
kind: Config
# added for post deploy 3p example
customActions:
- name: postdeploy-action
  containers:
  - name: predeploy-echo
    image: gcr.io/gcp-runtimes/ubuntu_18_0_4
    command: [«curl»]
    args: ["https://www.googleapis.com/pagespeedonline/v5/
runPagespeed?url=<Insert your website URL here>"]
build:
  artifacts:
    - image: scdongcp-app
      docker:
        dockerfile: Dockerfile
manifests:
  kustomize:
    paths:
      - kubernetes/dev
profiles:
  - name: qa
    manifests:
      kustomize:
        paths:
          - kubernetes/qa
  - name: prod
```

```
    manifests:
      kustomize:
        paths:
          - kubernetes/prod
```

The delivery pipeline configuration file, `clouddeploy.yaml`, also needs a stanza for the newly defined post-deploy action. In this example, the post-deploy action is called by the qa target. The name provided in the action must match the name used in `skaffold.yaml`:

```
    strategy:
      standard:
        postdeploy:
          actions: ["postdeploy-action"]
```

Here's the full `clouddeploy.yaml` file:

```
apiVersion: deploy.cloud.google.com/v1
kind: DeliveryPipeline
metadata:
  name: packt-deploy-pipeline
description: main application pipeline for Packt sample
serialPipeline:
  stages:
  - targetId: qa
    profiles: [qa]
    strategy:
      standard:
        postdeploy:
          actions: [«postdeploy-action"]
  - targetId: prod
    profiles: [prod]
---

apiVersion: deploy.cloud.google.com/v1
kind: Target
metadata:
  name: qa
description: qa cluster
gke:
  cluster: projects/${PROJECT_ID}/locations/us-central1/clusters/qa-
cluster
---
```

```
apiVersion: deploy.cloud.google.com/v1
kind: Target
metadata:
  name: prod
description: production cluster
requireApproval: true
gke:
  cluster: projects/riccardo-blog-test-v1/locations/us-central1/
clusters/prod-cluster1
```

Once the configuration files have been updated, you can create a new release. Perform the following steps to deploy the post-deploy image and view the results in the Google Cloud console:

1. Create a release against the pipeline you just defined:

    ```
    gcloud deploy releases create packt-deploy-release-004 \
      --project=${PROJECT_ID} \
      --region=us-central1 \
      --delivery-pipeline=packt-deploy-pipeline \
      --images=$Image_name_from_repo
    ```

    As the image deploys, you will notice an additional job called **Postdeploy**:

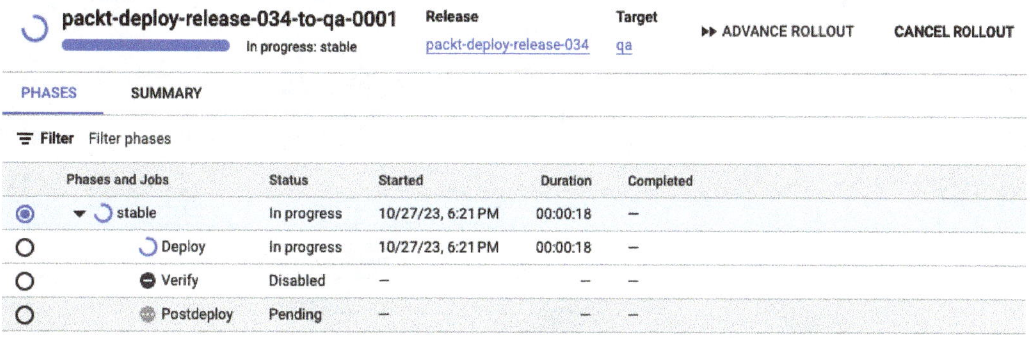

Phases and Jobs	Status	Started	Duration	Completed
▼ ○ stable	In progress	10/27/23, 6:21 PM	00:00:18	—
○ Deploy	In progress	10/27/23, 6:21 PM	00:00:18	—
● Verify	Disabled	—	—	—
◉ Postdeploy	Pending	—	—	—

Figure 11.15 – Cloud Deploy rollout details, showing the "Postdeploy" job

2. When the post-deploy job finishes, it will appear with a green checkmark next to it, as shown in the following screenshot:

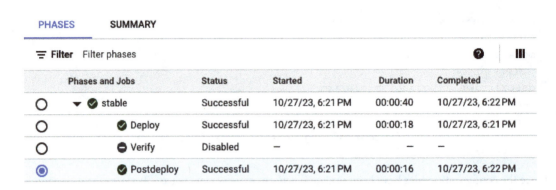

Figure 11.16 – Rollout details showing that the Postdeploy job was completed successfully

3.   Select the **Postdeploy** job.

The **Job runs** log will appear.

4.   Scroll through the log to see the results of the API call:

Figure 11.17 – Job run log entries, including results of the API call

Now that we've used the deployment verification and deploy-hooks features to integrate with external processes, let's learn how to use Pub/Sub to integrate with a workflow management tool.

Integrating Cloud Deploy approval with third-party workflow management tools

Cloud Deploy uses Pub/Sub to communicate with other applications, including applications for third-party providers.

Pub/Sub is often used in event-driven programming. With Pub/Sub, an application **publishes** information (messages) to a topic, and other applications **subscribe** to that topic to receive the messages. Those other applications can use these messages to invoke actions. In this section, we'll show you how to create a topic and subscribe to that topic via Pub/Sub.

Cloud Deploy publishes messages to the topics listed in the following table:

Topic	Description
`clouddeploy-resources`	Cloud Deploy sends a message when a resource is created, updated, or deleted – for example, when a delivery pipeline is created.
`Clouddeploy-operations`	Cloud Deploy sends a message upon render or deployment.
`Clouddeploy-approvals`	Cloud Deploy sends a message when an approval is needed for a promotion, or when a promotion is approved or rejected.
`Clouddeploy-advances`	Cloud Deploy sends a message when a rollout has advanced.

Table 11.1 – Cloud Deploy Pub/Sub topics

First, we'll use these messages to invoke an approval workflow using a third-party application.

Using a third-party workflow management system with Cloud Deploy approvals

Because each third-party (non-Google) application has its method of subscribing to Pub/Sub messages, this exercise only shows how to configure Google Cloud Pub/Sub to create a subscription that receives messages from Cloud Deploy.

Getting started

This exercise uses the Cloud Deploy delivery pipeline called `packt-deploy-pipeline` that you created in *Chapter 8*. The exercise also uses `scdongcp-app`, which was uploaded to `us-central1-docker.pkg.dev/${PROJECT_ID}/scdbook-repo/scdongcp-app`; you created this in

Chapter 2. Recreate these if you don't have them anymore. Similarly, the most recent release in the Cloud Deploy pipeline should have been completed successfully. If not, use the following command to deploy the container to the pipeline:

```
gcloud deploy releases create packt-deploy-release-004 \
        --project=${PROJECT_ID} \
        --region=us-central1 \
        --delivery-pipeline=packt-deploy-pipeline \
        --images=$IMAGE_NAME
```

For $IMAGE_NAME, use the name of the image in the artifact repository.

Your pipeline in the Cloud Deploy delivery pipeline visualization should look like this:

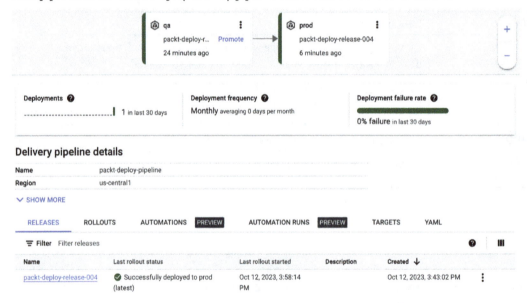

Figure 11.18 – Your delivery pipeline in the Cloud Deploy pipeline visualization

The first step in integrating with workflow management is to set one of the delivery pipeline stages to require approval.

Adding an approval to a pipeline stage

Approvals place a gate in front of the stage where it is called. With approval required, the release isn't promoted to this stage unless the approval is granted. Approval can be granted manually by logging onto the console, selecting the pipeline, and then marking the request as approved.

Approval can also be granted by a third-party application using Pub/Sub notifications. The application subscribes to the approval topic, `clouddeploy-approvals`. When the application receives the published request, that application uses its workflow to elicit approval or rejection. The application then returns that approval or rejection to Cloud Deploy programmatically using the Cloud Deploy CLI.

The approval requirement is configured in the target YAML. The `requireApproval : True` line was included in the `clouddeploy.yaml` file under the `prod` target, as shown in the following block:

```
apiVersion: deploy.cloud.google.com/v1
kind: DeliveryPipeline
metadata:
name: packt-deploy-pipeline
description: main application pipeline for Packt sample
serialPipeline:
stages:
- targetId: qa
profiles: [qa]
- targetId: prod
profiles: [prod]
---


apiVersion: deploy.cloud.google.com/v1
kind: Target
metadata:
name: qa
description: qa cluster
gke:
cluster: projects/riccardo-blog-test-v1/locations/us-central1/
clusters/qa-cluster
---


apiVersion: deploy.cloud.google.com/v1
kind: Target
metadata:
name: prod
description: production cluster
requireApproval: true
gke:
cluster: projects/riccardo-blog-test-v1/locations/us-central1/
clusters/prod-cluster1
```

Notice that the last target, `prod`, has `requireApproval` set to `true`. With this setting, the rollout to this target won't be executed until approval is provided.

Run the following command to apply the updated `clouddeploy.yaml` file:

```
gcloud deploy apply --file=clouddeploy.yaml --region=us-central1 \
--project=${PROJECT_ID}
```

The Cloud Deploy pipeline should now show a pending indicator between **qa** and **prod**:

Figure 11.19 – The delivery pipeline visualization showing "pending"

With your delivery pipeline now updated to require approval on the `prod` target, let's create a release.

Creating a new release

Follow these steps to create a release in Cloud Deploy:

1. From the main menu, select **Delivery pipelines**. Select your pipeline. Then, select **CREATE RELEASE**:

Figure 11.20 – The delivery pipeline visualization showing the CREATE RELEASE button

2. Under **Release details**, click **SELECT** to choose the container image you wish to use for this release:

← Create a release

Create and run a simple release by specifying a few resource names.

Creating a release in this way is useful for experimenting with Cloud Deploy. To create a fully functional release, see the Cloud Deploy documentation ⧉.

Release details

Choose a container *
registry.k8s.io/echoserver@sha256:5d99aa1120524c801bc8c1a7077e8f   SELECT

Release name *
release-bssq3bv

A release ⧉ represents the changes to deploy

Figure 11-21 – The Create a release dialog

3. Within the console, navigate to the scdongcp-app container.

The path for this is **ARTIFACT REGISTRY | us-central1-docker.pkg.dev/${PROJECT_ID}/ scdbook-repo | scdongcp-app**:

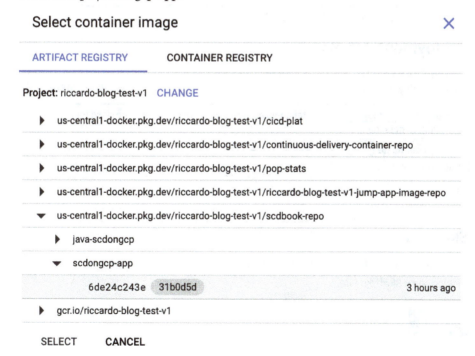

Figure 11.22 – Selecting the container image from under ARTIFACT REGISTRY

4.   Highlight the container image and click **SELECT**.

5.   Provide a brief description in the **Description** field:

 Create a release

Release details

Choose a container *

us-central1-docker.pkg.dev/riccardo-blog-test-v1/scdbook-repo/scdongcp   **SELECT**

Release name *

release-bssq3bv

A release ☑ represents the changes to deploy

Rollout name *

release-bssq3bv-to-qa

A rollout ☑ deploys a release to a target

Description

pub/sub demo

Optional description for the release and rollout

Deployment details

Deployment name (qa) *

packt-deploy-pipeline-qa   **VIEW MANIFEST**

The generated deployment ☑ will take this name. That configuration will be used for the following targets: qa.

Deployment name (prod) *

packt-deploy-pipeline-prod   **VIEW MANIFEST**

The generated deployment ☑ will take this name. That configuration will be used for the following targets: prod.

Skaffold

We generate the Skaffold configuration ☑ for you. You can edit this configuration by clicking View Skaffold File.

 CANCEL

Figure 11.23 – The Create a release dialog in Cloud Deploy

6. Click **CREATE**.

7. On the **ROLLOUT** page, monitor the progress of the release.

    While the rollout is in progress, there will be spinners next to the release name, the **stable** phase, and the **Deploy** job:

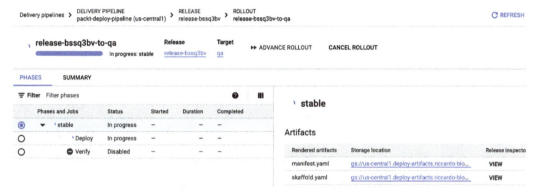

Figure 11.24 – The rollout details showing jobs in progress

8. Highlight the **Deploy** job, underneath **stable**, to see the logs in real time:

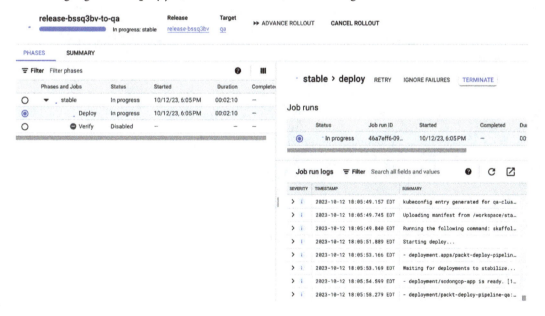

Figure 11.25 – The logs for the deploy job

9.   When the rollout is complete, all of the progress circles will become green:

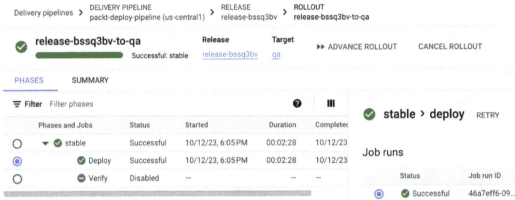

Figure 11.26 – The rollout details showing all applicable jobs in green

With that, you've created the release and seen it deployed successfully into the qa target.

Creating the Pub/Sub topic

Now, you'll need to create the Pub/Sub topic that will carry the approval notification. Follow these steps:

1.   Type Pub/Sub into the Google Cloud console's search bar and select **Pub/Sub** from the list of results:

Figure 11.27 – Searching for Pub/Sub in the Google Cloud console

2. Select **CREATE TOPIC** at the top of the **Pub/Sub** home page:

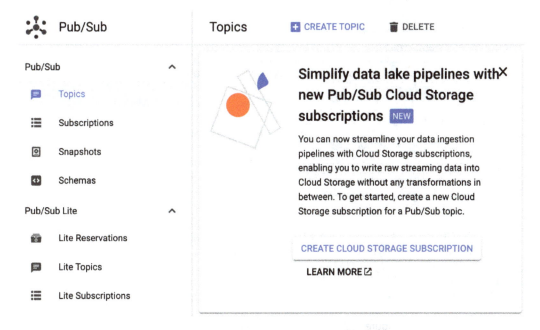

Figure 11.28 – The Pub/Sub home page

3. Type `clouddeploy-approvals` in the **Topic ID** field.

Important note

Users or service accounts require the `roles/clouddeploy.approver` role to approve rollouts to targets requiring approval. Recall that we set the `requireApproval : True` option in the pipeline configuration file earlier in this chapter.

---

4. Accept all the other defaults and click **Create** to create this Pub/Sub topic:

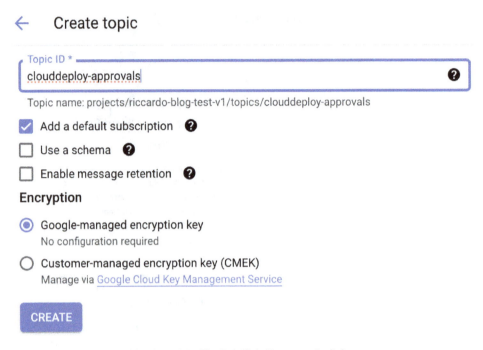

Figure 11.29 – The Pub/Sub Create topic dialog

5. Validate that the topic exists:

Figure 11.30 – Your new topic in the list of Pub/Sub topics

A subscription will be created alongside the topic.

With the Pub/Sub topic created, let's generate the Pub/Sub messages to publish to that topic by trying to promote to the target that requires approval.

Generating Pub/Sub messages

Cloud Deploy publishes messages on the topics listed earlier in this chapter. For approvals, when approval is required on a target, and when the release is pending approval on a promotion to that target, the approval-required message is published to the `clouddeploy-approvals` topic.

Follow these steps to generate that message:

1. Navigate to the pipeline.

2. Locate the QA stage in the delivery pipeline visualization and click **Promote**:

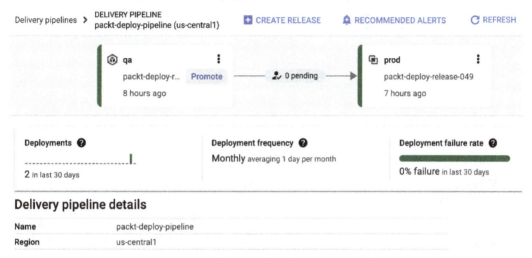

Figure 11.31 – The Promote button in the Cloud Deploy pipeline visualization

3. The destination target should now appear as **Approval required (0 pending)**:

Figure 11.32 – The Promote dialog with the destination target showing that approval is required

4. Enter a simple description in the **Rollout description** field:

Proposed deployment

Rollout name *
```
release-bssq3bv-to-prod-0001
```
Name for the rollout created by this promotion

Rollout description
```
pub/sub demo
```

Phase *
```
stable                                                              ▼
```
Phase to start the rollout at

Figure 11.33 – The Promote dialog showing the name, description, and rollout phase to start with

5. Click **PROMOTE** at the bottom of the screen.

6. Validate that the delivery pipeline visualization now says **1 pending**:

Figure 11.34 – The delivery pipeline visualization showing approval pending

With promotion to the `prod` target now pending approval, the message has been published to the `clouddeploy-approvals` topic. In the next section, we'll look at this message.

Viewing the message

In this section, we'll see if the subscription has received a message. Follow these steps from the Pub/Sub page in the Google Cloud console:

1. Type Pub/Sub into the Google Cloud console's search bar and select **Pub/Sub** from the list of results:

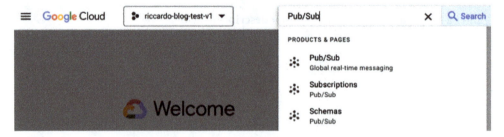

Figure 11.35 – Searching for Pub/Sub in the Google Cloud console

2. Select **Subscriptions** from the navigational panel:

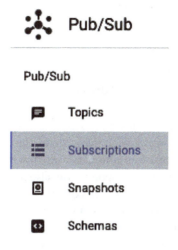

Figure 11.36 – The Pub/Sub menu

3. Select **clouddeploy-approvals-sub** under **Subscription ID**:

Figure 11.37 – Selecting clouddeploy-approvals-sub

4. Select the **MESSAGES** tab, then select **PULL**:

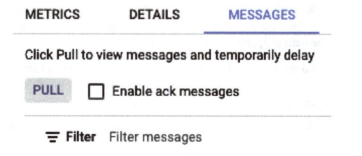

Figure 11-38 – Selecting PULL to pull Pub/Sub messages

5.   All the messages that are sent from Cloud Deploy should be present. Look for a message with **Required** in the **attribute.Action** column:

Publish time	Attribute keys	Message body	Ordering key	attribute.Action	Ack ↑	
Oct 12, 2023, 5:56:33 PM	Action		—	Required	Deadline exceeded	∨

Figure 11.39 – Pub/Sub messages from Cloud Deploy showing the "approval required" message

Your workflow management system will subscribe to messages of that type. Upon receiving such a message, it will initiate the approval workflow in that system. The output of that workflow will be a `gcloud deploy rollouts approve` command, which is the approval the rollout is waiting for to promote to the next target. Of course, the approval can also be rejected in the approval workflow, in which case the command would be `gcloud deploy rollouts reject`. The Cloud Deploy API automatically creates the Cloud Deploy Service Agent service account that's called upon its first use, enabling seamless service notifications through Pub/Sub. More information about the Cloud Deploy Service Agent service account and how to troubleshoot issues related to it can be found in the official Google documentation See *Receive Cloud Deploy service notifications* (`https://cloud.google.com/deploy/docs/subscribe-deploy-notifications#receive_service_notifications`) if needed.

Summary

In this chapter, we examined how to expand the capabilities of a CI/CD pipeline more in line with real-world needs. You learned how to create a Cloud Build trigger on an external repository, integrate a Cloud Deploy delivery pipeline with automated testing, and use Pub/Sub to initiate an approval workflow with a third-party workflow management tool.

You might not need these more advanced topics immediately, but once your DevOps pipeline is running, you could find these helpful when it comes to improving the overall experience.

Connecting the pipeline to third-party tools extends the range of what's possible. Many different third-party capabilities, such as Agile project management, metrics, source code repositories, and alerting tools, exist outside of the native capabilities of Google's first-party software.

This chapter also touched on some of the advanced first-party options in Cloud Deploy, such as automation. These advanced first-party options, when combined with third-party tools, can save time and increase productivity.

In the next (and final) chapter, we'll look at some best practices for continuous delivery and look ahead to future trends.

12

Diving into Best Practices and Trends in Continuous Delivery

In this chapter, we describe some best practices for continuous delivery on Google Cloud that we didn't cover exhaustively in previous chapters, and we'll also peek at some future improvements and development directions for Google Cloud software-delivery capabilities.

You can accomplish continuous delivery on Google Cloud using the tools and techniques mentioned in this book. We provided an overview of the pipeline in *Chapter 10*. After your pipeline is running, there are a few recommended practices for **observability**.

In addition to observability, **GitOps** has become a de facto standard methodology for deploying applications and configurations. Using these techniques, you should be up to the task.

The future of continuous delivery looks exciting, with new technologies being integrated into delivery pipelines. **Artificial intelligence** (**AI**) is poised to be integrated into almost every step in one form or another. From helping operators find new efficiencies to creating the YAML files used for configuring pipelines, AI can be hugely beneficial.

This chapter includes the following sections:

- Best practices for deploying secure delivery pipelines
- Anticipating the future

After reading this chapter, and having read the previous chapters in this book, you should feel more confident in being able to implement or improve continuous delivery in your organization.

First, let's examine some best practices for deploying software delivery pipelines.

Best practices for deploying secure delivery pipelines

This book includes many examples of how to accomplish goals related to setting up and operating a secure delivery pipeline. This section shares the following further tips:

- Using a host project for CI/CD infrastructure

- Using **VPC Service Controls** (**VPC-SC**)

- Using private pools for Cloud Build and Cloud Deploy

- Using Cloud Logging and Cloud Monitoring

- Enabling recommended alerts

- Using GitOps

Let's start by looking at using a dedicated project for your CI/CD resources.

Using a host project for CI/CD infrastructure

Google Cloud uses projects as a way to isolate workloads, credentials, and resources. Users, APIs, and billing are enabled and managed separately in each project. For one project to interact with another, explicit permissions must be granted on one or both of those projects. Using a host project for CI/CD infrastructure can save both time and money as you can consolidate all CI/CD functions in one place.

Many architectures isolate development environments into distinct projects as a way to limit the *blast radius* should something go wrong and bring down multiple services in a project. Without using a centralized project for CI/CD, each project would need a set of CI/CD tools to be configured, secured, and, in some cases, licensed. Billing alerts and API quotas can be managed at the project level, thereby increasing observability. There is less chance of a surprise in billing.

The following diagram illustrates how this works. The Google Cloud products that you use to build, store, secure, and deploy your applications are all enabled in one project. This project has the permissions it needs to deploy to runtimes in the three separate projects:

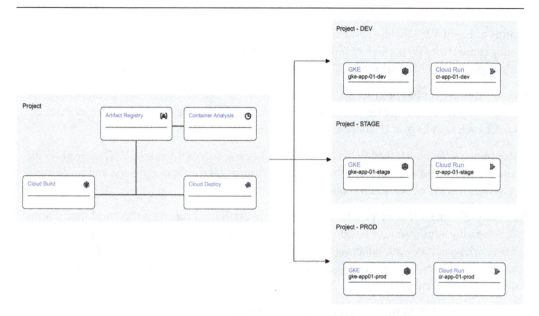

Figure 12.1 – Separate projects for CI/CD tooling and runtimes

Having a host project that provides CI/CD to multiple projects also makes it easier on operations staff since it simplifies the environment they need to work in. Less time spent tracking down errors in CI/CD systems in each project means more time to bring value to the organization by enhancing the availability and reliability of other systems.

Using a host project also simplifies how you implement the principle of the least privilege for access. Access controls can be configured such that developers have access to the dev and stage projects, but not to the prod project. Access to prod resources can be limited to service accounts, to limit or eliminate unapproved configuration changes for the most sensitive projects.

To dive deeper into host and service projects, we will discuss the networking side – that is, shared **virtual private cloud** (**VPC**).

A shared VPC empowers an organization to establish a common VPC network that multiple projects can tap into. This networking model offers a secure and cost-effective solution for inter-project communication via internal IP addresses.

Creating a shared VPC involves establishing the host project, configuring the VPC networks, and enabling connectivity for the service projects. The process begins by designating a project as the host. This host project will hold the shared VPC networks and serve as the central point of control.

Once the host project has been set up, VPC networks are created within it. These networks provide the underlying infrastructure for inter-project communication. Subnets are carved out within these networks, each with its own IP address range and configuration settings.

Service projects can be attached to the host project to gain access to the shared VPC networks. This attachment process involves enabling the shared VPC feature for the service projects and configuring the appropriate VPC network and subnets.

The beauty of using a shared VPC lies in its ability to establish a centralized control mechanism while delegating administrative responsibilities. Organization administrators retain overall control over network resources while adhering to the principle of least privilege. They can define consistent access control policies, ensuring that each service project has the necessary permissions aligned with its specific requirements.

Moreover, a shared VPC streamlines financial management since costs associated with the VPC networks are consolidated under the host project. This centralized billing model simplifies expense tracking and allocation within the organization.

Here are some of the key benefits of using a shared VPC:

- **Simplified network management**: A shared VPC eliminates the need to manage multiple VPC networks for different projects. Instead, all projects that are attached to the shared VPC network can use the same network resources and policies. This simplifies network management and reduces the risk of inconsistencies.

- **Secure communication across project boundaries**: A shared VPC allows resources in different projects to communicate securely and efficiently across project boundaries using internal IP addresses. This eliminates the need to use public IP addresses or NAT gateways, which can improve security and performance.

- **Consistent network policies**: A shared VPC ensures that all projects that are attached to the shared VPC network are subject to the same network policies. This helps ensure that all projects are compliant with security and regulatory requirements.

> **Important note**
> An in-depth discussion of networking is beyond the scope of this book. In this chapter, we'll talk about connecting to the host project and leveraging the network resources.

While a shared VPC provides cost consolidation and simplified billing, **VPC-SC**, a different service, offers enhanced security for sensitive data. It's described in the next section.

Consider using VPC-SC

In Google Cloud, VPC-SC offers a robust solution for safeguarding sensitive data by establishing a secure perimeter. This feature is exclusively available for builds within private pools, ensuring enhanced protection for your cloud-hosted applications. To effectively manage builds with VPC-SC protection, you can either use a machine within the perimeter or grant developers controlled access to the secure perimeter.

VPC-SC plays a pivotal role in minimizing the risk of unauthorized data transfer from Google-managed services. It empowers organizations to configure security perimeters around service resources and exercise granular control over data movement across the perimeter boundary. This approach enables organizations to isolate critical resources and services, reducing the attack surface and limiting potential security risks.

When using Artifact Registry and Google Kubernetes Engine private clusters within a service perimeter, you gain the ability to securely access container images. However, it's important to note that cached Docker Hub images hosted on **mirror.gcr.io** are not automatically included within the perimeter. To access these images, an egress rule must be explicitly added.

Additionally, to ensure comprehensive Artifact Analysis support, it may be necessary to include other services, such as Artifact Registry and Binary Authorization, within the service perimeter. By incorporating these services, you can establish a holistic approach to securing your cloud-based artifacts and maintaining compliance with industry standards and regulations.

Overall, VPC-SC offers a powerful and flexible solution for organizations seeking to protect sensitive data and enforce fine-grained access controls. By implementing VPC-SC, organizations can significantly reduce the risk of data breaches and unauthorized data exfiltration, enhancing their overall security posture.

Now that we've discussed VPCs, we'll go over private pools, which were first introduced in *Chapter 5*.

Using private pools with Cloud Build and Cloud Deploy

Cloud Build can use two types of pools – default pools and private pools. We mentioned this in *Chapter 5*, in the *Customizing your build workers* section. Default pools are publicly accessible and offer a secure, hosted environment with limited customization options. Private pools are dedicated, customer-specific resources that provide greater customization, including private network access. It's worth noting that Cloud Deploy, which uses Cloud Build to perform most of its operations, can be configured to use a private worker pool.

Another best practice for secure software delivery is to configure Cloud Logging and Cloud Monitoring, as explained in the next section.

Using Cloud Logging and Cloud Monitoring

Cloud Logging and Cloud Monitoring provide a comprehensive suite of tools for collecting, storing, analyzing, and acting upon logs and metrics from your Google Cloud resources and applications. **Cloud Logging** is a real-time log management solution that's offered by Google Cloud that has storage, search, analysis, and monitoring capabilities. In addition to automatically collecting logs from Google Cloud resources, you can also collect logs from your applications, on-premises resources, and resources from other cloud providers. To ensure compliance with regulatory and security requirements, you can specify where your log data is stored. Furthermore, you can set up alerts so that you're informed when specific events are reported in your logs.

The following are some of the features of Cloud Logging and Cloud Monitoring:

- **Viewing and analyzing log data**: You can view and analyze log data using the Google Cloud console via the Logs Explorer or Log Analytics page. Both interfaces allow you to query and view logs, but they use different query languages and have varying capabilities.

- **Logs Explorer**: The Logs Explorer is designed to troubleshoot and analyze service and application performance. It enables you to view individual log entries and find related entries. For example, if a log entry belongs to an error group, it's annotated with options for accessing more information about the error.

- **Programmatic access**: You can use the Cloud Logging API or the Google Cloud CLI to programmatically query log data and export it from your Google Cloud project.

- **Notifications**: Cloud Logging can be configured to notify you when specific events occur in your logs, such as a particular pattern appearing in a log entry, or a trend being detected in the log data. You can view the preconfigured Cloud Logging dashboard if you're interested in seeing the error rates of your Google Cloud services.

- **Log storage**: By default, all logs received by a Google Cloud project are automatically stored in a Cloud Logging bucket. You can customize various aspects of your log storage, such as which logs are stored, which logs are discarded, and where logs are stored.

- **Log routing destinations**: Log entries can be routed or forwarded to the following destinations, either within the same project or a different project:

  - **Cloud Logging log buckets**: Provides storage in Cloud Logging

  - **Google Cloud projects**: Routes log entries to a different Google Cloud project

  - **Pub/Sub topics**: Supports third-party integrations

  - **BigQuery datasets**: Allows log entries to be stored in BigQuery datasets

  - **Cloud Storage buckets**: Allows log data to be stored in Cloud Storage

Those are some of the features of Cloud Logging and Monitoring. Now, let's look at how logging works:

- **Log categories and Identity and Access Management (IAM) roles: Log categories** help describe the logging information available to you, whereas IAM roles control access to logs. You can grant predefined roles or create custom roles.

- **Log entry storage and deletion**: Log entries are stored in log buckets for a specified duration and then deleted.

Now, we will discuss the different types of logs.

Types of logs

Various types of logs are generated in Google Cloud that provide valuable insights into the behavior and performance of your applications and infrastructure. These logs include the following:

- **Platform logs**: Logs written by Google Cloud services

- **Component logs**: Logs generated by Google-provided software components running on your systems

- **Security logs**: Logs that provide audit information and help you answer *who did what, where, and when*

- **User-written logs**: Logs written by your custom applications and services

- **Multi-cloud and hybrid cloud logs**: These terms refer to logs from other cloud providers, such as Microsoft Azure, and logs from on-premises infrastructure

While logs are essential for troubleshooting and debugging, they only provide a partial picture of your system's behavior. To gain a deeper understanding of your system's performance and availability, it's crucial to use Cloud Monitoring.

Cloud Monitoring

Cloud Monitoring is a fully managed service that collects, stores, and analyzes metrics from your Google Cloud projects. It provides a comprehensive view of your system's health and performance, enabling you to identify and troubleshoot issues, optimize resource utilization, and ensure the reliability of your applications.

Cloud Monitoring seamlessly integrates with Cloud Logging, allowing you to correlate logs and metrics to gain a more complete understanding of your system's behavior. By combining the rich insights from logs with the quantitative data from metrics, you can quickly identify the root causes of issues and resolve them effectively.

Cloud Monitoring collects metrics, events, and metadata from Google Cloud, **Amazon Web Services** (**AWS**), synthetic monitors, and application instrumentation. Cloud Monitoring automatically collects and stores performance information for most Google Cloud services. You can collect Prometheus metrics by using Google Cloud Managed Service for Prometheus. Prometheus is a popular open source monitoring system that's used to monitor Kubernetes clusters. It collects metrics from Kubernetes components, including the kubelet, kube-proxy, and kube-scheduler, as well as from custom applications running on the cluster. If you install the Ops Agent on your Compute Engine **virtual machines** (**VMs**), then you can collect metrics and logs from your applications and third-party applications. The alerting, testing, and visualization services provided by Cloud Monitoring help you answer important questions such as the following:

- What is the load on my service?
- Is my website responding correctly?
- Is my service performing well?

Cloud Monitoring provides both Google Cloud console and API support for most of its services. Some services also support the Google Cloud CLI or Terraform. Google Cloud's operations suite uses dashboards, charts, and alerts to consume data and generate insights. The scoping project also includes a metrics scope, which defines the projects and accounts whose metrics are visible to the scoping project. Time series data from other Google Cloud projects and AWS accounts can be included in the metrics scope.

Monitoring lets you view and manage metrics in the following ways:

- For a single project
- For multiple projects within a single organization
- For multiple projects across multiple organizations
- For multiple Google Cloud projects and AWS accounts

Google Cloud's operations suite visualizes data and generates insights. The metrics scope defines which metrics a project can see. By default, a project can only see its own metrics. You can add other projects to the scope to expand the set of metrics.

To manage IAM roles for principals, you can use the **Identity and Access Management** page in the Google Cloud console. However, Cloud Monitoring provides a simplified interface that lets you manage your monitoring-specific roles, project-level roles, and the common roles for Cloud Logging and **Cloud Trace**.

Cloud Monitoring provides valuable alerting, testing, and visualization features that assist in answering critical questions, such as service load, website responsiveness, and overall service performance. The service offers both Google Cloud console and API support for most of its services, with some services providing additional compatibility with Google Cloud CLI or Terraform.

The collected data is ingested into Google Cloud's operations suite, which generates insightful dashboards, charts, and alerts. The scoping project, which serves as a host, also includes a metrics scope. This metrics scope determines the set of projects and accounts whose metrics the scoping project can access. This configuration enables the inclusion of time series data from other Google Cloud projects and AWS accounts.

Cloud Monitoring facilitates viewing and managing metrics in various ways, including single projects, multiple projects within an organization, projects across multiple organizations, and a combination of Google Cloud projects and AWS accounts. By default, a Google Cloud project has access to its own metrics, but the metrics scope allows for the expansion of accessible metrics through the incorporation of other Google Cloud projects.

The Cloud Monitoring pages in the Google Cloud console provide exclusive access to the time series stored within the scoping project. This project contains a repository for alerts, synthetic monitors, dashboards, and monitoring groups, allowing for centralized management and configuration. Google recommends using a new or resource-free Google Cloud project as the scoping project if you wish to view metrics for multiple Google Cloud projects or AWS accounts.

Cloud Monitoring is available globally, ensuring its services are accessible regardless of location. IAM roles can be managed through the Identity and Access Management page in the Google Cloud console. However, Cloud Monitoring provides a simplified interface specifically tailored to managing Monitoring-specific roles, project-level roles, and commonly used roles for Cloud Logging and Cloud Trace.

Cloud Monitoring automatically sets up dashboards when you create resources within a Google Cloud project. These dashboards provide metrics and essential information about individual Google Cloud services. Service-specific dashboards cannot be modified or copied, but their charts can be incorporated into custom dashboards.

Similarly, when configuring a supported third-party application that sends metric data to your Google Cloud project, Cloud Monitoring automatically installs dashboards. These dashboards offer metrics and general information specific to the third-party application. A list of supported applications can be found on the **Integrations** page. Moreover, you can import Grafana dashboards into Cloud Monitoring.

Custom dashboards, regardless of whether they're created or installed by users, offer a tailored viewing experience. They allow you to display relevant information meaningfully. Custom dashboards automatically update when new data becomes available, and they also let you analyze data from different sources within a single context, unlike dashboards for Google Cloud services and supported integrations.

As always, permissions play a part in how resources are accessed. To access dashboards in the Google Cloud console, you must have the Monitoring Viewer IAM role.

In conclusion, Cloud Monitoring offers a comprehensive platform for monitoring and visualizing metrics, logs, and traces. Its centralized interface, global availability, and integration with Google Cloud services and third-party applications make it an invaluable tool for streamlining monitoring tasks and gaining insights into system performance. With customizable dashboards, users can create personalized views of their data, enabling efficient analysis and problem-solving. By leveraging Cloud Monitoring, organizations can optimize their infrastructure, improve application performance, and ensure a reliable and scalable cloud environment.

While Cloud Monitoring provides a robust platform for monitoring, it is equally crucial to take proactive measures to respond to critical situations. Alerting mechanisms enable organizations to be notified promptly when predefined conditions are met, empowering them to address issues before they escalate.

Enabling recommended alerts

Tracking statuses across tens or even hundreds of pipelines can be challenging. Use the tooling provided to help stay on top of current deployments by leveraging the recommended alerts in Google Cloud services.

Google Cloud offers a variety of pre-configured alerts tailored for common scenarios across different services. With alerts, a message is sent, via a predefined channel, whenever the specified event takes place. For example, stakeholders might want to receive an email alert whenever a manual approval is required to advance a production release.

Cloud Deploy makes it simple to set alerts using the Google Cloud Console. The recommended alerts use Google Cloud Monitoring's notification system. This saves time for those already familiar with configuring Cloud Monitoring channels. For those unfamiliar with Cloud Monitoring, learning about it through Cloud Deploy alerts imparts a skill that can be transferred to other services in Google Cloud.

Neither Artifact Registry nor Cloud Build provides predefined alerts, but they do publish status changes through Pub/Sub topics, thereby emulating predefined alerts. Pub/Sub is Google's fully managed real-time messaging service. Subscribing to Pub/Sub topics allows you to monitor and use them as triggers for Application Integration, Google's solution for connecting SaaS applications and automating business processes. Application Integration provides several options for handling these messages, including triggering a workflow or sending an email.

Here are some examples of how you can use this integration:

- **Monitor Artifact Registry for new images**: You can create a Pub/Sub topic for each repository in Artifact Registry and subscribe Application Integration to that topic. When a new image is published to the repository, Application Integration triggers a workflow that can perform various tasks, such as deploying the image to a Kubernetes cluster or sending a notification to a Slack channel.

- **Monitor Cloud Build for build failures**: You can create a Pub/Sub topic for each Cloud Build trigger and subscribe Application Integration to that topic. When a build fails, Application Integration triggers a workflow that can perform various tasks, such as sending a notification to a developer or creating a bug report.

Using Application Integration and Pub/Sub to monitor Artifact Registry and Cloud Build can help you automate your workflows and improve your development process.

However, be careful when it comes to enabling alerts. Your initial impulse might be to enable all of them for every system surfacing every alert as it happens. When considering the alerts to enable, be aware that overdoing it can lead to alert fatigue. Alert fatigue occurs when IT professionals are overwhelmed by the sheer volume of alerts that are generated by monitoring systems, leading to a numbing effect and making it difficult to distinguish between critical and non-critical alerts. As a result, incidents may be missed or delayed, leading to potential system outages or security breaches.

Alert fatigue can have significant negative consequences for organizations:

- **Delayed incident response**: When IT professionals are constantly inundated with alerts, it becomes challenging to prioritize and respond to incidents promptly. This delay in response can result in prolonged system downtime and increased business impact.

- **Missed critical alerts**: The sheer volume of alerts can make it difficult to identify the truly critical ones. This can lead to missed opportunities to address potential security breaches or system failures promptly.

- **Reduced morale and productivity**: Dealing with constant alerts can be mentally and emotionally draining for IT professionals. This can lead to reduced morale, decreased productivity, and increased turnover.

Another avenue to address alert fatigue effectively is to adopt the recommendations provided by the **DevOps Research and Assessment** (**DORA**) team at Google. The DORA report highlights several strategies that can help reduce alert noise, prioritize alerts, and improve the overall incident management process.

DORA's recommendations to avoid alert fatigue

The DORA team at Google has conducted extensive research on alert fatigue and has provided several recommendations to avoid it:

- **Reduce alert noise**: Implement effective alert filtering and suppression techniques to minimize the number of non-critical alerts.

- **Prioritize alerts**: Use intelligent alerting systems that can prioritize alerts based on severity and context, helping IT professionals focus on the most important issues.

- **Automate incident response**: Leverage automation to handle routine tasks and escalate only critical incidents to human operators.

- **Foster a culture of learning**: Encourage a culture where IT professionals are continuously learning and improving their understanding of the systems they monitor. Those learnings from postmortems are then used to update the monitoring system.

By adopting these recommendations, organizations can significantly reduce alert fatigue and improve their overall incident response capabilities.

This discussion showed how to enable alerting as a method to monitor application delivery.

The last practice that we recommend in this chapter is to be flexible with your approach to GitOps, whether that be *push* or *pull*.

Using GitOps

GitOps comes in two flavors. There's the push-based approach, which was described in *Chapter 10*. There's also a pull-based model. The push model updates a target when a change occurs to a file in the source code repository. With the pull-based approach, the target checks the source code repository at a set interval, updating the target with any deltas between the target and the declarative configuration in the repository.

Cloud Deploy can be used alongside pull-based GitOps tools via the custom target feature. This capability is being described for those who may be curious about the capability.

Cloud Deploy has a feature called custom target types. It can be defined by customers so that they can work with targets that are not natively supported by the platform. The Google Cloud user community is encouraged to create and share targets in a GitHub repository. There are target types available for GitOps, Helm, Infrastructure Manager, Terraform, and Vertex AI.

Let's look closer at the GitOps custom target example provided in Google's GitHub repository. It can be found at `https://github.com/GoogleCloudPlatform/cloud-deploy-samples.git`.

The following is a description of the code provided in the `README` file in Google's GitHub repository:

"The GitOps deployer allows you to use Cloud Deploy to manage your delivery pipeline while using a Kubernetes git synchronization tool (such as Argo) to … apply changes to the cluster. This enables normal operation and use of Cloud Deploy features (such as progressions, verification, automation, etc…) with the difference being the deploy job writes the manifest to a git repository instead of applying to the cluster directly. From there, it is expected that a git syncing tool is running on the clusters which will synchronize its state."

The key part is that the Cloud Deploy custom target works in conjunction with a pull-based GitOps application. This pull-based application deploys the configuration changes.

We recommend using declarative configuration and **Infrastructure as Code** (IaC). There are advantages and disadvantages to each. A push-based model with Cloud Deploy provides less to manage and works well in situations with fairly static target clusters. Cloud Deploy's push-based model also works with target types other than Kubernetes, such as Cloud Run. The pull-based model usually requires additional management tools on one or more clusters, along with agents. The advantage, however, is that the pull-based model works very well in environments with a tremendous number of Kubernetes clusters that need to be configured centrally. This is especially true of environments that have inconsistent bandwidth, and the agent continuously polls for changes.

This chapter provided an overview of Google Cloud DevOps best practices for monitoring and logging, alerting, and GitOps. By following these best practices, organizations can improve the reliability and efficiency of their cloud-based applications. Monitoring and logging provide valuable insights into the health and performance of applications while alerting mechanisms ensure that critical issues are addressed promptly. GitOps enables teams to manage their infrastructure and applications using version control, providing a consistent and reliable deployment process. By adopting these best practices, organizations can improve the quality and reliability of their cloud-based applications while reducing the time and effort required to manage them.

Anticipating the future

The future of secure software delivery will focus on AI, simplicity, and interoperability. These changes will be encapsulated within the overall evolution of DevOps.

DevOps is a broad wrapper around people, processes, and technology. CI/CD is an integral part of the technology stack, and continuous delivery is a central process. The 2023 DORA report lists several **key outcomes** that organizations seek. These outcomes cover a wide variety of measures for organizations to evaluate, including elements from processes, capabilities, and culture.

Among those processes and capabilities are assessments related to AI use. The prominent inclusion of AI makes it clear that the DORA team sees AI as a way to improve overall performance and cultural aspects of an organization, such as burnout and job satisfaction. The idea is that for DevOps to evolve, the components within it must also grow and change to increase velocity. There is evidence, as presented in the DORA *Accelerate State of DevOps Report 2022*, that *"implementing software supply chain security controls, like those recommended by the SLSA framework, has a positive effect on software delivery performance when continuous integration is firmly established."*

Knowing that software-delivery performance is improved by integrating security controls, it follows that more security measures will be added and automated. We've already seen the beginning of that, with DevOps evolving into DevSecOps in most instances. This evolution underscores the importance of security being a natural part of the process. The term implies that security has equal status with development and operations.

AI will be a major technological driver of this transformation, helping DevSecOps become a ubiquitous and transparent part of the **software development life cycle (SDLC)**.

It must be said that these future trends make some assumptions. The most obvious assumption is that modern application workloads will continue to be created as **containers**, and that deployment often means orchestrating those containers and validating that the sources and tools used during the orchestration process didn't break the security contract.

Interestingly, the role of open source software in the enterprise continues to be defined differently among organizations due to several factors. Many of the major open source vendors have changed their software distribution models, so software developers need to be more aware than ever before about licensing upstream code. Similarly, code that's recommended by AI should be reviewed for source attribution.

It won't be the tools that slow down software deployment; it will be people. If developers continue to write software with intricate interdependencies so that they must be deployed as a batch to all be tested and verified together, then accelerating software delivery will be a challenge in their organizations. The 2023 DORA report shows us that smaller, more frequent updates are the way to improve DevOps overall.

The first major shift we'll look at is AI.

AI infusion

AI will evolve in a few different ways. Initial generative AI efforts will help automate the creation of YAML files, which will unlock a great deal of productivity. From there, we can imagine AI being used to bring disparate systems together to create a more consistent user experience. This will continue until we reach the point where AI creates the entire DevSecOps pipeline on the user's behalf.

Most pipelines today use YAML and/or JSON files to specify a declarative state for pipeline infrastructure, as well as to define application deployment. These YAML and JSON files can be very particular about syntax and structure and can fail if they're not aligned properly or if proper symbols aren't used when defining values. AI could help tremendously by providing the initial YAML structure and autocompletion of lines. This would help IT Ops personnel and save them time.

AI has already shown its value in DevOps, as reported in the 2023 DORA report: *"Evidence suggests that AI slightly improves individual well-being measures (such as burnout and job satisfaction)."* These encouraging findings likely predict an increased role for AI. The 2023 DORA report also includes a few AI-specific elements to track. Something that's explicitly AI-related is **AI contribution**, which tracks *"The importance of the role of artificial intelligence in contributing to a variety of technical tasks."* Less obvious but often included in AI chatbots in developer IDEs is **code review speed**, which tracks *"a single item assessing the time it takes from the pull request to the code change review."* This measure is almost always listed as an advantage when using AI pair programmers.

The following figure shows how an AI chatbot can help a user quickly learn a software delivery tool:

Figure 12.2 – The Duet AI chatbot giving instructions for creating a delivery pipeline

Summary

In this chapter, we discussed some of the best practices related to creating and monitoring CI/CD pipelines. This chapter also touched on predictions for the future of CI/CD and DevOps based on trends reported by industry analysts and the experience of this book's authors. Research from DORA tells us that successful teams constantly experiment with the combination of tools and personnel structures used, record the results of the experiments, and then analyze the results before deciding on the best parameters for the next experiment. You can use the information and examples provided in this book to experiment with your team.

References

To learn more about the topics that were covered in this chapter, take a look at the following resources:

- Google Developers. (2022, April 1). *Google Cloud projects: Tips and best practices.* Retrieved from `https://developers.googleblog.com/2022/04/google-cloud-projects-tips-and-best.html`.

- DeBellis., D., Lewis, A., & Villalba, D. (2023). *Accelerate State of DevOps Report 2023.* DevOps Research and Assessment (DORA).

- DeBellis, D., Peters, C. (2022) *Accelerate State of DevOps Report 2022.* DevOps Research and Assessment (DORA).

Index

packtpub.com

Subscribe to our online digital library for full access to over 7,000 books and videos, as well as industry leading tools to help you plan your personal development and advance your career. For more information, please visit our website.

Why subscribe?

- Spend less time learning and more time coding with practical eBooks and Videos from over 4,000 industry professionals

- Improve your learning with Skill Plans built especially for you

- Get a free eBook or video every month

- Fully searchable for easy access to vital information

- Copy and paste, print, and bookmark content

Did you know that Packt offers eBook versions of every book published, with PDF and ePub files available? You can upgrade to the eBook version at packtpub.com and as a print book customer, you are entitled to a discount on the eBook copy. Get in touch with us at customercare@packtpub.com for more details.

At www.packtpub.com, you can also read a collection of free technical articles, sign up for a range of free newsletters, and receive exclusive discounts and offers on Packt books and eBooks.

Other Books You May Enjoy

If you enjoyed this book, you may be interested in these other books by Packt:

Google Cloud for Developers

Hector Parra Martinez

ISBN: 978-1-83763-074-5

- Understand how to write, run, and troubleshoot code on Google Cloud
- Choose between serverless or GKE containers for running your code
- Connect your code to Google Cloud services using public APIs
- Migrate your code to Google Cloud flawlessly
- Build hybrid cloud solutions that can run virtually anywhere
- Get to grips with Cloud Functions, App Engine, GKE, and Anthos

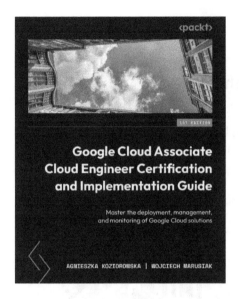

Google Cloud Associate Cloud Engineer Certification and Implementation Guide

Agnieszka Koziorowska, Wojciech Marusiak

ISBN: 978-1-80323-271-3

- Grasp the key topics needed to achieve ACE certification
- Import and export data to and from Google Cloud
- Implement and configure various networking options in Google Cloud
- Derive insights from data with Google Data Analytics
- Gain knowledge and experience in monitoring and logging
- Test yourself in various scenarios while reading the book
- Choose the optimal options to manage your solution's data

Packt is searching for authors like you

If you're interested in becoming an author for Packt, please visit `authors.packtpub.com` and apply today. We have worked with thousands of developers and tech professionals, just like you, to help them share their insight with the global tech community. You can make a general application, apply for a specific hot topic that we are recruiting an author for, or submit your own idea.

Share Your Thoughts

Now you've finished *Secure Continuous Delivery on Google Cloud*, we'd love to hear your thoughts! Scan the QR code below to go straight to the Amazon review page for this book and share your feedback or leave a review on the site that you purchased it from.

https://packt.link/r/1805129287

Your review is important to us and the tech community and will help us make sure we're delivering excellent quality content.

Download a free PDF copy of this book

Thanks for purchasing this book!

Do you like to read on the go but are unable to carry your print books everywhere?

Is your eBook purchase not compatible with the device of your choice?

Don't worry, now with every Packt book you get a DRM-free PDF version of that book at no cost.

Read anywhere, any place, on any device. Search, copy, and paste code from your favorite technical books directly into your application.

The perks don't stop there, you can get exclusive access to discounts, newsletters, and great free content in your inbox daily.

Follow these simple steps to get the benefits:

1. Scan the QR code or visit the link below

https://packt.link/free-ebook/978-1-80512-928-8

2. Submit your proof of purchase
3. That's it! We'll send your free PDF and other benefits to your email directly